NON-STANDARD COLLECTION MANAGEMENT

Non-standard Collection Management

Edited by
Michael Pearce

*a*SHGATE

Published by
Ashgate
Ashgate Publishing Company Ltd
Gower House
Croft Road
Aldershot
Hants GU11 3HR
England

Ashgate Publishing Company
Old Post Road
Brookfield
Vermont 05036
USA

British Library Cataloguing-in-Publication Data.
A catalogue record for this book is available from the British Library.

ISBN 1 85742 020 9

Typeset in 11 point Times by Plexus Design Consultants, Aldershot
Printed in Great Britain at the University Press, Cambridge

Contents

Illustrations

FIGURES

TABLES

Notes on contributors

Patsy Cullen (*Recorded sources, visual and audio*) graduated from Leeds University in 1971, then trained first as a librarian and later as a teacher. Awarded FLA in 1990, she worked in further education, including three years at HM Prison, Leeds, then moved to Sheffield City Polytechnic as Media Services Librarian. She taught for seven years at Leeds Polytechnic, Department of Library and Information Studies, specializing in media librarianship and educational technology. Patsy Cullen has taught extensively overseas, including courses for the British Council in Syria, India, Guyana, Kenya and Egypt. She has contributed articles and papers to many journals and conferences and for the past ten years has been co-editor of 'Seen and Heard' in *Audiovisual Librarian*. A former Chair and Secretary of the Aslib Audiovisual Group, and former Vice-Chair of the BUFVC, since 1989, she has been Director of Learning Resources at Bretton Hall College of the University of Leeds, Wakefield, with special responsibility for archives, staff development and research.

Eve Johansson (*Newspapers*) worked for 15 years in the British Library, beginning as a specialist in government publications and public service, and served as head of the Newspaper Library in Colindale for four years. From 1986 to 1989 she was secretary of the IFLA Working Group on Newspapers, and organized the 1987 IFLA International Symposium on Newspaper Preservation and Access in London. She has also been secretary of the IFLA Official Publications Section, chair of the Aslib Social Sciences Group, and a member of Aslib Council. She has published widely. Eve Johansson now lives in Sweden and works for the national newspaper *Svenska Dagbladet*.

John Kirby (*Slides, microfilms, microfiches*) was born in London in 1949. After obtaining a degree in classics from Liverpool University he gained a postgraduate diploma in librarianship at Aberystwyth. He started his working career with Northamptonshire Libraries, moving to Sheffield City Polytechnic in 1975. He is currently a member of the Polytechnic Library's management team and subject librarian for the School of Cultural Studies. He has produced a number of books and articles on librarianship, including *Creating the library identity* and, with Patsy Cullen, *Design and production of media presentations for libraries*. Their video for children on using libraries, *Let's find out!*, won the Library Association/TC Farries Award in 1985. He has also written extensively on the visual arts and worked on a number of exhibitions in the UK and Canada. His most recent work has been for the *Macmillan Dictionary of Art* and a bibliography of the 1951 Festival of Britain.

Albert Mullis (*Serials*). After a career in public and government libraries he moved to the British Library where he subsequently became head of the Serials Office in Bibliographic Services. He sat on the Governing Board of the International Serials Data Centre's International Centre in Paris, 1981–88, and was its Chairman. In 1983 he compiled and edited the *ISDS Manual*. In 1984 he moved to what is now the British Library Humanities and Social Sciences, where he is Budget Manager and Planning Officer, although keeping a close and keen interest in serials management. IFLA activities have included secretary of the Section on Information Technology, committee member of the Section on Serial Publications, member of the Working Group on an International Authority System and involvement (through his work on the *ISDS Manual*) with the ISBD(S) review. He represented the Library on the working party which led to the establishment of the Periodicals Barcoding Association and on the PA's Machine-Readable Codes Working Party. He has been a committee member of the UK Serials Group since 1986 and was its Treasurer, 1986–90. He has written a number of papers, articles and chapters for books on serials.

Michael Pearce (*Ephemera*) has a degree in Hispanic Studies from Liverpool University. He joined Nottingham City Libraries in 1956 as a graduate trainee and moved to Leicester City Libraries in 1964 as Central Lending Librarian. In 1965 he was appointed lecturer in the Department of Librarianship in Leeds College of Commerce, later incorporated into Leeds Polytechnic, and as lecturer and senior lecturer has been there since, teaching in the fields of library management, historical, analytical and descriptive bibliography, and information work, especially in the humanities. He obtained the FLA with a bibliography of John Drinkwater, and is currently working on a long-term project on the bibliography of Andrew Lang, and pursuing a Part Time MA in Art History at Leeds Polytechnic. *John Drinkwater: a bio-bibliography* was published by Garland, and a *Workbook of analytical and descriptive bibliography* by Clive Bingley. He also wrote the introduction to a reprint of Pollard's *Fine Books* published by EP.

Christopher Sheppard (*Manuscripts*) is Sub-Librarian in charge of the Brotherton Collection, Leeds University Library. After reading English and taking the B. Phil. in Modern English Studies at Oxford in the 1960s, he studied librarianship at Sheffield University (MA 1972). He was an Assistant Librarian at Leicester University Library, responsible *inter alia* for its comprehensive English Local History collection, from 1972 to 1979, when he took up his present post. He is directly involved in all aspects of the Brotherton Collection's work, its privately endowed funds allowing more active concern with the purchase of manuscripts and rare books than is currently possible in most comparable research collections in UK academic libraries. Creation of contemporary English literary manuscript collections and promotion of teaching based on research resources have been amongst his priorities and he is now engaged in planning extensive new accommodation for all Leeds University Library's special collections.

Andrew Tatham (*Cartographic materials*) is College Map Curator at King's College London. He was educated at Charterhouse and Durham University where he read geography. After a period in commercial map production, he joined King's in 1973. In 1984 he obtained a doctorate for work on marine charts of the Napoleonic period and he continues to teach the history of cartography to undergraduates and postgraduates. Dr Tatham is also involved in tactile cartography, being the Vice-Chairman of the International Cartographic Association's Commission on the subject and co-editor of the forthcoming 'Guide to maps and diagrams for visually handicapped people'. In the field of map care he co-authored 'Keyguide to Cartography' and has a long association with its national organization, the Map Curators' Group of the British Cartographic Society, currently being Group Convenor and its representative on BRICMICS (British and Irish Committee on Map Information and Cataloguing Systems) and on Groupe des Cartothecaires de LIBER (Ligue des Bibliothèques Européennes de Recherche).

John R. Turner (*Out of print books*) is a lecturer in the Department of Information and Library Studies at the University College of Wales, Aberystwyth. He teaches courses in historical and analytical bibliography, and in the preservation of library materials. Formerly he was Managing Editor of Scolar Press Ltd. and then worked for a short time for the Brotherton Library at the University of Leeds.

Stuart Waumsley (*Sets*) is Librarian of the Yorkshire Libraries Joint Music and Drama Service which holds one of the largest collections of music and drama sets in Great Britain and is the only regional service of its kind. He was previously Music Librarian of the West Riding County Library (1970–74) and the London Borough of Hounslow (1967–70). He studied music at Birmingham University and librarianship at University College, London. He is the author of *The organ music of Olivier Messiaen* (Paris, 1968) and is currently working on a book for Ashgate designed to guide the inexperienced listener on a variety of pathways in a graded and systematic way through the maze of classical music.

Introduction

The rationale of this work is based on the fact that as a lecturer in librarianship, and more specifically, in collection management, I have regularly been involved in, or have heard of colleagues being involved in, advising ex-students whose *cris de coeur* have included criticism of our not lecturing them on the finer points of managing collections which are out of the usual run of a librarian's experience. It is not unusual, when practising librarianship, to come across small to medium collections within the library which are not being properly exploited because of ignorance on how to manage them, or of some unsureness of the subject itself, or because they contain material which is new enough not to have much written about it.

Thus this volume contains chapters on what might appear to be a range of material historically, but all are types which are united by a certain rarity in the experience of most librarians. It is aimed at those who need to know how to progress from scratch with a collection, but not necessarily to take it into the realms of complete specialization. Also it contains information about the various types as well as guidance on how to manage them. There is a note of important collections, and of further readings. Other titles have appeared on collection management, although usually on fairly specific aspects such as cataloguing and classification, but nothing which attempts to guide the beginner in the control and management of collections in order that they may be properly exploited. In this sense, the volume should be useful for students of librarianship, and those recent and not so recent students who find themselves having to deal with unfamiliar types of material. No doubt the *cris de coeur* will continue, for some types of collection have not been covered here as yet – for example, photographs and trade literature. It is, however, hoped that this will form a *vade mecum* which librarians can use to set them on the path to exploiting the unusual and/or unfamiliar parts of their general collections, and if they wish, pursue the subject further by way of the bibliographies attached, and, if necessary, visits to the collections mentioned.

Michael Pearce
April 1992

1

Manuscripts

CHRIS SHEPPARD

MANUSCRIPTS

The number of manuscripts that has been created throughout the ages is incalculably vast. Behind virtually every printed book there lies not only one manuscript, latterly perhaps a typescript or word-processor print-out, but also beyond that, normally, earlier drafts and notes and related correspondence. Then, separately for those manuscripts associated with subsequent publications, there is the greater number which were never intended to be for publication: every literate person now and for thousands of years is or has been a potential and probably actual maker of manuscripts of some description.

Little less enormous has been the variety and complexity of manuscripts produced, particularly great in comparison with printed books, which have remained relatively homogeneous in conception during some five and a half centuries of production. Manuscripts have been written on clay tablets, stones, leaves, in the margins and in between the lines of printed books (all too often, librarians might say), on the backs of envelopes and bus tickets and on their authors' hands. In 1980, the planners of *The Location Register of English Literary Manuscripts* declared their intention to record all fragments they discovered of the papers of literary authors, 'even including their laundry bills' and in the Register's *Annual Report 1988–89* the fulfilment of that promise was proudly announced following the recording of an endorsed tailor's bill of Edward Gibbon, the eighteenth-century historian of the Roman Empire's decline and fall.

How large a repository might have been filled with laundry and tailoring bills no longer extant can scarcely be conjectured. Certainly collections of manuscripts that have been preserved differ greatly in size, from the accumulation of millions of manuscript items in the archives of the Public Record Office to the single letter cherished by some private individual. For every single manuscript that has been preserved, countless more have been destroyed and, all being well, are yet to be created.

These observations point to some of the particular problems and opportunities which manuscripts present to librarians. There are so many which might be preserved, even compared with the plethora of printed books. In their great variety, they present peculiar difficulties for disciplined description. Each manuscript is to a greater or lesser degree an individual production and many, in fact the great majority, are unique, thus most manuscripts are irreplaceable, unlike a healthy proportion of printed books, which means that their use must be particularly carefully controlled and that exceptional measures to ensure their continued physical well-being must be taken.

The librarian's work with manuscripts can be deeply satisfying: it involves, frequently, the provision of information which cannot be acquired from any other source and allows a uniquely intimate sense of contact with intellectual and other human activity of the past, be it a thousand years ago or yesterday.

ACQUISITION

Unlike an archivist whose task is essentially to receive the documents created by the institution or organization which his or her archive serves, the librarian, especially with some access to funds, is a collector.[1] Potentially the manuscripts librarian may acquire material by purchase and by gift and the practicalities of both of these processes will be considered in some detail.

Purchasing

There are broadly three sources from which manuscripts may be bought: firstly, from private individuals or organizations owning manuscripts which may or may not be of their own making; secondly, from professional dealers in manuscripts, who are frequently also booksellers, and thirdly, from auctions. Of course, dealers in manuscripts will have acquired their stock from private owners and from auctions, and both dealers and private owners sell at auction, but so far as the purchaser is concerned, the three sources have distinct characteristics.

However, whatever the manner in which manuscripts are offered for sale, the librarian's initial response will be the same, to consider whether the manuscript material, whether it be an individual item or a large body of manuscripts, is desirable for the library's collections. A judgement must be made on whether the material offered represents a worthwhile end in itself, a self-sufficient resource, appropriate to co-exist with the other holdings it would join; or whether it will add a new element to relevant or closely-related collections already held, extending their significance. The latter kind of judgement may often be made relatively easily, but deciding to develop a new interest for the library, even when it will clearly serve established purposes, is more difficult. A good deal of consultation with colleagues and potential users of the material may be necessary and a measure of imaginative anticipation of how material might be used, when it is not obviously related to the known demands made on the library.

If the desirability, in principle, of the purchase is established, the second fundamental question of whether it can be afforded immediately follows. The question has several aspects.

Does the library have or have access to sufficient money to buy? It may be possible, particularly if the purchasing decision is not urgent, to supplement the library's own resources by raising additional funds, for example by application to a grant-making body such as the Purchase Grant Fund administered from the Victoria and Albert Museum on behalf of the Museums and Galleries Commission. Generous friends of the library may wish to be associated with a particular purchase by giving financial support and even some public appeal for funds may be appropriate. Above all, if an acquisition seems particularly desirable, a library's parent institution or organization should be encouraged to support it with special funding.

Does the purchase have sufficient priority to justify the commitment of funds which may be necessary or desirable for other purposes in future? The question applies even if funds are specifically reserved for manuscripts purchasing. While the opportunity to make a particular manuscript purchase will often be unique and a manuscript in the hand is worth two still to enter the competitive arena of the auction room, the librarian will be aware that other unpredictable opportunities will surely come.

Is the manuscript material available at a price which seems reasonable and appropriate, as well as being affordable? There is no firm, objective measure of the value of manuscripts, since they are unique or virtually so. It may be possible to compare their prices with those of other material of comparable extent, scarcity and significance, by reference to past sales, but demand varies and no index of inflation applies accurately to manuscript prices. A price which seems reasonable to one potential purchaser may not to another; for example, a private collector of manuscripts may be prepared to pay much more, for personal reasons of pride and satisfaction in ownership, than a library for an item the research possibilities of which have already been exploited extensively. In short, a manuscript may simply seem too highly-priced for what it is. Indeed, it may be possible to try to negotiate a lower figure and it is by no means uncommon for an over-optimistic price to be reduced, especially if the librarian's view is subsequently endorsed by the failure of the manuscript to sell elsewhere.

Another less obvious but significant factor affecting the affordability of a potential purchase is the likely expense of processing and otherwise caring for the material involved. The first inclination of many librarians will be to acquire first and worry later about the costly, long-term implications of acquisition, but these expenses cannot simply be ignored.

Purchasing from private owners

It is much more common for libraries to buy manuscripts rather than books from private individuals, certainly as a proportion of their total collections of each class. The reason is, of course, that virtually every person is a private owner of unique manuscripts which may be of interest to libraries, whereas only a few have printed material of comparable potential. Whether such manuscripts as fill the filing cabinets, boxes and cupboards of private owners will have a market value naturally depends on whether anybody wants them. Their appeal may derive from the perceived importance of the people or organizations responsible for producing the manuscripts or of the documented events in which otherwise unremarkable people or organizations have become involved. Their interest need not be universal: if it comes from just one source other than its owners, then the material has a potential market.

When owners of manuscripts decide to sell them, this can be for many reasons. They may no longer be interested in them, or having acquired them from some other source, they may never have been particularly interested. They may still prize the material, but want or need the money it can realize, or they may feel that it should be kept in better circumstances then they can provide.

Having decided to try to sell manuscripts, the owner may, suitably or not, turn to a professional dealer in manuscripts or to an auction house and, if so, the material may enter one of the other categories considered here. However, through advice or of their own accord, the owner may offer the material directly to a library, perhaps with sound reasons for doing so. Typically the library involved may have an established reputation for collecting a particular type of material, or the owner may have strong reasons for wishing to see the material preserved, if possible, in a library of his or her choice. However, there may be no well-developed logic behind a private vendor's approach; an offer may simply be made speculatively

4

to the nearest library supposed to be likely to show any interest in manuscripts, especially if it is believed to have money for making purchases of the kind.

When an offer of manuscripts is made to a library in this way, it may or may not be accompanied by an indication of their price: the would-be seller may name a price, or suggest some rough figure, but equally likely may ask the potential buyer to make an offer. Some vendors will be well-informed about the value of their possessions, especially if they have come by their manuscripts by purchase or have sold similar material before, but in the writer's experience, the less knowledgeable owners are more likely to over-estimate than to under-estimate their manuscripts' market value when they suggest a target price. The most tactful way of responding to a worthwhile but overpriced offer – and tact will normally be especially in order when dealing with a private vendor – is probably to plead the inadequacy of available funds and to indicate a sum which is manageable. Equal tact is needed in rejecting an offer outright on qualitative grounds and the most effective way to avoid giving offence will be to plead that no money to purchase is available. If in such circumstances it seems possible that another library might wish to acquire the material, then a more promising kind of library might be suggested, but a specific institution should only be named with its prior approval.

If the material offered by a private owner would certainly be desirable and the library is asked to suggest a price, a figure must be calculated, as we have seen, by reference to the most relevant records available of past sales. As a guide, the prices set by dealers for similar manuscripts in their catalogues should be regarded with caution. Firstly, they will include a significant amount added to the dealer's own buying price, to reflect the costs of maintaining staff, business premises and capital tied up in stock, as well as profit, costs which the private owner does not generally have to meet in relation to a sale. Secondly, the appearance of manuscripts in dealers' past catalogues does not necessarily mean that they have sold at the prices indicated, or indeed sold at all. Prices achieved at auction are a much more reliable guide and the better basis for calculation. Thus in making a financial offer, the librarian should aim at the figure he or she would have been prepared to pay at auction for the same material, including the auctioneer's premium (around 10 per cent). As the seller of manuscripts is thus offered more than he or she might expect to receive from an auction (avoiding also the seller's premium and associated costs) and the buyer pays no more than the supposed 'going rate' (while also saving on costs and with the potential certainty of acquisition), both parties should be satisfied. The seller also stands to gain more than by sale to a dealer, whose buying price has to be low enough to allow a selling price that is not

5

excessively high; likewise the library pays less than a dealer would ask. Having set prices on request for some dozens of private purchases of this kind, the writer's offer has been rejected on only one occasion, which it would be entertaining but improper to specify.

A librarian can play a more active role in the acquisition of manuscripts from private sources by actually approaching their owners with a view to purchasing. The librarian may actually know that a particular individual or organization has desirable manuscripts, or may simply hope so. A courteous enquiry setting out the library's relevant acquisition policy and hinting at the availability of some funds for purchase is likely to receive a courteous and perhaps productive reply: as we shall see, gifts rather than purchases may result.

It would again be invidious to mention some of the individuals whom the writer has contacted to buy manuscripts in their possession for the Brotherton Collection at Leeds University, chiefly in the English literary field. However, it has been the policy to contact possible owners of material which is not widely collected elsewhere, as it will probably be too expensive and too late in the day to set up a rival or even complementary collection, and in any case users of the manuscripts will not welcome the necessity to work in a succession of repositories. One may benefit when established relations between an institution and a source of manuscripts break down. Thus in 1981, when the outstanding journal of the arts, the *London Magazine*, was faced with a libel case which threatened its existence, its editor Alan Ross announced that the financial crisis was worsened by the inability of a particular American library to continue to purchase the magazine's archives. The Brotherton Collection intervened and has bought the archives regularly ever since; the Collection has benefitted enormously from this association, with many associated literary and publishing papers also being acquired, and at the same time a major contribution has been made to the continued well-being of the *London Magazine* itself.

Purchasing from dealers in manuscripts

With so many manuscripts in existence and the supply potentially inexhaustible, it is not surprising that there is a very large number of professional dealers in manuscripts, ranging in the United Kingdom from the great London booksellers to remote, one-person concerns. The value of a single manuscript to be sold by one of the former may exceed that of the entire stock of one of their more modern contemporaries. Some dealers specialize in manuscripts to the general exclusion of books and some in manuscripts of a particular period or kind, such as autograph letters. Most dealers issue catalogues of their stock, or more frequently parts of their stock, being recent acquisitions or material assembled on some coherent, unifying theme. Some dealers produce a regular and stately series of catalogues, others only occasional listings as manuscripts come their way. Many libraries will have links with the trade and receive catalogues as a matter of course; dealers new to the business often appear and frequently acquire mailing lists for their catalogues from established firms.

When responding to a dealer's catalogue, it is essential that the librarian acts promptly. Still more than with rare printed books, the opportunity to buy particular manuscripts may never come again and while the librarian makes the necessary judgements and decisions about the desirability and possibility of purchase, any number of other librarians, private individuals and others can be assumed to be acting similarly from their different perspectives at the same time. Only the first purchaser buys. Perhaps inevitably, speed of reaction may adversely affect the quality of decisions and lead to some mistakes being made, but there is at least the consolation, not enjoyed in the case of many printed books, that a duplicate is most unlikely to be acquired inadvertently!

Clearly, a library's procedures must be designed to ensure that without delay catalogues reach the appropriate member of staff, whose duties should allow for swift consideration of them, even at inconvenient times. Most librarians' tasks are divisible into the immediate, the deferrable and the 'same day if possible', and if catalogue scrutiny is not placed in the first of these categories, a library will soon become aware of the obvious consequences for collection building. However, there are circumstances in which some of this urgency in the face of unknown competition can be mitigated. If one has become a valued customer of a dealer, one may receive advance copies or proofs of catalogues ahead of some other libraries; the situation is still likely to be competitive, but at least some advantage is gained. Dealers may also offer material before it is publicly catalogued at all, especially when a library is thought to be very likely to want to acquire it. This can save the dealer the considerable expense involved in publishing a description of the material and lead to a quicker sale, thus giving a quicker return on investment than would otherwise be possible. Hence, it is worthwhile for the library to ensure that key dealers are well-informed about its major collecting interests. Some offers of this kind must be viewed with scepticism, as it may be that the dealer has almost despaired of making a particular sale and hopes the direct approach will be a successful tactic; but this will not matter to the library approached, if the opportunity is considered entirely on its merits, which may include some reduction in the asking price. Undoubtedly, however, there is a measure of genuine goodwill and indeed of scholarly responsibility in some direct offers from dealers; they have even been known virtually or actually to give manuscripts away to appropriate places to clear their shelves. One may also gain extra time, as well as welcome help in making up one's mind, when considering a purchase if it is possible to see the material involved on approval before buying or rejecting. Naturally a dealer will want to give precedence to the definite sale over the potential, but it will normally be accepted that some inspection time is reasonable, particularly for material hard to assess from descriptions alone, if the service is not abused by over-long pondering by the customer.

Anyone who has compared a dealer's buying price for a manuscript at auction with the subsequent selling price in a catalogue appearing only weeks later will know that startling differences are seen: well over 100 per cent is not at all unusual as a mark-up. However, as we have seen, dealers' costs before clear profit is shown may be considerable and though many good manuscripts can be acquired without dealer involvement in the transaction, many more only become available through the dealer's ingenuity in seeking them out or his presence as an acknowledged middle-man. As with private owners, the librarian can try to bargain over a price, but how sympathetically this is received even once, let alone repeatedly, will depend on how good a case for reduction is made and on whether some other potential buyer is prepared to pay what has actually been asked.

Purchasing at auction

Many manuscripts are sold at auction, both by the well-known London auctioneers, notably Sotheby's and Christie's, whose sales are well-publicized and who produce highly informative advance catalogues, and by more obscure provincial auctioneers, who may only rarely include manuscripts in their programme of sales, with rudimentary descriptions. The former are easy to get to know about, the latter usually extremely difficult, in the writer's experience, though they may offer remarkable bargains. Sales in the vicinity of a library may be advertised locally, but hearing of those further afield is often a matter of luck, the good fortune, frequently, of notification coming through some grapevine.

The auction is a most effective medium for selling unusual or unique items such as manuscripts, the monetary value of which is simply what the highest bidder is prepared to pay at the particular time: the mechanism of escalating offers tests what the market actually, rather than theoretically or speculatively, will bear. The librarian, like other bidders hoping to buy manuscripts at auction, suffers the uncertainty of not knowing what price a lot may actually realize (the auctioneer's own advance estimates often being well off the mark), but when a bid does prove successful, there is the satisfaction of knowing that, unless all rivals were also bidding for their own permanent collections rather than for resale, essentially a wholesale rather than a retail price has been paid.

Most librarians would normally be well advised at auction to employ professional agents. Many, if not all booksellers and dealers in manuscripts, besides attending auctions to add to their own stock, will buy as agents on behalf of libraries in return for a commission charged on purchases, usually around 10 per cent, with no fee if bids are unsuccessful. Having been alerted to a library's interest in a particular auction lot, the agent will first view it well before the sale to advise on its condition and other features about which the librarian may enquire. Though ideally the librarian should view for him/herself, in the real world of innumerable calls on one's professional time and of expensive travel, the only practical course open is to rely on the agent's expertise as a substitute. Very importantly, the agent will also give informed advice on the likely price at which the material will sell; besides having extensive records of past sales, the agent is likely to know more than most librarians about other potential buyers. If the librarian decides to proceed with a bid to an agreed level, it is an essential understanding that the agent undertakes not to bid on his own account, at least until the client's maximum figure has been passed in the bidding. Occasional conflicts arise between different clients of the same agent, but then one must either rely on the even-handedness of the agent, advising all customers equally well in confidence, or else use a different agent's services. In any case, the final decision about whether and what to bid must be the librarian's own. Sometimes one learns that another library comparable to one's own, in a sense another branch of the same national research enterprise, is a potential rival bidder; one must then think about whether bidding competitively will be in the best interests of scholarship and one may decide to forego an opportunity.

If required, the agent will bid at the sale in his or her own name, a skilled process in its own right. If the bid is successful within the library's maximum figure (or close above it, as allowing some flexibility to respond to sale-room developments is often wise), the agent handles the actual purchase and delivery to the client. A payment of commission to the agent may seem generous in relation to the service given during a particular transaction, especially if it was expensive but straightforward; but over a series of transactions, many of which may not lead to purchase because no bid is proceeded with or because one is outbid, the agent's services are very good value for money. There is much to be said for developing a close relationship with one agent of proven skill and integrity, though some libraries prefer to use different specialists for different kinds of material.

Gifts

The generosity of private individuals and institutions to libraries can be astonishing. The writer's working life is spent at Leeds University in a magnificent library built some fifty years ago at the expense of a local industrialist, Lord Brotherton (1856–1930); if today the necessary materials and craftsmanship could even be found, it would cost many millions of pounds to build. At its heart is the Brotherton Collection, the nucleus of which was Lord Brotherton's companion gift to the university, an assembly of books and manuscripts for research valued at many more millions. Generosity on such a scale is rare in British libraries, if not unique, but libraries have received and continue to receive countless other gifts, many perhaps no less impressive if reckoned in relation to the means of those who have given them.

Gifts in kind are more frequently made than gifts of money and the kind is most commonly manuscript, as manuscripts are so plentiful and possessed by so many people. Still more than those who offer manuscripts for sale privately, donors of manuscripts normally wish to see them preserved in a particular place, usually because of a personal connection with it or because it is considered the right place for material of a particular kind to be kept. While some donors will always wish to give to the largest and most prestigious of libraries, many prefer to approach smaller places where their gifts will receive more personal attention and will enjoy a relatively higher significance. Thus, at the time of writing, the Brotherton Collection has just received a vast collection of the papers and correspondence of a late professor of Leeds University who had an extraordinary range of eminent literary and artistic friends, a collection which must be valued at tens if not hundreds of thousands of pounds. Leeds was given the material, rather than other possible destinations for the papers, both because of the professional connection and because of the strength of its related manuscript collections.

The most welcome gifts will be those which the library would gladly pay for in other circumstances, assuming funds to be available; less desirable, but still very welcome, will be those which the library would not choose to buy, with limited resources, but which still make an actual or potential contribution to the library's purposes. However, problems lie with those gifts which are of no real apparent interest, no matter how imaginatively one tries to assess their potential, or which, while intrinsically worthwhile, are for some reason inappropriate for the library.

Every effort should be made to accept even unwanted gifts conscientiously offered, if to do so will not be positively damaging to the library: the offence given by refusal might thoroughly outweigh the inconvenience of acceptance and no library will want to alienate even the most misguided well-wisher. However, in some cases, rare one hopes, the costs of storage, conservation and cataloguing material offered will be out of all proportion to the contribution it may make to the library's resources and do actual harm: the offer of a physically enormous body of archives to a small library would cause insuperable difficulties, for example, and even if space could be found for them they might remain virtually unusable for an indefinite time. Such gifts will have to be politely declined, stressing the library's inability rather than unwillingness to accept. Taking this course may be necessary even if the material is relatively desirable, though it will need a good deal of resolution on the librarian's part to resist the inclination to acquire regardless of the practical problems that will ensue.

Another potential difficulty which may attend an offer of manuscripts is that the donor may wish to impose certain conditions. For example, copies of the material may be asked for, or a catalogue of the gift, or access to the manuscripts may be denied for a specified period of time. The librarian should do all possible to allow the necessary commitments to be made, but should only agree to the terms if certain that all obligations can be fulfilled. If, however, the terms are likely to prove impractical or impossible to meet, the librarian should seek to modify them – denial of access for 25 years may seem acceptable protection of confidentiality, for example, but not 250 years – but if no reasonable compromise can be reached, almost any gift could prove more trouble than it is worth.

Frequently, the possibility arises of material being placed in a library 'on deposit' or, to use the rather curious phrase, 'on permanent loan'. Here, the material is available in the library as if it belonged to the library (though perhaps subject to its own special terms), but actual ownership remains with the lender. Before accepting such an arrangement, it is very desirable for the librarian to secure binding assurances on the minimum period of deposit; if the library is to bear the considerable expenses of administering the material, it must be confident that it can enjoy the benefits of such investment for a time that represents sufficient recompense. Other relevant issues, such as responsibility for insurance, if any, must also be carefully investigated in advance. It may emerge that a potential donor opts for lending primarily to ensure that the receiving library will not at some future date attempt to sell the material involved, but it should be possible to give undertakings on the future security of outright gifts which will satisfy the donor; in any case, if a deposit can be retracted, it may be at risk of future disposal by a donor's successors which the donor did not intend should happen.

A sensitive matter for the librarian's consideration when manuscripts are offered as gifts is the question of whether the donor is aware of the value of the material involved. Does the person responsible for an act of generosity of this kind realize how generous he or she is being by foregoing the possible benefits of sale? While librarians will be delighted to buy manuscripts on the open market at what proves a bargain price, many would feel uneasy at accepting gifts which may be worth far more than their owners realize. How to proceed most tactfully will vary with specific circumstances, but there have been several occasions in the writer's own experience when it has been possible to pay for 'expenses' associated with a gift, in a way that preserves the essential nature of the gift but somewhat eases the owner's sacrifice.

Gifts do have their limits, and it should be remembered that the presentation of manuscripts as physical objects does not normally include the gift of their copyright. Indeed, donors will often want specific assurances to this effect, whether or not it is they themselves who actually own the copyright, and the position should be clarified for them. When gifts are made, it will also be prudent to enquire about the donor's attitude to copying of manuscripts. The Copyright, Patents and Designs Act 1988 (in force since August 1989) gives libraries considerable freedom to copy manuscripts for purposes of research or private study, if the copyright owner is not known to have prohibited such copying. When manuscripts are purchased, it may be reasonable to regard it as the copyright owner's responsibility to make any prohibition known, but if one is given manuscript material it is a courtesy, if possible, for the librarian actively to discuss the situation with the donor.

Thus far we have considered gifts that are 'offered', but there are many instances of gifts being solicited successfully. Some organizations, for example, destroy their older archives and would readily allow their preservation in libraries which expressed an interest. Likewise, individuals made aware of a library's interest in their manuscripts may be ready to make gifts of them, rather than to sell, if the reason for the approach is well-argued and the request is not over-ambitious; contact may be so worded that the owner may without embarrassment offer material for sale if he or she prefers. Recently, for example, the Brotherton Collection approached the outstandingly successful novelist Barbara Taylor Bradford in the hope of acquiring some example of her work in manuscript to preserve in Leeds, the city of her birth. Her unexpected response was to give her entire literary archive, fascinating and happily still-growing manuscript evidence of the way in which she has delighted millions of readers. It is also often the case that after manuscripts have been bought from a private owner, supplementary material will later be given, which is welcome tangible assurance that the initial transaction, thus enhanced, was handled satisfactorily.

CATALOGUING AND CLASSIFICATION

Cataloguing

The aim of library cataloguing is the consistent and accurate description of a library's possessions in accordance with prescribed rules in order to provide a permanent record of them and to facilitate their identification and retrieval by users requiring works of particular kinds. This holds good for manuscripts as for any other material in a library's care. Cataloguers will be aware of the great variety of problems which printed books pose, but as a generalization it is fair to say that in their comparative heterogeneity, manuscripts pose more, even the single, distinct manuscript item that exhibits many of the characteristics of the printed book.

For most printed books of the last 500 years or more, the search for cataloguing data begins with the title-page, but for most manuscripts, unless very narrowly conceived in anticipation or simulation of a publishable form, no such conveniently disciplined source of basic information is available: the elements of a catalogue description must be assembled from a range of sources within and probably external to the manuscript itself. The characteristic descriptors for the printed book are its authorship, its title and its publisher, place and date of publication. However, the authorship of a manuscript is much more likely to be obscure or unknown and it may well have no formal title; obviously it has no publisher, but also its place and date of composition are quite probably impossible to establish precisely and indeed it may have been created at several locations and at a series of times. Information on the edition of a printed work is likely, for all the tortuous publishing history of some works, to be relatively easy to present compared with elucidating the analogous relations of a manuscript to other manuscripts or printed versions. The language and perhaps typography of printed material may be obstacles to their cataloguing, but the difficulties of reading modern handwriting, let alone the script of older manuscripts, may be much more considerable and illustrations and other features of manuscripts may have to be described in a detail which would not normally be contemplated in conventional book cataloguing.

Furthermore, to the extent that each manuscript is unique, it will require a unique, custom-made formulation for its description: compared with printed books the opportunity to use, even with extensive modification, the cataloguing data produced elsewhere is very restricted, if not non-existent. In any case, the nature of the content and format of catalogue records for manuscripts will often be governed by the precedents established within particular libraries, rather than by reference to standard, published codes such as the Anglo-American cataloguing rules.[2] These precedents may have been set at a progressively more remote stage of the library's development and a present desire to catalogue new manuscript acquisitions in a manner shared by other libraries may conflict with the library's wish that its own records should at least be self-consistent over different constituent collections, old and new. The goal of comprehensively recataloguing existing manuscript collections to conform to new principles of description is likely to be less practically attainable than is the case with printed books, because of the greater amount of original labour that will be involved and quite probably the smaller share of a library's resources that can be committed to such an enterprise.

The contrast of the manuscripts cataloguing process with that of printed books becomes still more marked in relation to those manuscripts or groups of manuscripts which are more strikingly different in nature from books. For practical purposes, the approach to the task of cataloguing a large group, or archive, of interrelated manuscript materials, many of which may be single leaves or fragments, must differ from the treatment of the single, distinct entity. The normal approach to such larger groups of manuscripts will be to formulate a generalized description for the catalogue of the nature and extent of the group, emphasizing some of its major features, and to reserve more detailed analysis of its contents for a separate listing maintained with the material; frequently this list will be reproduced for wider distribution to interested parties. Just how authoritatively detailed this listing can be will depend on practical circumstances, chiefly how much of the librarian's time can be devoted to it in the face of other demands. It may be that readers are generally better served by more material, more rapidly being made accessible through comparatively rough listings than by the provision of minutely researched records of some collections while others lie untouched and unusable. This is not positively to advocate inadequate and shoddy listing of material, with speed of production the only virtue, but just as a librarian dealing with a reader's enquiry must constantly assess and re-assess quite how helpful he or she can afford to be at the expense of other legitimate and pressing activities, so the manuscripts cataloguer must consider where the provision of necessary and sufficient information changes to the pursuit of research which may reasonably be the province of the user of the manuscripts. It should be remembered that most libraries will be very reluctant, for reasons of security, to allow readers access to manuscripts which are wholly or substantially uncatalogued, even though their would-be user has no alternative source for the information they contain; librarians, therefore, have a considerable obligation to bring their manuscripts to a state which allows their open consultation as rapidly as possible.

Classification

There may be libraries which classify their manuscripts using the same classification systems as are applied to their general collections of printed books – Dewey, Library of Congress and so on – but if so, their practice is far from the norm. Doubtless, many manuscripts could be so classified, for example those which are drafts of works subsequently printed, the intellectual substance of which is indistinguishable from that of their published counterparts. However, there are several reasons why conventional library classification is not really appropriate for manuscripts.

Firstly, as manuscripts are most unlikely to be available to readers without the librarian supplying them, let alone on open access alongside cognate printed works, the function of classification in physically collocating related works for browsing and other retrieval purposes does not apply. Secondly, as we have seen, manuscripts, particularly in groups, are likely to be particularly heterogeneous in nature, thus defying useful classification on similar terms to that of printed books. Even the practicality of classifying more homogeneous examples, when they are old, is open to question. There has been considerable unresolved debate, which can apply equally to manuscripts, as to whether older printed books of the kind commonly sequestered in rare book collections should be classified on the same basis as modern ones: on the one hand, it has been argued that distinguishing older books from their modern relatives in the classification process needlessly segments recorded knowledge chronologically, denying the library user important access to the subject matter of earlier works and guidance on their relationship with modern literature, while on the other hand it is countered that the most significant elements of earlier works cannot be indicated in terms of modern classifications of knowledge without unhelpfully distorting their meaning as it was for their original readership.[3] Thirdly, there are in any case other approaches to providing subject access to the contents of manuscripts which are appropriate and applicable to them as they are not, generally, to printed material and there would be danger of misleading readers if only some of a library's manuscripts were classified like books, while others were differently treated.

The whole process of sorting a group of related manuscripts, be they an individual's literary papers, the records of a religious house or a business enterprise, or whatever else, is itself an exercise in classification.[4] The whole group is sorted into coherent smaller sub-groups of related material, which may in turn be divided into smaller groups again; within these groups, manuscript items are ordered according to suitable features, with chronology commonly a major ordering principle, always bearing in mind the compromise necessary between ordering the material as logically and helpfully as possible and maintaining the original order imposed on it by its creators or former owners. (This inherited order may best be recorded independently of the actual physical arrangement chosen for the material within a library rather than preserved in the order of the documents themselves, particularly when the original arrangement appears to reflect no conscious principles.) The systematic order established is controlled by some form of notation added to the documents. Thus the sorting process, which may vary greatly in complexity, involves in effect the creation of a classification of the elements of the manuscript group and its nature evolves organically from the particular material in hand, rather than being imposed from outside.

The application of computers to the recording of manuscripts has now provided the potential for giving subject access to the contents of the manuscripts which can be considerably superior to that for printed books provided by libraries. Book classification and the assignment of subject headings in their cataloguing will generally fall well short of a comprehensive indexing of their contents: quite properly, that detailed indexing is left to the producers of books themselves, backed up by general abstracts and indexes in hard copy or machine-readable form. However, most manuscripts are created with no indexes of their own and increasingly librarians are using computers to index the manuscripts in their care in a way more consistent with the indexing within printed books than with library cataloguing and classification of them; the process will also facilitate the creation of lists of manuscript material of the kind already observed to be supplementary to their basic, general catalogue description.

How comprehensively this indexing is done varies with the staff time and expertise that can be devoted to the task and with the adequacy of the computing facilities available to the library, but major projects currently in progress, such as the recording of the Wellington Papers at Southampton University and of the Hartlib Papers at Sheffield University demonstrate what is possible.[5] These projects are backed by considerable special funding (the credit for securing which must go to the institutions concerned), but progress can be made with far more modest means. Thus the Brotherton Collection at Leeds is creating a computer database of descriptions of its holdings of seventeenth- and eighteenth-century verse as part of its normal activities. Most of the poems involved appear in bound miscellanies and commonplace books, manuscript anthologies in effect, which were formerly catalogued only as entire volumes, rather than in terms of the diverse, individual entities by a great many authors appearing within them; had it been felt desirable to classify them, single broad class marks telling the user very little would have been the result. Now, not only is each poem recorded by its first lines and author and title if known, but details of subject matter, format and many other features appear, almost any of which can be searched for singly or in combination using a free-text information retrieval system. The body of material so treated thus becomes immeasurably more accessible to users, not only to students of poetry but also to those interested in any of the numerous topics to which the poems refer, and not only locally but to anybody who can access the database from elsewhere. Initiatives of this kind should increasingly become possible even in quite small manuscript repositories and with small collections their benefits may be exploited particularly rapidly. The fact that such developments may be parallel to, rather than fully integrated with, other established cataloguing and indeed classifying operations means that they need good publicity to ensure general awareness of their availability and uses.

CONTROL OF USE

Because manuscripts are unique or virtually so, most are effectively irreplaceable. Almost invariably, therefore, even if they are of negligible value, manuscripts will not be available for loan to individuals and will have to be consulted within the repository which preserves them. Occasionally, arrangements may be made for their temporary transfer from one library to another to assist a scholar or for exhibition purposes, but such arrangements are complex, involving agreements about special transportation, insurance and circumstances of display or consultation. These processes are likely to be expensive and time-consuming and put a considerable burden of responsibility on the receiving institution, while the lender, no matter how carefully matters are handled, experiences anxiety, so the norm is undoubtedly that manuscripts remain unequivocally in the safekeeping of their owners.

Manuscripts are in libraries to be seen and used, whether for advanced research and teaching or simply to inform or entertain quite casual observers. Access to them should therefore be as easy and open as possible: the greater the obstacles between manuscript and audience, the more the very reason for the library having the manuscript is undermined. However, this maximization of accessibility must be balanced with the necessity to ensure the physical security of manuscript material: clearly, if a manuscript is lost or damaged, accessibility will be totally compromised.

When a manuscript is literally in the hands of a reader, it is at risk of accidental and deliberate harm: at risk of being stolen or maliciously damaged, of being torn or soiled or thoughtlessly defaced or taken away inadvertently; a group of manuscripts seen together may be disarranged, thus hindering future use.

The first precaution against accidental or deliberate mishap must be the provision of a secure reading area, access to which is controlled entirely by library staff. If the area must also serve as a place for the storage of library materials, they should if necessary be inaccessible to readers. In addition to enforcing normal library regulations, one should insist on the use of pencils for note-taking; some readers will think that prohibitions on pens relate to steel nibs and ink wells, but the risk of ink from more modern types of pen getting on to a manuscript is still unacceptable. One may even ask users to wash their hands before consulting a manuscript. Such requirements as this can best be incorporated in written regulations governing the use of manuscripts, which can be given to the would-be user, preferably in advance of a visit. Indeed, one can make the prior notification of a visit a prerequisite of granting access, as this helps ensure that one can make all necessary preparations for the visit. However, although experienced or even sensible researchers usually do make appointments to pursue their work, not everyone will and if such people are turned away as a matter of course, it may be for no better reason than one's own convenience. The practical possibility of serving the unannounced visitor should at least be investigated sympathetically.

Whatever the circumstances of a reader's visit, one needs to establish who the potential user of a manuscript is, by asking for a reference or some other form of personal identification. Unfortunately, knowing precisely who the user is does not necessarily guarantee their honesty or competence, but it does have an obvious security dimension and also helps identify the kind of assistance the reader will need. Because of what should be librarians' intimate knowledge of the manuscripts they preserve and the close personal contact with readers inevitable in such supervised collections, it should be possible to give very valuable guidance appropriate to the needs of different kinds of reader and this possibility represents one of the most satisfying elements in the manuscripts librarian's work.

Ideally it should be possible to maintain constant observation of readers when they are using manuscripts. However, in practice, in a busy or understaffed manuscripts collection such observation can be very difficult to maintain and a moment's inattention can be enough for mishap to occur. A useful strategy can be to have closed circuit television surveillance of the reading room, linked to a screen elsewhere, preferably with recording facilities. This has the advantage that if constant observation is not practically possible, at least the user of manuscripts will not know exactly when observation is taking place. Clearly, this is not a substitute for personal presence and irregular inspection, but if the reader's attention is drawn to the additional means of control, its salutary effect can be constant.

Ideally, also, it should be possible to ensure in fine detail that the manuscripts received by a reader are exactly the same and in the same condition as those returned after use. This counsel of perfection implies that every square centimetre of manuscript used and every blemish on it should be inspected with the reader before use, with a full agreed record kept, and corresponding joint inspection be made after use. How practical a possibility this will be in working circumstances depends on various incidental factors, notably the nature of the material in use. At extremes, the joint inspection of a single leaf manuscript is a very different matter from the inspection of a large manuscript of many loose and varied leaves. Similarly, the processes possible when a single reader is involved may be compromised when there are several readers requiring simultaneous attention from a small number of staff. Wise expedients are to ensure that no reader is given a greater number of manuscript pieces at one time than can reasonably be accounted for, even if this means more labour of piecemeal fetching for the librarian, and for the librarian to be alert to any specially vulnerable features of the material involved, either in terms of value or condition, and to draw readers' attention to the librarian's awareness of them. A signed declaration of what is being consulted must always be secured and time must be allowed for the librarian to check and be seen to check what has been used before the reader leaves; this will often necessitate concluding the reader's visit before he or she would ideally want to finish or extending a visit beyond that time.

Besides these observations and checking measures, additional security for manuscripts in use is commonly afforded by marking them, stamping, embossing or perforating them in some way. These markings may be a combination of the clear and obvious, for deterrent effect, and the concealed. However, besides being time-consuming to apply on large collections, any fragment of which could be at risk, it may be difficult to mark manuscripts adequately without disfiguring them in a way which detracts from their readability, thus, the more closely a mark is associated with a valuable, distinct element of a manuscript (a signature, for example, which needs protection) the more likely it is that the essential feature will be damaged. But, of course, the less closely the marking is associated with what it most seeks to protect, the more it can be cut away or otherwise neutralized by a thief. The conclusion is that while both visible and invisible marks on manuscripts contribute to their security, they can only be one imperfect element, in a broader protection strategy.

A further very valuable course of action is to microfilm or otherwise copy manuscripts for security and also conservation purposes. Such copies provide a kind of insurance against any kind of loss of all or part of a manuscript, while providing invaluable evidence in the case of theft. Indeed, many researchers can be served adequately by the provision of a copy of the manuscript rather than the original which is thus protected from unnecessary handling and exposure to risk. A negative microfilm master can be used for producing any subsequent copies of the material that are required, avoiding more handling. However, even the minority of libraries which have immediate access to microfilming facilities will find the comprehensive, systematic copying of large manuscript collections a very considerable burden: priorities will have to be set, reflecting the likely volume of use of particular groups of material and their vulnerability to damage in repeated consultations, and libraries will have to ensure that the copying does not infringe copyright.

Whether or not copies have already been made by the library, readers will frequently ask for them to be made for them to buy, often as a substitute for travelling to see manuscripts at first hand for themselves. As with printed books, copying must only be undertaken subject to copyright regulations and to the material itself being physically suitable for copying. If microfilming is requested, the library with no microfilm camera will have to consider whether the risks involved in arranging for outside filming of the material are acceptable. Virtually all libraries will have photocopying facilities, but only a minority the special archival copiers which do not require the inversion of material being copied and which regulate its exposure to light; such equipment is relatively expensive. Besides taking copyright and physical condition into account, librarians will individually decide the other terms on which copies will be provided. For example, because of the comparatively complex handling often involved in manuscript copying, higher charges may be set for them than for other classes of material. It may also be stipulated that, notwithstanding the charge, copies should be returned to the library after use, that they be leased to users in effect; this may help to ensure compliance with the copyright regulation that copies of certain manuscripts should only be made for the exclusive use of the requesting individual and in any case the library may wish to maintain some on-going control over who has access to its manuscripts, even in copied form.

Independently of restrictions imposed by copyright, libraries will normally wish to secure undertakings from purchasers of copies of their manuscripts (and indeed from hand-copiers) that they will not publish or otherwise reproduce them without specific permission. In many cases, such permission will freely be granted, if the manuscripts' source is acknowledged, particularly if no facsimile reproduction of material is involved. In other cases, however, when the would-be user clearly seeks to derive significant financial advantage from use of the material, it is quite legitimate for the library to seek to share in that profit by charging a fee. While it is very rare, perhaps illogically so, for a library to charge a fee for verbal transcription of manuscript material, it is common for fees to be charged for facsimile use of material as plates or illustrations, in television programmes, advertising and elsewhere. There is little consensus established between libraries on what levels of fee should be charged and on the rights so conferred, although members of the Consortium of University Research Libraries (CURL) have recently had discussions on this, and arguably, each proposed use had its unique characteristics anyway, *ad hoc* negotiation being most appropriate. If a library has no experience of such matters, it would be well-advised when necessary to seek advice from colleagues in other institutions, which may have considered and proven policies and scales of charges.

Increasingly, microfilm publishers are interested in copying whole collections of manuscripts for commercial sale, offering some kind of fee or royalty for the use of manuscript raw material. In responding to proposals of this kind, libraries have to weigh against each other the advantages of having security copies of their manuscripts made at the publisher's expense, of getting some income from the enterprise and participating in a form of service to scholars, with the disadvantages of irrevocably losing a great measure of control over their collections, thus losing contact with their users, and of deriving, frequently, very little financial benefit indeed from doing so, while experiencing considerable hidden costs in preparing material for the copying process.

CONSERVATION AND PRESERVATION

Though manuscripts are usually at risk of loss or damage when in use by readers, they are vulnerable at all times. As with all ills, prevention is better than cure, with the latter being the regrettable recourse following some failure of the former, which must therefore be the librarian's first priority.[6]

Security of manuscripts from theft is a fundamental element in their preservation. Aspects of this when they are in use have already been considered, but also the place in which the manuscripts are stored must be effectively protected from unauthorized intrusion. Just how well protected will greatly depend on how much money has been and can be spent on appropriate measures. Good locks on all entry points are a bare minimum; beyond that, cumulatively, further physical strengthening such as grilles on windows, electronic alarms and personal surveillance by librarians or security staff can be added. A safe or strong-room gives additional protection, but if large collections of papers are to be protected, such accommodation fills very rapidly unless provided on an improbably grand scale. Any set of security measures can be compromised by negligent operation, so access to keys and security codes must be strictly controlled and standard procedures always followed.

To some extent the unique nature of manuscripts gives them some built-in protection from theft. The more valuable an individual manuscript is, the more likely it is to have been recorded and described in detail, its ownership will be widely known and the market in which it might most readily and profitably be sold will be aware of this provenance. However, this is no reason for complacency, as many manuscripts are comparatively unknown, others can be dismembered and disguised (more easily than printed books) and the frustrated thief may simply destroy material that proves difficult to sell.

The librarian cannot be complacent, either, when considering the various environmental and natural factors which put manuscripts at risk. Ideally, manuscripts should be stored in an air-conditioned environment in which temperature, humidity, air circulation and lighting levels can be closely controlled. Alas, for many librarians such provision is an ideal they despair of achieving. However, whatever the given environment, it is a basic essential that some means of measuring and recording the prevailing conditions should be used. Spot checks are better than nothing, but much inferior to the constant monitoring night and day, every day, that can be achieved using recording thermohydrographs. Even within small areas, the recorded evidence will show the best and worst locations for the storage of vulnerable material and provide the basis for trying to make improvements. There will be evidence, also, if necessary, of the harm that can be done by shutting down heating during periods of library closure or otherwise economizing on services; as with security precautions, even the most sophisticated means of environmental control will be comparatively ineffective if it is not allowed to function consistently. At least the protection of manuscripts from prolonged exposure to light should entirely be within the librarian's power; the danger is particularly to be avoided when manuscripts are on exhibition or display.

Of all environmental dangers, the one most to be feared is fire. The most likely accidental cause is some electrical defect and not only should wiring be checked, even renewed, periodically, but care should be taken to ensure that all electrical equipment, photocopiers for example, is observed when in use and switched off and unplugged when not. Smoke detectors should be placed strategically, which will receive immediate response if activated. As methods for controlling fires can be more widely damaging than the fire itself, fire extinguishers using dry processes should be readily available as a first resort. As with security precautions, expert advice should be sought. Water damage other than in fire control is also a potential hazard, so the librarian should watch for roof damage, cracked glass and vulnerable pipes, and position manuscripts accordingly in storage.

Even within the most satisfactory environment possible, the physical composition of the materials of which manuscripts are made contributes to their deterioration. The problems of stabilizing the condition of printed books, which were always intended in some degree to be kept for some time by their owners, are well known and the problems of manuscripts are the same writ large. Most manuscripts have not been created with any thought of their indefinite preservation in mind and accordingly they involve a haphazard mixture of poor quality, brittle papers with unstable or corrosive inks. Methods of mass deacidification of large quantities of paper at low cost are in their infancy. The librarian with limited funds may have to think hard before investing in the treatment of the paper of a single book, so how much greater is the problem of considering the treatment of a box of late nineteenth-century autograph letters, when dozens more such boxes wait nearby in the librarian's care.

The custodian of many such manuscripts must therefore try to ensure at least that they are stored in ways that retard their deterioration, even if it cannot practically and comprehensively be arrested. They should be placed as individually as possible in acid-free enclosures – envelopes, folders and boxes from specialist suppliers, designed for the preservation of manuscripts. If custom-made enclosures into which manuscripts will fit precisely can be afforded, so much the better. Any paper-clips or staples should be removed carefully from papers. Boxes should be shelved flat to ensure the stability of their contents.

Despite sound and comprehensive measures preventative of damage to, or undue deterioration of, materials being put into effect, there will remain manuscripts which need repair, if only because they needed it even before acquisition. Only a small minority of librarians in the United Kingdom have adequate repair facilities available to them in their own institutions and most will have to employ specialist help elsewhere. Inexpert attempts at conservation, however well intentioned, risk exacerbating rather than curing problems; the only amateur methods that can be sanctioned are those which beyond any doubt use harmless materials and are totally reversible. Indeed, many manuscripts that were professionally conserved in the past now need remedial treatment, as standards of practice have changed and improved; for example items protected by being 'tipped-in' in guard books may be contaminated by inferior materials in contact with them and by tearing at the hinges created where they are glued in place at the edge. We would be arrogant to suppose that today's conservation methods will never be improved upon, so reversibility of present action must be a priority in professional work, too. Libraries with comparatively little experience in conservation would be wise to consult others which have, before entrusting material to conservators for treatment; it will be expensive, requiring skilled labour and special materials and equipment, so value for money will be vital.

Given these costs, almost every library will have to exercise alert judgement on which manuscripts in its care should have priority in the competition for conservation expenditure. There is no simple rule to follow here. It is reasonable that material which is to be used intensively should be conserved before the little used, but predicting patterns of use in a large and varied collection is difficult and of course conservation measures may put material out of use at inconvenient times. Possibly very valuable items should be conserved before more modest ones, but if the former are little used, their research potential having been realized or their interest highly esoteric, arguably it is they that should wait. Again, very badly damaged material may seem to require treatment more urgently than less damaged, but if the former's condition is comparatively stable, it may be better, for a given sum of money, to arrest the deterioration of sounder materials in greater quantities, before their condition worsens.

IMPORTANT MANUSCRIPT COLLECTIONS

In seeking to identify the important collections of manuscripts in the United Kingdom, one inevitably thinks first of the British Library. Over centuries of manuscripts acquisition by purchase and by gift, the British Library has pursued its ambitious aim, in Arundell Esdaile's words, 'to assemble, preserve and make available the written sources of the main intellectual and historical activities of the world, and especially, of course, of this country'.[7] Another library would gain great distinction from possessing any one of numerous British Library collections – the Cotton manuscripts (despite many being burnt in 1731 after being consolidated in Ashburnham House, partly because of its supposed comparative safety from fire), the Harleian MSS, the Sloane MSS, the Lansdowne MSS, the Egerton MSS, the Arundel MSS, the Stowe MSS, and many more. Still today, the British Library has the means to purchase manuscripts which virtually no other library in the United Kingdom could contemplate acquiring; for example, at the time of writing, it has just secured the Trumbull papers at a price far exceeding the total annual expenditure on staff and acquisitions of almost any other academic library in the country.

No less beyond dispute is the importance of the manuscript collections of the National Libraries of Scotland and of Wales, of the libraries of the Universities of Oxford and Cambridge and of other institutions belonging to the Consortium of University Research Libraries. None will consider their funds for manuscripts purchasing adequate, but they are nevertheless comparatively strong and they receive gifts consistently with the first principle enunciated in Matthew 25:29, 'For to every one who has will more be given, and he will have abundance; but from him who has not, even what he has will be taken away'; less well-endowed libraries will be glad that for the present the second principle of that verse does not yet apply to their manuscript holdings. The large libraries also have the great advantage for readers of having large collections of relevant printed books which may be used in comparatively convenient association with their manuscripts.

One could proceed further with sketching this notional stratification of libraries and other repositories possessing manuscripts and in a sense such an account of the relative importance of collections, in terms of their size, range and no doubt financial value, would be valid. However, it disregards another facet of 'importance' at least as significant and legitimate: that for the user of manuscripts, the important collection is the one, however grand or modest, that has the manuscripts he or she wishes to see for a particular purpose. The uniqueness of manuscripts means that in the context of a need to consult certain manuscripts in its care, any library can enjoy the experience, however rare or transitory, of being the most important of libraries. In their invaluable book *British Archives*, Janet Foster and Julia Sheppard list well over 1000 different libraries, record offices and other establishments currently holding collections of manuscripts in this country, and the list is not exhaustive.[8] Though the difference in scale of these places is evident, each has material that is indispensable for certain kinds of enquiry; thus, for example, for the study of Thomas Hardy, an essential centre is Dorset County Museum, for Winifred Holtby, Hull Local Studies Library, for Gilbert White, the Gilbert White Museum at Selbourne, rather, in the first instance, than any vast and celebrated treasure house. In its different way, arranged by the names of writers of manuscripts rather than geographically, the *Location Register of Twentieth-Century English Literary Manuscripts and Letters* likewise attests to how widely manuscripts which may be important to research are dispersed.[9] If one considers those, for example, of Walter de la Mare, undeniably *the* important collection of his papers is at the Bodleian Library, Oxford; but one can readily infer the circumstances in which it may be Buckinghamshire County Record Office or Northamptonshire Record Office that really matters to a particular researcher, Gloucester Public Library or Bath Reference Library, Somerville College, Oxford, or Cheltenham Ladies' College. Thus manuscripts can constantly be a great leveller of libraries.

NOTES

1 The generalized distinctions often drawn between librarians concerned with manuscripts and archivists are seldom, in fact, very helpful. In practice, many libraries possess collections of manuscripts which can properly be termed archives and many archives have individual manuscripts which can be studied in their own right; it is not the titles of the persons dealing with them that matter, but the appropriateness of the skills and methods they bring to bear. However, the characterization of receiving archives and collecting libraries is made in Robert H. Balmer's entry 'Archives' in *Encyclopaedia of Library and Information Science*, edited by Allen Kent and Herbert Lancout, vol 1, New York: Dekker, 1968, p. 517.

2 Chapter 4 of *Anglo-American Cataloguing Rules*, 2nd edition, 1988 revision, gives a detailed insight into the features of manuscripts with which cataloguers must be concerned, even if not professionally committed to using those rules.

3 The case for conventionally classifying older, 'rare' books is argued in John Feather, (1982), 'The Rare-Book Librarian and Bibliographic Scholarship', *Journal of Librarianship*', **14** (1) January, pp. 30–44. In part, Feather specifically takes issue with the opinion of Roderick Cave expressed in his *Rare Book Librarianship*, London: Bingley, 1976, especially p. 81; Cave replies to Feather in a letter to *Journal of Librarianship*, **14** (3) July 1982, pp. 218–20.

4 The process of sorting, or classifying, a large collection of related documents is vividly described in J.H. Hodson (1972), *The Administration of Archives*, Oxford: Pergamon, pp. 123 ff. This is a particularly readable example of the numerous works on archive administration highly relevant to manuscripts librarianship, classic studies being T.R. Schellenberg's *Modern Archives: Principles and Techniques*, Chicago: Chicago U.P., 1956, and his *The Management of Archives*, New York: Columbia U.P., 1965.

5 For a detailed account of the work at Southampton University, see C.M. Woolgar, (1988), 'The Wellington Papers Database: An Interim Report', *Journal of the Society of Archivists*, **9** (1), January, pp. 1–20. The article following it in the *Journal*, 'Introducing computers in the record office: theory and practice' by John Walford, Henry Gillett and J.B. Post, loc. cit., pp. 21–29, indicates something of the potential of computers in less experienced hands than those of Woolgar and his team.

6 There is a large and growing specialist literature on the security, conservation and preservation of library materials. *Caring for Books and Documents* by A.D. Baynes-Cope, London: British Museum, 1981, is simple but authoritative. For an account of repair methods, though best not attempted by most librarians, see Arthur W. Johnson, *The Practical Guide to Book Repair and Conservation*, London: Thames and Hudson, 1988. Wide-ranging expert discussions of contemporary issues and practice in the field appear in the series of Seminar Papers issued by the National Preservation Office since 1987.

7 Arundell Esdaile, (1946), *The British Museum Library*, London: Allen and Unwin, p. 226 ff. Esdaile's account of the earlier manuscript collections is valuable, though one needs to see, notably, the *Index of Manuscripts in the British Library*, 10 vols., Cambridge: Chedwyck-Healey, 1984–86, to form a full impression of the awe-inspiring extent of the collections.

8 Janet Foster and Julia Sheppard (1989), *British Archives. A Guide to Archive Resources in the United Kingdom*, 2nd edition, London, Macmillan. In a pragmatic way, the authors take a broad view of archives to embrace 'any primary source material in a variety of media whatever its origin' (p. vii).

9 *Location Register of Twentieth-Century English Literary Manuscripts and Letters*, 2 vols, London: British Library, 1988. This union list is derived from a computer database compiled at Reading University which is to be steadily updated; a second phase to cover manuscripts of the eighteenth and nineteenth centuries is in progress.

2

Out of print books

JOHN TURNER

THE MATERIAL AND ITS PROBLEMS

In this chapter an out of print book means, quite simply, one that can no longer be obtained from the original publishers. New editions, reprints or facsimiles of a relevant title will often be available but for this kind of material the text must be in an earlier form and must also be contained on those earlier printed sheets rather than some later copy. Thus, the chapter will deal with material which is normally kept in 'special' or 'rare book' collections excluding those categories (manuscripts, ephemera, periodicals, etc.) which are covered in other chapters.

In other contexts because of the long time scale involved it is usual to divide out of print books into three groups: incunables or books printed before 1501; the remaining books from the hand-press period, from 1501 to about 1800; and books from the machine-press period from about 1800 to the present. However, there are sufficient common features as far as collection management is concerned for all the groups to be discussed together and distinctions will be made only where necessary, particularly in relation to classification and cataloguing, and conservation and preservation.

ACQUISITION

Many authorities[1] advocate that a policy on acquisition of out of print books needs to be written down. Even if the main areas of the policy are self-evident and completely obvious there will always be areas of apparent secondary importance that need pondering over and that can produce unexpected conclusions. Of course the National Library of Finland, for example, will collect all Finnish books. It will also collect some, although not all, Swedish, Norwegian and Russian books and once the objective becomes anything less than complete coverage the uncertainties begin. What kind of Swedish books will be collected and will the same limitations be applied to Norwegian and Russian books, and what about Danish books? The very act of writing down the policy in a logical sequence forces the author to confront these uncertainties.

The policy on out of print books will follow most closely the acquisition policy for the library as a whole. It will also take account of the present constitution of the collection in order to maintain the strength of those subjects which are already well represented and to fill in gaps wherever they are found. At the same time the policy should never be seen as a rigid set of rules. Unique opportunities arise occasionally when a library is perhaps offered an almost complete collection on a subject which has hitherto not been of importance to the institution. The acquisition policy should be flexible enough to allow this new subject to be accommodated if the collection on offer is thought to be too good to miss.

A clear acquisition policy is probably more important for out of print books than for newly published material because the conditions for acquiring out of print books are much more uncertain. Two factors, when to buy and how much to pay, essential factors for accurate financial control, are usually completely unpredictable. Anything from single titles to large collections can come onto the market at any time without warning. Whereas new books are published fairly regularly throughout the year with predictable peaks (before the academic year, before Christmas, and so on), in the case of out of print books the librarian may have found nothing worth having for six months and then be faced with six expensive items in one week. Similarly, despite records of prices in *Book Auction Records* and *American Book Prices Current*, there can never be absolute certainty that the price being asked for a particular item is fair. The price often depends on condition and provenance and these features are not always mentioned in the price records.

In addition to the unpredictability of when an acquisition can be made and how much it should cost, the location of any item which may become available is also subject to the same uncertainty. It is not too much of an exaggeration to claim that a copy of a desired title may turn up anywhere in the world where there is a second-hand bookshop or an auction.

Perhaps even more important than a written policy is an awareness by the librarian that difficult decisions are part of the job, occur regularly and cannot be avoided. For example, a knowledge of the collection and the acquisition policy will show that specific titles are missing – it is possible that the librarian has lived with this list for years. A title which would fill a minor gap then comes up for sale at, say, £200 more than the last recorded copy. Do you buy this copy or continue waiting for a cheaper one to turn up? The decision is complicated further because copies are rare and come onto the market one at a time. Any hesitation will mean that the book has already been sold to another customer. Missing this copy or deciding not to buy may condemn the librarian to waiting many more years.

Still more difficulties arise if the title would fill a major, rather than a minor, gap in the collection and if the price is very high indeed. The cost of such a book could equal the annual budget of a whole department in the same institution – and still be a bargain. Since troubles do not come singly, the offer of this title could arrive in the same post as a separate offer of a large collection of books, no one title of similar importance to the previous expensive book, but a collection which the library needs and at a total price roughly the same as that of the single book. As before, the greater the time taken to arrive at a decision, the greater the chance of losing both offers.

Because of working more or less continuously with such dilemmas many practitioners feel that a written policy is not strictly necessary. In arriving at each decision the librarian is forced to confront the implications of acquiring any title and among the first questions to answer are how that title fits the existing collection and how it helps to achieve the purpose of the institute as a whole. In the example above it would certainly be wise to have thought of all conceivable objections before meeting the head of department whose total budget you have just exceeded in buying one book.

Sources for the acquisition of out of print books

Having decided what to acquire, the next problem is acquisition itself. There is a wide range of sources which can be divided into two main groups since all material coming into a collection has either been bought or donated. Items can be bought from second-hand or antiquarian booksellers, from auctions, or through personal negotiations with a private owner. These sources will be considered in turn below, followed by a few comments on donations.

The distinctions between second-hand and antiquarian booksellers has never been clear and it is a matter for the individual dealer to choose how to describe the business. Antiquarian is a more up-market title and antiquarian stock usually contains more rare books, although not necessarily older books, than a second-hand bookseller. In practice there is a range of dealers in a continuous progression from general second-hand shops with a few shelves of books among the furniture and bric-à-brac to exclusive organizations selling nothing but books and then only the rarest and most expensive. There is a similar range in the size of the operations, from part-time businesses conducted from the owner's home to multi-storey shops with stock and turnover to match. There is a further similar range in specialization from the narrowest to the most general, either by subject, period or both.

Because dealers can be located almost anywhere many of them overcome geographical separation by producing catalogues which they send to potential customers. Consequently it is important that the dealers know in advance if you are likely to be interested. It is sometimes difficult to provide this advance information because the librarian, in turn, does not know that the catalogue is being prepared. However this is not a major problem and it is easily limited because despite the world-wide distribution of dealers, British librarians will buy mostly from British dealers. Established libraries and their needs, not to mention their available cash, are also well known to the book trade. There are also a few publications which can help: directories of second-hand dealers often contain an index by subject specialization so that where a librarian's subject interests coincide the dealers can be informed in advance. Such indexes can be found in *Sheppard's Book Dealers in the British Isles*, Old Wokingham: Martins Publishers; *Driff's Guide to all the Secondhand and Antiquarian Bookshops in Britain*, London: Driffield; and The Provincial Booksellers Fairs Association *Membership list*.

Being known to the dealers is only one of the difficulties of buying from catalogues. Because the books are out of print, the titles listed in catalogues are single copies and it is this fact which brings the urgency already mentioned above to the decision to buy. There will often be several buyers chasing the single copy of the most desirable titles and the only way to secure such a title is to telephone the dealer immediately. It is therefore important to arrange a postal delivery as early each morning as possible. The Post Office may well be fulfilling their obligations in this and the librarian should ensure that delays in receiving the post are not being caused by the system of distribution within the institution. It is galling to lose a purchase at the last minute, after winkling out a catalogue from a dealer in the backwoods, after fighting to get at the post before anyone else, and after suffering agonies before deciding to spend the money. If, on putting through the call to the dealer the line is engaged, you can only hope someone is ordering a different title altogether from the one you want. All the same, hunting down missing titles, even if the hunt is unsuccessful provides real excitement, and if successful provides enormous satisfaction as well.

Each issue of the periodical *Antiquarian Book Monthly Review* contains

31

a list of the latest catalogues with short descriptions of their contents, as well as a section of reviews and comments on catalogues received. Unless the library is already included on a dealer's mailing list it is unlikely that a catalogue will be received in time to purchase much from it if it is requested after the announcement in the periodical. However, there is always a slight chance and at least the list in this periodical gives an indication of the dealers whose subsequent catalogues could be useful to the librarian. Each issue also has numerous dealers' advertisements which often reveal subject specialization and can supplement the indexes in directories. The main advantage of information in the *Antiquarian Book Monthly Review* over the directories is that it is more up to date.

Some dealers do not produce catalogues and in those instances the librarian has to rely on personal visits to go through the stock. As a result, purchases not made from catalogues usually take place only from booksellers in the vicinity of the library. Book fairs have been in existence for some time but a recent development has been their systematic organization. Fairs are particularly suited to dealers who do not produce catalogues or who do not own shops. There is now a Provincial Booksellers Fairs Association, founded in 1974 and with about 650 members in 1990. The Association is run as a co-operative and operates through local committees which arrange about 180 fairs a year in various towns throughout Britain. Many of the fairs are single events arranged once only while others have become annual meetings at a fixed location, for example, at York, at Edinburgh to coincide with the Festival and at the Mentmore Antiques Fair. There is a two-day fair in London in June each year which has now become a major event and many of the provincial fairs are important, not least as places where the librarian can meet a large number of dealers.

Meeting dealers is always useful because it is much easier to arrive at mutual understandings in face to face discussions rather than in letters or by telephone. On the other hand, it is debatable if time spent simply browsing in second-hand bookshops is worthwhile as far as the results it brings in acquisitions is concerned. However, almost all librarians find the lure irresistible and rare book specialists are usually hopeless addicts. Discoveries can be made and a single find compensates, in satisfaction if not in cost-effectiveness, for countless hours with nothing to show.

It is possible to give dealers, whether producers of catalogues or not, a list of titles which you are especially interested in obtaining. There is then always the added possibility that the price of anything on the list will be slightly higher than it would have been if you had not declared an interest. However, most dealers are fair and honest and all of them are bound to earn a living by charging more than they paid in every case. The periodical *The Clique*, which was once widely recognized as the place to advertise wants, is now defunct. Other periodicals carry wants lists, notably *The Bookdealer*, but none has yet completely taken the place of *The Clique*.

Buying at auction involves different problems. In the first place there is no rush to decide whether to purchase as there is with dealers' catalogues. Auction sales are advertised in advance and announcements appear in *Antiquarian Book Monthly Review* and frequently in the national and local press. Catalogues are prepared for most auctions and these too are usually ready in advance of the sale. The librarian therefore has much more time and can be quite certain what to do before spending any money. Sales exclusively of books are organized regularly by the large, well-known auction houses (Sotheby, Christie, Bloomsbury Book Auctions, Bonham, and Phillips) at their premises in London. There are also regular book sales in Bristol by Taviner, in Crewkerne, Somerset, by Lawrence, and in Swindon by Dominic Winter. The London houses hold occasional book auctions in provincial cities. Books can also be included along with furniture and other household belongings in almost any general sale. In these cases, however, the advance warning can be brief and perfunctory; the advertisements for the auction may simply mention 'books' and the catalogues are sometimes no better, with lot after lot listed just as 'a collection of (any number) books'.

All auctions allow the goods to be viewed, usually on the day before and the morning of the sale. It is essential to see what you intend to bid for, particularly at auctions in which books are not the most important items or where they are poorly catalogued. Those auction houses which hold regular book sales will have examined the books themselves and will describe them fairly carefully, if briefly, in the catalogue. Imperfect copies will be noted or there will be strong hints that something is wrong by statements that a lot is to be sold 'with all faults' or is 'not subject to return'. Nevertheless, even the best auctioneers make mistakes and a careful check of the bibliographical details including author, title, date, edition and collation should always be carried out before bidding. The reason for such careful checking depends on one of the essential differences between buying from a dealer and from an auction. If a book from a dealer turns out to be anything other than its description in the catalogue, or its verbal description by the dealer, the buyer has a legal right to a refund of the full purchase price. Exactly the opposite applies to goods bought at auction and the small print in sale catalogues goes to some length to point out that descriptions of lots are opinions only, that the auctioneer cannot be held responsible for the descriptions, and the goods carry no guarantee whatsoever.

The necessity for viewing, then, let alone attending the sale and waiting for your lot to be called, would appear to rule out auctions for any librarian working outside London. The solution is to contact one of the many dealers, and particularly one of the long-established firms, who accept commissions to bid on your behalf for specific lots. The commissioned dealer would then attend the viewing, report any imperfections and suggest a reasonable price for your chosen lot, and attend the sale to bid for you. Before the sale you would have made clear what the upper limit of your bid was to be although the dealer would, of course, try to buy the lot for as low a price as possible. Once such arrangements are seen to be working and trust has been established it may be possible for the dealer to bid higher than your limit at his discretion. The normal charge for this service is 10 per cent of the hammer price. An alternative to commissioning a dealer, if you are satisfied about the nature and condition of a lot, is to send in a postal bid to the auction house. Sale catalogues include a blank form for this purpose. There is no charge for the service and lots will be bought for the lowest price below your limit.

The practice of selling goods in lots can be a nuisance because the auctioneers, understandably, tend to include a few dull titles with one or two more interesting books. Most buyers would inevitably be bidding for the interesting books and would have no use whatsoever for the rest of the lot. Occasionally there can be pleasant surprises when a purchase is delivered to the library and one of the dull titles in the lot turns out to be not dull at all.

There are some hidden costs in buying at auctions. To begin with, unlike dealers' catalogues which are free, sale catalogues have to be paid for and the annual subscription for the complete range of sales that include books or manuscripts at one of the large London houses, for example, was £212 in 1990. Second, successful bids incur a buyer's premium of 10 per cent on the hammer price and Value Added Tax is payable on the premium. Thus, if bidding through a dealer to a limit of £200, a successful bid would cost £20 for the dealer's commission, £20 buyer's premium and £3 VAT, making a total of £243. Finally, delivery and insurance charges would probably take the figure over £250.

The third source of acquisition mentioned at the beginning of this section was buying directly from the owner through a private arrangement. The owners are usually private individuals, but it sometimes happens that commercial dealers approach the librarian in this way with a special offer if they think something would be of more benefit in that collection than elsewhere. As before, and in all such instances to follow, the offer can be anything from one book to a whole collection. The approach will be made before the book or books have been listed in a catalogue or advertised for sale. In fact, this element is usually part of the deal – you have been given the chance to buy before anyone else. The price is lower than it will be later because the dealer will get a quicker return for his money, if several books are involved, they will all be sold together rather than piecemeal, and the dealer will be saved the expense of preparing and mailing a catalogue. The dealer cannot wait long for an answer but there is less urgency about the decision than when buying from catalogues.

Offers from private individuals do not happen frequently and negotiations tend to be straightforward because it is very rare to be offered anything of interest and discussions soon come to an end. Awkward moments can arise over prices when the librarian has to explain that what is obviously a priceless heirloom in the eyes of the vendor is worthless to anyone else, nor is its value much enhanced by the inclusion on the end-papers of the owner's family tree. Occasions when valuable and useful books are brought in by a vendor who is also ignorant of their worth happen only on television. The chance of an outsider arriving at the library and wanting to sell precisely the book you have been looking for is obviously remote. The chances are much better from people within the organization – professors on the point of retirement, for example.

The transaction need not begin with the vendor. In the case of professors who are about to retire, the librarian probably knows each of them and through conversations over the years knows not only that some of them have collected books since their student days, but also the high spots of their collections. A few tactful questions from the librarian would soon determine the plans they have for their books.

Donations, the final aspect of acquisition to be considered, are subject to the same drawbacks as unsolicited offers to sell, in that the donor seldom has any idea of matching the gift with your acquisition policy. Much more diplomacy is required in telling a potential donor that the library does not want the books than in saying the same to a prospective vendor. It is imperative, even at the risk of appearing churlish, to explain to the donor that the library cannot always accept everything that is offered. Further-more, if the gift is accepted, the librarian should avoid all preconditions. He or she alone needs to decide whether to keep the collection together, how to catalogue, how to shelve, what to repair, what to discard, and so on. All gifts impose some costs on the library, such as the cost of accessioning, any immediate repairs, and future maintenance. Sometimes these extra costs are sufficiently high to be the main reason for turning down an offer. The same costs should also be kept in mind when deciding on an auction bid, particularly if the books are less than perfect. The earlier suggestion that a bid of £200 is in reality a bid of £250 could easily rise to £500 if extensive conservation work is needed.

The librarian can take a similar initiative in approaching possible donors as was suggested with possible vendors. It may be that what begins as an announcement to a professor on the point of retirement that the library would be in the market if certain items were put on sale, ends with an offer from the owners to present them free of charge. Collectors within the institution or in the local area are often known to the librarian and by making the first move the librarian has already decided that what is being asked for is what is needed and does not conflict with the acquisition policy.

A further method of supplementing a collection almost free of charge, albeit in a modest way, is to use BookNet. The BookNet service is run by the British Library from the Document Supply Centre and is the descendant of the Gift and Exchange Scheme. Librarians send in their discarded books and periodicals to Boston Spa where the material is sorted, classified and lists prepared. Participants receive two free lists every month from which they can request whatever titles they wish to take into stock permanently. The requests are dealt with in the order they are received and the books are then dispatched free to the successful applicants except for a service charge of £3.50 on each item supplied.

CLASSIFICATION, CATALOGUING, RETRIEVAL

Classification and cataloguing

Many of the principles for cataloguing and classifying rare books were agreed by the beginning of this century and what has happened since then has been a gradual refinement of the principles according to the needs of scholarship. An impressive number of refinements and changes came about before scholarship made its demands, so that it was the application of cataloguing and classifying in bibliographies which opened up lines of enquiry and research never attempted or never even possible before.

The problems are tackled here, by and large, in chronological sequence beginning with incunables. Incunables have always been seen as a separate category, different to all other printed books, and because printing with movable type began in Germany, German bibliographers have tended to concentrate on the earliest period, but important work has also been achieved by other scholars. By 1908 the British Museum had begun the *Catalogue of Books Printed in the Fifteenth Century now in the British Museum* which was based on the work of Robert Proctor and particularly on his *Index to the Early Printed Books in the British Museum from the Invention of Printing to the year 1500*, 1898. Proctor aimed to show how printing had spread through Europe, or to describe 'the natural history' of early printing, and for this purpose he arranged the books chronologically by country, town and printer. This arrangement became standard for incunables and is known as 'Proctor order'. Proctor established the sequence by close analysis of the typography of the books and it was this method of treating books as historical artefacts, each one obviously holding a text, but also holding historical evidence in its physical make-up, which has formed one of the cornerstones of bibliographical investigation.

Methods of bibliographical description for later periods were then devised by several scholars but most notably by Walter W. Greg, Fredson Bowers and G. Thomas Tanselle. They were all concerned with the accuracy of the descriptions and were attempting to provide written accounts of books which could be used, as far as possible, as substitutes for the original copies. In this way a scholar with access to only one copy of a particular book could use the bibliographical descriptions of similar copies elsewhere to decide if all copies were identical or to isolate copies in which there were likely to be variations in the text.

Once the descriptive method was established it was possible to arrange descriptions in some classified order to bring out certain features of the books, in the same way that Robert Proctor illustrated the expansion of printing from Germany through the arrangement of the catalogue entries. The simplest examples are found in author bibliographies which are often arranged chronologically to show the development of the author's work, such as D. Gallup *T.S. Eliot: a Bibliography*, 1969; and Richard L. Purdy *Thomas Hardy: a Bibliographical Study*, 1954. Similar results can be obtained through the use of indexes and David F. Foxon's *English Verse 1701–1750*, 1975, for example, includes a complete volume of indexes of first lines, chronology, imprints, bibliographical notabilia, descriptive epithets and subjects.

At the same time as work on cataloguing or bibliographical descriptions was proceeding attempts were being made at comprehensive listings of every known title within certain catagories. The best known of these are the various short-title catalogues: A.W. Pollard and G.R. Redgrave, *A short-title Catalogue of Books Printed in England, Scotland and Ireland, and of English Books printed Abroad, 1475–1640*, 2nd edition, 1976–(in progress); D.G. Wing, *Short-title Catalogue of Books Printed in England, Scotland, Ireland, Wales and British America, and of English Books printed in Other Countries, 1641–1700*, 2nd edition, 3 volumes, 1972–1988; and now the *Eighteenth Century Short-title Catalogue* and the *Nineteenth Century Short-title Catalogue* about which more will be mentioned later. The aim of comprehensiveness and the large number of titles involved in all these catalogues made it impossible to give full bibliographical descriptions as well. There have, however, been a few attempts to do both, for example, *Gesamtkatalog der Wiegendrucke*, 8 vols, 1925–40.

All the above examples and many others besides are now standard reference works. There is therefore no necessity for full descriptions of more copies of books which have already been described and it is normal simply to give the basic details and to include a reference to a standard work. If a particular copy differs from all existing descriptions, then of course, a full bibliographical account is required.

Retrieval

The use of computers for retrieval has completely changed previous methods. Huge amounts of bibliographical data on out of print books are already held in computer stores and more records are added every day. There has been no attempt as yet to store full bibliographical descriptions, but in the last ten years there have been great advances in the enumerative records.

The immediate advantage of searching an electronic database is that all the intricacies and limitations of printed indexes become superfluous. Each search is unique and search terms can be combined or excluded at will so that the arrangement of entries, such as Proctor order, or printed indexes, such as the array in Foxton's bibliography mentioned above, would be merely starting points. Furthermore the answers to electronic searches can be produced in seconds and the vast amount of information available for investigation would be quite impossible to assemble together using any other method.

One database in particular, that of the *Eighteenth century short-title catalogue (ESTC)*, has been an outstanding success. After several years of planning, work began in 1977 to enter the records of all eighteenth-century books and printed documents held in the British Library after each copy had been examined and re-catalogued. Records have continued to be added and up-dated ever since at the British Library and also at the University of California. In 1990, thirteen years after the project began, new records were still being added at a rate of about 2000 each month and the file contained a total of over 261 000 records.[2] The holdings of eighteenth-century printed material in many libraries throughout the world are now included.

The success of *ESTC* suggested a similar scheme for incunables and since 1982 the *Incunable short-title catalogue* has been available online. *ISTC* has a file of slightly less than 23000 records.

Some academic library catalogues are accessible electronically through JANET (Joint Academic Network) as OPACS (Online Public Access Catalogues) although they seldom include many out of print titles and often simply list the current loan stock. However, a much more important source, the catalogue of the British Library, is also accessible online through Blaise. The complete catalogue is not yet in the database but in early 1900 all records from A to Saint (more than 2.8 million entries) were included and new entries are added regularly. The British Library catalogue is also in the process of being published on CD-ROM[3] and *ESTC* and *ISTC* are under consideration to appear in this form.

Online union catalogues of out of print material are also available. The *ESTC* is probably the most comprehensive within the limits of its historical period although the American OCLC (Online Computer Library Center Inc.) claims to be 'the world's largest bibliographic database' with 22.1 million entries. The file is a union catalogue of the holdings of over 10 000 libraries.[4]

The *Nineteenth Century Short-title Catalogue (NSTC)* differs in several respects from the sources mentioned so far. In the first place, when complete it will undoubtedly be the largest of the short-title catalogues and for this reason alone would seem to be potentially the best candidate for computer storage and retrieval. The plans, however, are to publish in print only. Second, the results have become available very quickly, as work on the project did not begin until 1983 and already seventeen large volumes have appeared. Third, the work is being compiled at Newcastle University but the whole project is being published commercially by Avero Publications. Fourth, the information is being taken directly from the catalogues of a group of large libraries rather than from copies of the books themselves because, it was argued, a start had to be made quickly and to examine millions of copies would have swamped the scheme. This last factor, together with the lack of computer access, would appear to reduce the usefulness of the project to an unacceptable level. Nevertheless, in general the work has been well received and the argument that it is only a starting point, and that is better than nothing at all has been accepted.[5]

CONTROL OF USE

Closed access is the only moderately secure system for a valuable collection of out of print books. The size, rarity and value of the collection will determine the degree of security measures taken but a full range of precautions would include the following.

Areas of the library where the public are not allowed must be made inaccessible by doors which are kept locked with as few keys as possible issued to known members of staff. Both members of staff and readers must be issued with passes including a photograph of the owner. Staff passes should be worn like badges visible at all times and should be obviously different from readers' passes. Readers' passes should have an expiry date, two to five years after the date of issue, and nobody must be allowed into the reading room without showing a pass.

The readers should fill in application forms for books, the top copy to be retained by the library and another copy returned to the reader when the book is brought back to the issue desk. All books and documents must be examined when they are returned by the reader. If fire precautions allow there should be only one entrance to the reading room controlled by, and under the observation of, the issue desk. Bags or cases should not be allowed in the reading room and on leaving, the reader's personal books and papers must be checked.

The reading room itself should be as open as possible with no pillars or corners which could create areas not visible from the issue desk. Large windows through which the readers can be seen from outside the reading room are an added deterrant. There should be no access to toilets from inside the reading room.

All books, and preferably all documents, must be clearly marked as belonging to the library. The marks should be obvious to the readers and should be made with indelible ink. Indelible marks on books are regrettable but the damage can be kept to a minimum by making them fairly small and by avoiding important pages such as the title-page; the verso of the title-page or a similar regularly marked page in the preliminaries may be an acceptable compromise.

Considering the building as a whole, all outside doors and windows must be secure and particular attention must be given to any doors or windows in quiet side alleys away from a main thoroughfare. If possible the whole building should be clearly lit from the outside at night so that people approaching or leaving are visible. The local police are always willing to help with advice on security and should always be consulted.

If a thief or vandal is caught the advice of the police would undoubtedly be to prosecute. Unfortunately the experience is usually every bit as harrowing for the librarian as the thief, with the librarian almost inevitably forced to play a ruthless, unbending, pitiless role. Even more disturbing is the fact that the majority of thefts are committed by members of staff.[6] Trust nobody from the part-time cleaners to the security staff to the chief librarian!

CONSERVATION AND PRESERVATION

Throughout the 1980s conservation has been very popular and treated with great respect among librarians. A vast literature on the subject has grown up, some of it excellent and much of it technical and scientific. Despite the popularity and all that has been written there is still a great deal of uncertainty and it is still difficult for librarians to know what to do in a given situation.

Even the title of the subject is misunderstood. Conservation means the process of making [a book] safe and reasonably stable. Preservation means the process of keeping [a book] in a reasonably stable condition. It is possible to speak only of reasonable stability because all books, being mainly organic, will one day rot away.

The causes of deterioration can be internal or external to the book. In general, internal causes need some conservation work by an expert and external causes can be dealt with by the librarian. Causes of deterioration, whether internal or external, can be due to chemical, physical or biological factors. The chemical factors are chiefly the presence of acid and the action of ultra-violet light. The main physical factors are the effects of temperature, humidity and dust. The main biological factors are the action of fungi, insects, rodents and other small mammals, readers and librarians. Each factor has its remedy and they will be considered in turn below. After the causes of deterioration have been considered the techniques for repairing books will be discussed.

The most difficult problem for the librarian in dealing with acidic books is knowing that they are acidic in the first place. Acid can be present internally in brand new books in the paper or the binding materials and this has been increasingly common at least since the early nineteenth century. As with all factors causing deterioration, the action of acids is fairly slow in human terms and even the worst examples of acidic paper will last for twenty-five years or more. When new, of course, the paper looks like any other paper, but then it will lose its flexibility, become brittle and finally crumble to pieces. But the whole process takes many years and there will be no dramatic sudden changes. The problem for the librarian is that there is nothing to see at first and the loss of flexibility will not normally be noticed. It is not until the paper has reached the brittle stage that it becomes clear that something is wrong. Another warning sign of acid is that paper will gradually become discoloured if it contains lignin from wood pulp. A yellow tinge will become apparent which will slowly deepen to light brown as the paper becomes brittle.

There is no simple rule for the detection of acid in books but loss of flexibility and yellowing become easier to recognize with practice. Acid is also more prevalent in nineteenth and early twentieth-century books than in older ones. It was then that new materials and methods were introduced in papermaking that seemed to be advantageous at the time but the long-term effects of which could not be foreseen. There are scientific methods for the measurement of acids in books which involve the use of either chemical tests or pH meters. The methods are not difficult but they are so far removed from the day to day activities of ordinary librarians and they are required so infrequently as to be not worth the trouble. In most libraries they are not necessary and should be left to trained conservators.

Acid makes the librarian's life still more complicated because it can be transferred from one place to another and can migrate into acid-free books. Neutral paper in books can be contaminated by acidic binding materials, inserted press cuttings, book plates, neighbouring acidic books and a host of other sources. It is important therefore to remove the source of the acid or at least to isolate acidic books from the rest of the stock. Isolation is most easily achieved by putting each acidic book in its own acid-free box and returning it to its usual place on the shelf.

There are several reliable methods for removing acid from books and new ones are under development. Some do-it-yourself methods are available which give only temporary protection and all the methods which provide something approaching permanent protection have to be carried out by qualified conservators. There is a pressing need to discover a method by which large numbers of books can be treated in bulk, quickly, safely and cheaply. Ideally the bulk method should provide paper strengthening as well as deacidification because simple deacidification leaves the paper just as brittle as it was before treatment. The ideal sounds as if it would be an impossibility but progress is being made and there is a good expectation that the ideal will be achieved. The most encouraging results have been achieved using the process of graft co-polymerization[7] which is being developed by the British Library and the University of Sussex.

The second factor causing books to deteriorate which was mentioned above was the action of ultra-violet light. Besides causing the colours of bindings to fade, ultra-violet light also starts a chemical reaction in paper with results similar to those due to the presence of acid – the paper slowly becomes brittle and discoloured. Ultra-violet light is present to some extent in all light visible to humans so it is not possible to protect books completely from its effects. The damage can be kept to an acceptable minimum by taking a few simple precautions. Relatively high levels of ultra-violet light are emitted from fluorescent tubes used for lighting but plastic shields can be fitted which effectively reduce the levels. Books should never be stored in direct sunlight and if they cannot be moved, the windows can be fitted with protective plastic film or painted with clear protective varnish. None of these shielding methods is permanent and the treatment for windows is expensive. A cheap solution for windows is simply to fit blinds.

The harmful effects of temperature and humidity, two of the physical causes of deterioration, operate together. High humidity weakens water-soluble glue in bindings and also provides good conditions for the growth of fungus, while low humidity drives out moisture from paper making it less flexible. Either of these conditions combined with high temperature exacerbates the effects caused by the level of humidity and also speeds up all chemical reactions. Only low temperature is beneficial to books. For the storage of books the recommended temperature is between 16° and 20° C (or 60° and 68° F) with relative humidity between 50 and 60 per cent and the best way to achieve these recommendations is through an air conditioning system. The best air conditioning systems not only control temperature and humidity but also extract dust, although the dust extraction must be done either by activated carbon or ceramic pellets.

Temperature and humidity should be measured and recorded whether or not the library has air conditioning. The most satisfactory procedure is to use a thermohygrograph which constantly records both figures. The records are important because they show patterns of change which would not otherwise be noticed, for example, a steep rise in temperature every Friday evening in summer when the air conditioning is turned off, a similar steep rise in humidity every Friday evening in winter, and so on.

If there is no air conditioning the first priority is to avoid high temperatures in order to reduce the possible damage from the wrong humidity and to slow down harmful chemical reactions. Having brought the temperature down to an acceptable level the next priority is to avoid fluctuations in either temperature or humidity. Such fluctuations cause the books to expand or contract as the changes take place and consequently the bindings are under constant strain. It is therefore better to settle for a steady temperature or humidity outside the recommended figures rather than to aim for a recommended level and to keep missing. Humidity can be controlled by portable humidifiers and an even cheaper answer may be simply to keep the room well ventilated. Problems with humidity can also sometimes be alleviated by fitting double glazing.

Few libraries will be equipped with automatic dust extractors and those without must therefore rely on dusting and cleaning by hand. There is little point in redistributing dust inside the library by flicking it off the tops of books with cloth or feather dusters and the use of small hand-held vacuum cleaners is much more efficient. It is important to remove dust from books because it causes discolouration of the pages, it is an abrasive and can damage the pages and the sewing in the bindings, and a layer of dust holds moisture on the surface of books.

Fungus was the first of the biological factors mentioned above which cause deterioration. Even when fungus has been removed from paper it often leaves a persistent stain and the fungus itself can be very difficult to eradicate because each plant releases millions of microscopic spores into the air which can lie dormant for long periods of time until the right conditions and germination occur.

The presence of fungus in books can attract insects that feed on the fungus. The larval stage is probably the most dangerous because the larvae, like small caterpillars, eat the fungus growing on the pages but, of course, they do not stop at the fungus and eat the paper as well. There are more than 160 species of beetle with such larvae, usually known as 'book worms'. A further problem with all small organisms like fungi and insects is that they have a short life cycle and therefore over the years there is an accumulation of debris from decomposing dead bodies. Eradication of either fungus or insects usually requires the help of experts.

Small mammals, and particularly mice, rats and cats, can be even more destructive of books. Mice and rats build nests by tearing up paper if they have access to it, and all three animals excrete, give birth and die wherever they choose. Cats, being the largest, are the easiest to keep out but it is necessary to maintain basement doors and windows to ensure that there are no gaps large enough to provide an entrance. Small holes which could be used by mice and rats should also be blocked although the professionals should be called in for any infestation no matter how insignificant it appears to be.

Book repairs

Repairs become necessary as a result of disasters, normal ageing and the wear and tear of use. It is, however, neither possible nor desirable to repair everything and the librarian must decide which books to try to keep and which to allow to wear away. The decision, of course, must be taken in light of the acquisition policy. Other considerations before deciding are the cost of repair compared with the cost of replacement, and the possibility of using a copy or a later edition as a substitute. The money which has been set aside for repairs must also be used to the best advantage and it will sometimes be preferable to pay for several small repairs rather than a few big ones.

If possible some money should be saved for emergencies. The need for a disaster plan is now widely accepted and there are special requirements for books during the clean-up operation after a disaster has happened. The main hazards are fire and flood, and in a fire, smoke damage and the water used to extinguish the flames usually cause as much trouble as the fire itself.

The sheer numbers of books involved in a disaster is often the first obstacle. The stock should already have been graded according to value and the most valuable should be dealt with first but this could still run to thousands of books. Very wet books can be frozen in order to hold them in a stable state. Work can then be carried out on them one by one at a later date when the initial urgency has passed. Books which have not had a soaking can be dried by standing them upright with the pages fanned out. To speed up the drying, fanned out books can be placed in a make-shift wind tunnel constructed by hanging a plastic sheet over a line and using an electric fan to direct a current of cold air underneath. Special care must be taken with wet art or coated paper because if the sheets are allowed to dry in contact with each other the surfaces will bond together and be impossible to separate. A useful pamphlet on the clean-up operation is Peter Waters, *Procedures for Salvage of Water-damaged Library Materials*. Once these initial emergency procedures are complete most wet, smoke-stained and damaged books will need to be dealt with by trained conservators.

When arranging with conservators for less urgent repairs caused by ageing or careless use the following recommendations should be kept in mind. Each repair should be only the minimum necessary to prevent further deterioration. Sometimes damaged books which are not in frequent use do not need to be repaired at all. Books with broken bindings can be kept in acid-free boxes and detached boards can be kept with the book by tying round with unbleached tape. Re-bind only as a last resort.

No attempt must be made to 'restore' a book to its original state but at the same time repairs must not radically change the appearance or structure. Thus, a book issued in paper boards should remain in paper boards and should not be re-bound in full leather to give it a 'better' or more expensive binding. It would be just as mistaken to try to save money by replacing original full leather with a cloth binding.

All materials used for repairs should be of good quality and free from acid. All repair procedures carried out should be reversible and easily removed without causing further damage to the original. As much of the original as possible should be preserved, for example, an original leather spine can sometimes be removed intact from a damaged binding which can then be replaced over the new leather spine. All repairs must be weaker than the original so that under stress the repair would break before the original.

Trinity College, Dublin, have published an excellent pamphlet, *Preserving our Printed Heritage*, on their non-stop conservation programme.

IMPORTANT COLLECTIONS

Britain has an overwhelming range of important collections of out of print books, the full extent of which still remains to be discovered. The British Library and the national libraries of Scotland and Wales contain the official collections but there are hundreds of other libraries with collections of national importance. Some idea of the scope and variety of institutions where the books are to be found can be seen from the introduction to the Library Association's *Directory of Rare Book and Special Collections* which includes 'collections wherever they have been located in public and national libraries, in libraries of universities, colleges and schools, cathedrals and churches, societies and institutes, and a limited number of private libraries where there is likely to be some continuity or permanence'.[8] The range of types of library is mirrored in the subjects collected and it can be seen from the subject indexes to the library guides mentioned below that the areas of knowledge covered are almost without limit.

In this chapter there would obviously be little purpose in picking out any collections for special mention from such a vast range. There are several published guides to collections which contain sufficient information for most needs and which include the following selection.

Moelwyn I. Williams (ed.), *A Directory of Rare Book and Special Collections in the United Kingdom and the Republic of Ireland* London: Library Association, 1985.

Aslib, *Aslib Directory of Information Sources in the United Kingdom* ed. E.M. Codlin, London: Aslib, vol. 1 *Science, technology and commerce*, 5th edn, 1982; vol. 2 *Social sciences, medicine and the humanities*, 5th edn, 1984.

Libraries, Museums and Art Galleries Year Book, Cambridge: James Clarke, intermittent publication.

British Library, *Guide to Government Department and Other Libraries*, 28th edn, London: British Library, 1988.

Paul Morgan, *Oxford Libraries Outside the Bodleian: a Guide*, 2nd edn, Oxford: Bodleian Library, 1980.

An attempt is underway to list the subject strengths of all libraries and to indicate the level of collecting in those subjects at the present time. The system was developed in the United States in the late 1970s and is known as Conspectus. Conspectus data for Britain is being co-ordinated at the British Library and some information is available now. When the scheme is in full operation it will be possible to list collections within a given geographical area at, say, 'research' level in any subject, or to list all the collections in Britain at 'comprehensive' level in a given subject, and so on.

BIBLIOGRAPHY

General works

R. Cave, *Rare Book Librarianship*, 2nd edn, London: Bingley, 1982.
M.V. Cloonan (ed.), 'Recent trends in rare book librarianship', *Library Trends*, **36** (1), Summer 1987.
A.M. Scham, *Managing Special Collections*, New York: Neal-Schuman, 1987.

General periodicals

Antiquarian Book Monthly Review
The Book Collector
The Library
Library Association, Rare Books Group, *Newsletter*
Papers of the Bibliographical Society of America
Studies in bibliography

Acquisition

General policy

E. Futas (ed.), *Library Acquisition Policies and Procedures*, 2nd edn, Phoenix: Oryx Press, 1984.
G.E. Gorman and B.R. Howes, *Collection Development for Libraries*, London: Bowker-Saur, 1989.

Bookselling guides

Sheppard's Book Dealers in the British Isles, Old Wokingham: Martins Publishers, 1989.
Driff's Guide to all the Secondhand and Antiquarian Bookshops in Britain, London: Driffield, 1984.
Provincial Booksellers Fairs Association, *Membership List 1989–1990*, Cambridge: PBFA, 1990.

Classification, cataloguing, retrieval

F. Bowers, *Principles of Bibliographical Description*, Princeton, NJ: Princeton University Press, 1949.
M.J. Crump, *Searching ESTC: Factotum* Occasional paper No 6, January 1989.

W.W. Greg, *Collected Papers*, Oxford: OUP, 1966.

G. Groom, 'Bibliographies of older material', in G.L. Higgens (ed.) *Printed Reference Material*, 2nd edn, London: Library Association, 1984, pp. 454–501.

G.T. Tanselle, 'Descriptive bibliography and library cataloguing', *Studies in bibliography*, 30, 1977, 1–56.

G.T. Tanselle, 'A sample bibliographical description, with commentary', *Studies in bibliography*, 40, 1987, 1–30.

Factotum is the newsletter of the *ESTC* which often contains articles of general interest for librarians.

Control of use

L.J. Fennelly, *Museum, Archive and Library Security*, London: Butterworth, 1983.

Conservation, preservation

General works

A.D. Baynes-Cope, *Caring for Books and Documents*, 2nd edn, London: British Museum, 1989.

G.M. and D.G. Cunha, *Conservation of Library Material*, 2nd ed, Metuchen, NJ: Scarecrow Press, 1971, 2 vols.

F.W. Ratcliffe, *Preservation Policies and Conservation in British Libraries*, London: British Library, 1984.

S.G. Swartzburg (ed.), *Conservation in the Library: a Handbook of Use and Care of Traditional and Non-traditional Materials*, London: Aldwych Press, 1983.

S.G. Swartzburg, *Preserving Library Materials: a Manual*, Metuchen, NJ: Scarecrow Press, 1980.

G. Thompson, *Museum Environment*, London: Butterworth, 1978.

A. Wilson, *Library Policy for Preservation and Conservation in the European Community*, Munich: Saur, 1988.

Repairs and bookbinding

S.A. Buchanan, *Disaster Planning: Preparedness and Recovery for Libraries and Archives*, Paris: Unesco, 1988.

C.C. Morrow and C. Dyal, *Conservation Treatment Procedures: a Manual of Step-by-step Procedures for the Maintenance and Repair of Library Materials*, 2nd edn, Littleton, Colo: Libraries Unlimited, 1986.

Trinity College, Dublin, *Preserving our Printed Heritage: the Long Room Project at Trinity College Dublin*, Dublin: Trinity College, 1988.

P. Waters, *Procedures for Salvage of Water-damaged Library Materials*, 2nd edn, Washington: Library of Congress, 1979.

Important collections

See the directories listed on p. 46 and

A. Matheson, 'Conspectus in the United Kingdom' *Alexandria* **1** (1) 1989, 51–9.

NOTES

1 See, for example, E. Futas (ed.), *Library Acquisition Policies and Procedures*, 2nd edn, Phoenix: Oryx Press, 1984, or G.E. Gorman and B.R. Howes, *Collection Development for Libraries*, Munich: Bowker-Sauer, 1989.

2 All Blaise file statistics were obtained from Blaise Help Desk in March 1990.

3 Available from Chadwyck-Healey at £9000.

4 OCLC *Annual Report*, January 1990.

5 See, for example, C. Hurst, 'Tackling the big one: cataloguing the books of the nineteenth century: a review article', *Journal of Librarianship* **18** (1), January 1986, 71–7.

6 M.P. Wyly, 'Special collections security: problems, trends, and consciousness', *Library Trends* **36** (1), Summer 1987, *Recent Trends in Rare Book Librarianship*, 241–56.

7 M.L. Burstall, C.E. Butler and C.C. Mollett, 'Improving the properties of paper by graft copolymerisation', *Paper Conservator* **10**, 1986, 95–100.

8 Directory of Rare Book and Special Collections, Library Association, page x.

3

Newspapers

EVE JOHANSSON*

THE MATERIAL AND ITS PROBLEMS

Newspapers as a part of a library's stock are characterized above all by their large size, difficulties of handling and storage, the preservation problems created by cheap, wood-pulp based paper, and their immense popularity as research material. The sight of vast, decaying volumes in inadequate storage, impossible to clean; of fragments of brown paper on the floor; and of libraries struggling to cope with demand and the rate of growth of the current stock, are only too familiar. Since the growth of interest in local history and the expansion of academic research in the 1960s, newspapers have been a heavily-used source of information, covering as they do all subject fields, and providing a record of the ordinary life of communities which speaks more directly to the future researcher than any other original source material. They are used by a public which is wider than that for any other source material, for interests ranging from local history to sport, fashion, theatre, hobbies and puzzles. Whether in a public library with a collection of local newspapers or an academic library with an international research collection, they attract an enthusiasm from their users that is not often found, and heavy use compounds the problems of handling, exploiting and preserving this invaluable part of our heritage. In professional terms, newspapers have attracted lively interest in recent years.

Two other characteristics, less immediately apparent except to those who

* I am grateful for help and comments to Geoffrey Hamilton, Geoff Smith, Stephen Lester, Mike Western and Kelvin Ithell at the British Library Newspaper Library, Dr Ann Matheson of the National Library of Scotland, Dr Lionel Madden at the National Library of Wales, Julian Roberts at the Bodleian Library, Oxford, Dr Fred Ratcliffe at Cambridge University Library and Peter Fox at Trinity College, Dublin.

work closely with newspapers, are the absence of satisfactory indexes to most of them and the difficulty of adopting a subject approach to the material: it is usually necessary for the user to hunt through long runs of material for what he requires (finding innumerable compelling distractions as he does so).

ACQUISITION

Issues of selection as well as acquisition are covered in the following comments. A library's selection of newspapers for stock is an integral part of its general collecting policy, and will depend crucially on its degree of specialization. Newspapers, unlike most other materials, are selected both for their information content (reporting of news, share price information, arts and book reviews, for instance) and for their inherent significance as a primary record of the national life and development of different countries, and in both ways will complement a library's other stock. In selecting, whether current titles or retrospectively, information is required on both aspects: first, an expert assessment of their reliability and coverage is needed; second, assessment of their political stance, circulation and geographical coverage, and even design. This information is difficult to assemble for many parts of the world. No single published source provides it. *The Encyclopaedia of the World's Press* (see Bibliography), although published in 1982 and now out of date, provides an interesting historical commentary on the principal established titles and figures for circulation, and remains the only such guide. The most comprehensive current guide is *Benn's Media Directory*, but it does not give sufficient information about circulation figures, and is intended to serve more as a guide to advertisers than as a library reference tool. Help from experts and library users is an essential part of selection decisions, and it is possible, particularly in academic libraries, to enlist the help of visiting scholars or of the institution's own researchers when they are visiting other countries.

A vital aspect of selection is the question whether to purchase the original newspapers or microfilm. Selection and preservation decisions are interrelated. If the newspapers that are acquired are intended to be part of the permanent stock, and if microfilm is the library's preservation medium, it is usually more economic for a library to purchase microfilm originally as its only copy rather than to pay the double costs of purchase of paper originals and preservation microfilming or the purchase of replacement microfilm later. A decision will depend on the speed with which titles are required and speed of supply of microfilm from a commercial source or a national library or equivalent in the country of origin. In the UK, film of many UK current titles is quickly available from the British Library bureaux that are filming for the newspaper publisher or a library. For overseas newspapers, where speedy supply of the original is expensive, the larger commercial micropublishers and some library sources can supply some titles within months of publication. Microfilm is normally the only practical means of acquiring back files of newspapers, and it is increasingly easily available.

There are many suppliers, both in the UK and overseas. They divide into:

   (i)   micropublishers, selling widely from a regular list of titles (though sometimes quite small companies)
 (ii)   microfilming bureaux whose principal business is in the supply of a service to microfilm documents, and who sell copy film as a by-product of their main activity
(iii)   libraries which are microfilming and sell their film, and
(iv)   individual newspapers or newspaper groups.

In the UK the library suppliers are many, including the British Library Newspaper Library and others, particularly county libraries, which can supply film of current titles or back files. In addition, newspaper publishers are often able to supply, either on a current basis or back files. Today about 1000 titles are filmed currently by the British Library Newspaper Library, and over 800 by other bodies. Overseas, the national library in a particular country may have a regular microfilming activity and sell its film, the major micropublishers such as Research Publications Inc. and University Microfilms Inc. have lists of their titles, and the Library of Congress in Washington, DC and the Centre for Research Libraries in Chicago are reliable and extensive suppliers of film of other countries' newspapers on a standing order basis.

There is unfortunately no single comprehensive listing of microfilm suppliers or of the microfilm available. The directories listed in the Bibliography at the end of this chapter are not complete. All titles filmed by the British Library Newspaper Library are listed in its catalogue of microfilm (see Bibliography) and the Newspaper Library is happy to help with information about sources of other titles. However, the British Library's *Register of Microform Masters* does not include the Newspaper Library's catalogue of microfilm, nor the microfilm of newspapers made by many other agencies. The Library of Congress *Newspapers in microform* is not being kept up-to-date, and the Meckler *Microforms in print*, though its coverage of UK titles is good, is not comprehensive.

Where UK newspapers are concerned, the acquisitions needs of most libraries will be met by an order to an ordinary newsagent, who can delivery directly. The most difficult newspapers to identify and acquire will be the less well-established free or community newspapers, which spring up, merge and cease publication in a way that the established local 'paid-for' titles do not. There is no easy way of discovering which new titles are appearing, circulation managers are not used to handling subscriptions or dealing with requests for missing issues, and titles are bought and merge in a confusing way. Most libraries find that it is essential to enlist the help of staff resident in the areas of circulation, to report and bring in copies of new titles, and even to keep and donate the copies delivered to their homes, and are resigned to gaps in sets so long as representative coverage of their areas is achieved. The libraries collecting community newspapers from larger areas, such as the National Library of Scotland and the National Library of Wales, ask staff on visits to other libraries to look out for new titles. Deposit in the British Library is impossible to secure.

For acquisition of overseas newspapers, the librarian faces a choice between an ordinary order with a local newsagent, direct subscription for paper copy with the newspaper publisher, and the use of a subscription agent. The decision depends on the speed of supply required, costs, and the degree of specialization of the library. As to costs, it is difficult to give general guidance beyond saying that they have to be investigated case by case. A regular order to a local newsagent, particularly in London, may be the most economical and reliable source of the national newspapers of the US and the European and Commonwealth countries, depending on the newsagents' charges, and many are happy to supply particularly if a library is a valued customer for other newspapers such as circulation copies. Local newsagents however can probably not supply the less well-known titles, and direct subscription to the newspaper publisher may be necessary. Subscription charges vary. The customer can usually choose between bulk mailing (for instance, of a month's issues), the cheapest form of supply, and mailing by air of single issues. Unfortunately, not all newspapers have efficient and service-oriented subscription departments: library subscriptions are probably a minor interest to them. There is a case for using a specialist library agent in another country if a library's collecting needs are particularly specialized, for instance in covering countries where on-the-spot knowledge about new titles is needed (South Africa at the present time is an example). For the regular running of an order, use of an agent has the advantages that missing issues will be checked and claimed by him and that invoicing and payment will be more efficient (sterling invoices can be requested, and the costs of newspapers included on invoices for other materials), but there may be delays in processing, so this method is probably not suitable where speed of availability to the user is a priority.

The processing of newspaper acquisitions is usually straightforward, though typically it demands more space and larger working surfaces than the ordinary book and periodical intake, but it should be remembered that missing issues need to be claimed as quickly as possible, and that checking of microfilm purchases is essential. Newspaper publishers consider their product as ephemeral, and do not keep stocks of back issues. Microfilm acquisition can be specialized work: it is important to know your suppliers and to keep in touch with them. Microfilming bureaux may change ownership and newspapers or libraries may change the bureaux they use. It is of the greatest importance to check film quality from any but the best-known suppliers, as soon as film is received, on a sample basis if need be. Frame-by-frame checking is probably impossible for most busy acquisitions sections. The contents of boxes should be checked against the labels, at both the start and the end of the reel, and the run checked for completeness and for breaks at appropriate dates. The film should be inspected with the naked eye for any signs of spotting, water damage, flecks in silver halide film, or incorrect practices such as the splicing of the user copy of a film or the presence of rubber bands (which should always be replaced by acid-free paper tags). Finally, sample reels should be examined on the microfilm reader for gaps, errors such as pages filmed upside down, legibility, exposure, lighting and reduction (see also p. 64) and general neatness. All faults should be followed up with the supplier, and replacement reels requested where necessary: suppliers are usually helpful, and value their reputation for quality.

An incorrectly-labelled box not identified as soon as it is received will create a problem that it may not be possible to solve a few years later: and if there has been a decline in the overall quality of a supplier's or a bureau's product it is essential that it be spotted soon.

CLASSIFICATION, CATALOGUING AND RETRIEVAL

Storage requirements alone normally mean that newspapers will be kept as a physically separate stock, so that library classification systems do not apply. Typically, they are housed as part of the local studies collection in a public library or as part of an area studies collection in an academic library.

There are no generally-accepted rules for the cataloguing of newspapers. A good general guide, though it is not intended as a set of cataloguing rules, is the *International Guidelines for the Cataloguing of Newspapers*, produced by the IFLA Working Group on Newspapers and published by the IFLA UBCIM office in 1989. The Library of Congress published its

Newspaper Cataloguing Manual for the guidance of the very important US Newspaper Program in 1984, but it is not generally used elsewhere. Some libraries in the UK have adopted the practices of the British Library, which still uses the former British Museum cataloguing rules (last revised in 1961); but these are now quite inadequate for the complexities of cataloguing holdings of originals and microfilm. The Anglo-American Cataloguing Rules for serials are not felt by those responsible for the larger collections to be appropriate for newspaper work: in particular, newspaper specialists generally prefer the principle of single entry, with all changes of title reflected in one entry, to that of successive entry contained in the AACR rules, and the IFLA *Guidelines* reflect this preference.

The cataloguing of newspapers presents difficulties and demands specialist knowledge where changes of title, the complexities of editions and the cataloguing of runs held partly on film and partly in the original are concerned. Changes of title need to be recorded in detail, and may be complex where long runs are held or with some less-established newspapers, particularly free newspapers. It is important to record the popular title of a newspaper where this is not derivable from the masthead. Editions statements involve both editions in the sense of time (earlier and later editions of the same title published in the same place on a single day) and editions in the sense of place (newspapers published in a group, covering different towns, and often with different titles, but containing much of the same copy). It is important to establish which is the 'main' edition, which will generate the main catalogue entry, and the precise relations between editions. The newspaper publishers can often provide information as to what they consider to be the main edition, and this can be important where microfilm made for or in co-operation with the publishers is being catalogued. Microfilm of the local editions as currently published will normally, for reasons of cost, consist of the whole of the main edition but 'change' or 'changed' pages only of the local editions or titles; and it is important that the catalogue directs the user, when he is looking for a 'local' edition, to the title where the rest of the text can be found. (This choice of 'main' entry may not however be that which the librarian would choose as being bibliographically correct: the edition which has been published for the longest time would be preferable in theory.)

Not all libraries will have complex entries, but some examples can be given from the British Library Newspaper Library catalogue:

Bridgewater Journal vol. 1. no. 2–   13 April 1984–   . Wells Somerset 1984–   . Microfilm: 1986 onward

Frome Journal vol. 1 no. 1–   29 May 1980–   . Wells Somerset

1980– . Microfilm: 1986 onward. Changed pages only. A variant edition of *Bridgewater Journal*

The Journal vol. 1 no. 1–vol. 2 no. 17 1 May 1985–26 April 1986 [continued as:] *The Mid Week Journal* vol. 2 no. 18– 3 May 1986– Wells Mid-Somerset Newspapers Ltd. Microfilm: 1986 onwards. Changed pages only. A variant edition of *Bridgewater Journal*

The Mid-week journal vol. 2 no. 18– . 3 May 1986– . *See* The Journal.

Subject access to the contents of newspapers raises extremely difficult sets of questions. Indexes are lacking to many national and most local newspapers. The well-known published indexes, such as those to *The Times* and *Economist*, can be pressed into service to provide dates for tracing nationally-reported events or reviews in other newspapers.

On-line access has made some difference. PROFILE is one host for the principal UK newspapers on line, and includes *The Economist* from December 1981, the *Guardian* from May 1984, *The Financial Times* from January 1985, *The Times* and *Sunday Times* from July 1985, *Today* from March 1986, *The Daily Telegraph* and *Sunday Telegraph* from January 1987, *The Independent* from September 1988 and the *Washington Post* from January 1984. The databases are not full text. Reuter Textline, however is about 85 per cent full text and at the time of writing holds, among other titles, *The Economist*, the *Aberdeen Press and Journal*, the *Belfast Telegraph*, the *Daily Mail*, *Glasgow Herald*, *Liverpool Echo*, *Mail on Sunday*, *Manchester Evening News*, *The Times* and *Sunday Times*, *Western Mail*, and the *Yorkshire Post*.

There exist surprising numbers of indexes to UK local newspapers in libraries: a survey carried out by the British Library Newspaper Library has identified over one thousand; but they differ widely in their coverage and are difficult to maintain. Cuttings services maintained by local newspapers can help, but are not normally accessible to the public.

CONTROL OF USE

Correct handling by staff and users is one of the most important aspects of managing a newspaper collection, and demonstrates the value of having a specialized staff with a knowledge of all aspects of newspapers. Space and appropriate provision of equipment are essential. Large tables and stands for bound volumes are needed: it is much easier to read a large volume on a stand than on a flat table, and it avoids users leaning on volumes and writing their notes on top of a volume. Staff handling heavy volumes in the stacks need adequate space, and large trolleys for moving and delivering them. Security is an important consideration when dealing with copies that are unbound, boxed or parcelled. Newspapers are exceptionally vulnerable to misuse and abuse, which can range from people filling in the crosswords to columns and pages being cut out. Users should be given guidance in the correct handling of volumes and the correct way to open them and turn fragile pages, and will usually respond if it is pointed out what precious materials they really are. Where microfilm is held, it should always be the microfilm that is offered first to the user, the original being treated as what it is – rare and fragile – and issued to the public only in case of special need.

Demand for photocopy from newspapers is high. Above all, photocopying should be controlled, and done by staff, not readers. Unbound issues of newspapers can be copied on ordinary office copying machines, with care. Large copying machines with a screen which reaches to the edge of the machine, so that the text can be read into the gutter, and which copy up to A3 size, can be used if volumes are sound and handled with extreme care: one suitable machine is the 1603 Archivist copier. However, copies from larger pages should be made from microfilm wherever possible: a frame of microfilm is made from the pages wanted, the film developed and paper copy made from that. Suitable machines are the REGMA AR2, 3MS 630 and others available from OCE, Rank Xerox, and Minolta, which can produce copy up to A2 size. It can be helpful to have the reader–printer machines, for copying from microfilm, available in the reading-rooms for readers' own use, though the machines are expensive and likely to be in heavy demand. The Fuji FMRP30AV is of a more compact size for reading-room use, but cannot produce copies larger than A3.

CONSERVATION AND PRESERVATION

The characteristics of newsprint

Since the great expansion of the newspaper press in the developed world at the end of the last century, when the newspaper industry began to seek a source of cheap and plentiful newsprint to meet the new demand, most newspapers have been printed on low-grade, wood-pulp based paper, mostly imported from Scandinavia and Canada, and intended as a throw-away product. It contains cellulose fibres – normally sulphite pulp – added to increase the mechanical strength of the paper, and an internal size based on aluminium sulphate rosin, which when exposed to atmospheric humidity undergoes hydrolysis, producing sulphuric acid. This acid decomposes the cellulose molecules, thus reducing the strength of the lignin fibres and the paper. Atmospheric pollutants such as sulphur dioxide and nitrogen oxide can also be absorbed. Paper turns brown and brittle, corners of pages break off, and paper in bound volumes breaks away from the sewing. It is striking to compare the state of preservation of a newspaper from the eighteenth century or before about 1850 with one of more recent date: the older title, printed on rag-based paper, will usually still be white and solid to handle while one of 1900 or more recent date will be brown, crumbling at the edges and with little or no resistance to folding. The newspapers printed in the last hundred years are not intended to last: they are intentionally ephemeral, and libraries have the task of slowing the course of their self-destruction as best they can.

Storage

Correct storage and handling of newspaper originals is the most important factor in assisting their preservation, and incorrect storage has been shown by the NEWSPLAN projects (see below) to be the factor most commonly hastening their deterioration. The most effective way of ensuring the survival of newspaper originals would be to store them, flat, sealed from air, in a dark store with constant humidity and temperature, to purchase microfilm and not allow the originals to be used. Ideally, light in the stores should not exceed 50 lux., preferably not natural light, and temperatures should be controlled at 13° C and a constant relative humidity of 40 per cent. Atmospheric conditions should be properly monitored with the use of thermometers and hygrometers. These conditions should be the objective for libraries planning new buildings, and for all with the responsibility of permanent preservation. Few established libraries however, can afford such ideal conditions. The more modest points which follow are however of great importance: correct handling and good management of stock will go a long way to ensure the survival of working copies of the originals.

Newspapers (including bound volumes) should always be stored flat, not vertically, on shelves large enough to hold them and with space allowed so that volumes or boxes can be removed by library staff and delivered to users. Newspapers should never under any circumstances be folded. Basic cleanliness is essential. Shelves and volumes, boxes or parcels should be cleaned at least once a year, using a soft cloth on parcels and the backs and spines of volumes, but a feather duster only on the edges of pages. All staff handling newspapers in stacks and reading rooms should be trained in the handling of heavy volumes, provided with adequate working space and manoeuvring room, and with overalls to protect clothes.

Newspaper originals may be bound parcelled or boxed. From the preservation point of view there is little advantage of one method over the other. Ensuring correct handling, as indicated above, is a more important factor. The decision to bind, parcel or box will depend on available funds and the relative importance of security. If newspapers are bound, the pages are held flat and air is excluded between them; but it is important that volumes are not too large because then their sheer weight can destroy the paper along the sewing, and difficulty of handling for the staff increases the risk of accidental damage. Boxes and paper and all materials used should be acid-free. Parcels should be tied, not tightly, with flat tape, not twine or string, which can cut into the edges of the paper.

Planning a preservation programme

The long-term planning of a preservation programme is essential. It must be based on the overall objectives of a library, a systematic assessment of the degree of deterioration of stock, agreement as to the criteria for establishing priorities, the establishment of policy as to the relative shares of microfilm and conservation of originals in the programme, and on retention of originals, and realistic costing including the costs of space, and it should take into account the activities of other relevant libraries and the potential for co-operation.

The systematic assessment of need demands good information on the physical state of the originals in a collection, the number of volumes involved, the use they receive, their rarity, and their relative importance. In most libraries this information is well known to the experts in charge of the collection, but it must be documented in order to secure agreement to the allocation of resources. It will be well worthwhile to carry out a survey of the stock to establish the number of volumes and number of pages requiring conservation or replacement, and the number of occasions when individual titles are used. Examination of bindings is not enough: the state of the paper inside is of even greater importance. Various tests can be used. The paper-fold test for the robustness of paper is a useful one and can be used to rate titles in groups: if the corners of a sample of pages can be folded over and back without breaking off three or more times, the title can be rated as Group 3, if the corners break off when the paper is folded once then the title can be rated as Group 1, and so on. Chemical tests of the acidity of paper provide a more scientific guide, and can be carried out with simple equipment. Individual titles should be examined at different periods and divided up into the most deteriorated years for which preservation is most urgent, and those for which treatment is less urgent: typically, the years before 1870 will be in sounder condition than later years, and there will be 'black-spots' of more serious deterioration owing to heavy use, very often of the newspapers from the First and Second World Wars. Volumes should also be sampled for local problems such as water damage, mould, insect attack, and damage to first and last pages which suffer most in use. Lists of sections of the stock should be prepared, with a rating of the degree of deterioration and information on the treatment recommended – minor local repairs, rebinding, replacement of missing pages with photocopies, deacidification and paper strengthening, micro-filming, withdrawal from use, and so on – and an estimate of the number of volumes and number of pages in each section.

Next, how are priorities to be assessed? The local importance of a title, the degree of use, and its rarity should be borne in mind, as well as the physical condition of sections of a library's stock. Decisions will sometimes be difficult. Does rarity or local importance have greater weight than short- or medium-term user demand? Is it more important, in a situation of shrinking resources such as most libraries now face, to replace a heavily-used set of a national newspaper such as *The Times*, which is readily available in many libraries, or a rare local newspaper of which the library in question holds the best set? These are policy questions on which it is important to secure management agreement.

It is important to bear in mind the policies of other libraries. There have been cases of libraries duplicating expensive microfilming effort, and of local newspapers investing in microfilming of their titles while nearby libraries were doing the same. Libraries can co-operate to ensure that all local newspapers are available locally, that the best originals and the most complete possible set is being microfilmed: they can also co-operate to ensure that one set of the originals is conserved in a given area. British Library policy is an important element (see below), and means that local libraries can rely on it to meet the archival needs of the country in so far as it holds and preserves all newspapers in the original and can almost always be relied upon to supply microfilm. There is however still a strong case for planning at local level by public libraries, academic libraries and others.

The NEWSPLAN programme, at present being actively promoted by the British Library and the library Regions of the UK, and described below, will provide much more of the information that is needed about libraries' policies, and about the contribution being made by the newspaper industry itself. The full-time researchers for the NEWSPLAN programme are working in such a way that local libraries will be able to build on to their reports the detailed information on their own collections.

If other libraries' plans and priorities are known, the assessment of priorities becomes much simpler. The experience of the NEWSPLAN researchers, part of whose job has been to make recommendations on priorities, is that with detailed examination of individual titles in different libraries' stock the priorities to a great extent fall into place.

Policy on the conservation of newspaper originals is a difficult area. Should a library rely on the conservation of the original or on microfilm replacement? Should it conserve the originals after microfilming, or discard them to secure savings on accommodation costs? The objective must be the most cost-effective mix of treatments within available resources, taking into account detailed examination of the use and the importance of individual titles and bearing in mind the policies of other libraries. It may for instance be desirable to ensure that one set of the originals of all local titles is preserved locally, rather than relying on the British Library to do this: if this is decided, it becomes a question of identifying the best set held locally, assigning the resources to its preservation if possible, and of other libraries in the area relying on microfilm.

The costs of a preservation programme include not only the obvious direct costs of binding and microfilming or purchase of microfilm, but also the full staff costs of preparation and checking, and the consequential costs. Experiments should be carried out to estimate the staff time required for preparation of volumes. A major microfilming programme will require the purchase and fitting of microfilm reading machines and copiers, and will result in extra cataloguing work. There may be savings, for instance in service to readers (microfilm is cheaper and quicker to deliver to readers than the originals, and cheaper to photocopy) and potential sales of microfilm that can be taken into account.

Costs of conservation of originals, binding and microfilming should be established in detail, with estimates from bureaux or from in-house facilities, and these costs should be mapped on to the lists of priorities for treatment. The existence of other microfilm of titles on a library's desiderata list should always be investigated: where a microfilm is already being made by another agency, so long as it is made to a good standard (and the master correctly preserved), purchase of the film is likely to be a cheaper alternative to filming in house, and is strongly recommended in principle: we waste scarce resources by duplicating microfilming effort. Acquisitions and preservation budgets and staff resources should be adjusted accordingly. The best ways of investigating what microfilm is available was mentioned above.

As an interim step, some sections of the stock may need to be withdrawn from use and left, wrapped in acid-free paper and correctly stored, to await treatment. This is a big step and will require the agreement of library

61

management, but it may be necessary, for instance in the case of rare originals not being conserved elsewhere.

In all this, the value of small-scale, local repairs should not be neglected. Missing, torn and damaged front pages can be replaced with photocopies, tears repaired with acid-free tape, and damaged bindings repaired. Single volumes can be deacidified, laminated and re-bound (for instance, volumes from the years 1914–1918 and 1939–1945, which receive very heavy use). Repairs required can be identified in reading rooms, as volumes are delivered to readers, and implemented if resources permit; and a separate list of smaller, urgent repairs would be a valuable by-product of the kind of survey being recommended, worth planning and implementing separately.

If the scale of a preservation problem seems daunting, the assessment and planning at a detailed level and the establishment of concrete fact will usually put it into perspective: and as a general rule the single most important step towards securing resources for preservation is good planning based on good information.

Microfilm

Some general points

Policy questions that lie behind a microfilm preservation policy, including the availability of film for purchase, have been dealt with above. This section concerns the more technical aspects, and aims to set out what a library with little or no experience of implementing a microfilm preservation policy needs to know.

Microfilm is the single most important preservation medium for newspapers. It is an established technology, the photographic miniaturization of documents and engineering and architectural documents. Microfilm was probably first used during the seige of Paris in 1870 to send photographic negatives of documents, 'pellicules', by pigeon post and it has been used commercially since the early years of this century. The first use of microfilm to replace newspaper originals was probably made during the 1930s in the USA as part of work creation programmes under the New Deal. Standards for microfilming evolved relatively late and are listed in the bibliography.

In implementing a microfilm preservation policy, many questions need to be asked. Is microfilm or microfiche to be preferred? If microfilm, should it be 35 mm. or 16 mm., positive or negative polarity, silver halide or diazo film, black and white or colour? Is in-house filming to be preferred and should the organization aim to set up its own filming unit, or can outside facilities be used? Which offers the best use of available funds?

Film and fiche

Thirty-five mm. cellulose triacetate silver halide film is the film recommended by the international standards for newspaper preservation. 16 mm. microfilm is sometimes used, but can produce problems with too large a reduction, particularly for some older, large-size broadsheet newspapers. (The reduction ratio should never be more than ×22.) Fiche is also used from time to time, and is known to be used by some UK newspaper publishers for preservation of their current newspapers. Silver halide fiche is archivally permanent, and any reduction can be accommodated by varying the number of frames on a standard A6 fiche, but in general fiche is not to be recommended. There are difficulties in using standard fiche readers for larger-than-usual frames and security problems when handling and filing large amounts of fiche in a library context. (A year's run of a broadsheet newspaper on fiche might for instance occupy 640 fiches as opposed to around 15 reels of microfilm.)

Silver halide and diazo film

Diazo film is sometimes preferred for the user copy, as silver halide user copies are more vulnerable to mishandling and scratching. Its life is not so long (around 25 years before the chemical composition begins to change), so replacement costs must be borne in mind if diazo film is being considered; but, since diazo copy can be made from a silver halide master, so long as the master is correctly preserved, diazo is a valid choice for heavily used titles.

Polarity and colour

Some libraries prefer a positive polarity (black print on a white background), and others a negative polarity (white print on a black background) for their use copies, and a case can be made for either. Negative film is felt to be more comfortable in use, as less light is reflected back to the reader's eyes from the screen; on the other hand, if illustrations and photographs are felt to be an important part of the text, a negative polarity gives a very odd effect. Black and white film remains the standard for newspaper microfilm. No colour film is of archival permanence, though a life of up to 100 years is claimed for one product.

Preparation for microfilming

Preparation of materials for microfilming is of vital importance, and can make the difference between good film and unusable film. It will not normally be undertaken by a bureau, but has to be done by the customer, and is time-consuming – one reason for thorough forward planning of a preservation programme. It is very risky indeed to rush newspapers through to filming by a bureau at the end of the financial year if money unexpectedly becomes available! The British Library Newspaper Library produces a free leaflet on *Newspaper microfilming. Some guidelines for libraries and newspapers* which gives useful guidance on the preparation of newspaper originals for microfilming, and is available from the Newspaper Library (see address on p. 70).

Some libraries (for instance, the French Bibliothèque Nationale) disbind newspapers before filming, and may re-bind after filming or simply wrap the original in acid-free paper for storage in the knowledge that the micro-film will be the copy delivered to readers in future. This has the advantage of reducing shadow in the gutter of volumes, but is probably more costly, and does not simplify the task of handling the material during filming: indeed, it can increase the risk of damage to paper.

Technical considerations

It is essential for any library buying or planning to make its own microfilm to appreciate the technical aspects of microfilming – film density, illumi-nation, resolution, reduction ratios, the correct positions for filming and order of filming, the use of 'targets' (the eye-readable information given at the start and end of each film), the correct division of reels and the method of processing. They are not daunting, are familiar to anyone with a knowledge of photography, and with closer acquaintance are fascinating. Space does not permit more detail here, but they are explained in some of the bibliography items (see particularly Michael Gunn, *Manual of Document Microphotography*, and the paper by Johan Mannerheim in *Newspaper Preservation and Access*).

After filming and processing, the master negative is checked frame by frame for technical quality and for completeness and correct filming. Mistakes should be spotted at this stage, and re-filming and splicing-in undertaken. (The user copy should never be spliced: if errors or omissions are found, the corrected film to be added should be spliced into the master negative, and a complete new user copy produced. For this reason it is of the greatest importance to ensure that quality control in any outside bureau is satisfactory: it is very inefficient to discover errors later.) At this stage, the users' copy is made. The master negative – the film which actually comes off the camera – should now be stored, in theory never to be used again, and should never be delivered to users. Ideally, a second negative should also be made, to be used for generation of further copies.

Storage of microfilm

Microfilm storage is as important as the storage of originals. For the master negatives, air should be filtered to remove dust, temperatures should not rise above 20° C, and relative humidity should be controlled at 30 per cent. The user copy should be stored at an ambient temperature similar to that of the areas in which it will be used, to avoid risk of condensation when film is brought out to be used in reading rooms, in acid-free boxes and in low light. The master and the other copies should as a security measure be stored in different locations. The spools on which film is stored and the cans or boxes in which it is to be kept should be acid-free and of archival quality, and the film should be secured inside the can or box with acid-free paper tags – never rubber bands. Master negatives should be stored in reels horizontally, so that no pressure is put on the film.

Setting up and running your own microfilming unit

The requirements to be borne in mind when a library considers setting up its own microfilming unit are set out in the British Standard 6660, and in the paper by Terry Ilbury in *Newspaper preservation and access* (see Bibliography). It is a very considerable undertaking. Suitable equipment, including cameras with high columns and sliding platforms, is likely to cost at present-day prices over £20 000 per work-station, and a suitable location may be expensive to provide. Microfilming cameras must be free from vibration, with cameras absolutely rigid, and the environment dust-free, without natural light, and with sufficient working space for large volumes. An investment can only be justified if a steady workflow can be ensured and specialist staff employed.

The alternative is the use of a bureau. The importance of checking film quality, and even of examining samples of work from well-known regular suppliers, has been stressed above. Occasional visits to bureaux may be worthwhile. Precise specifications for the microfilm burea to be used must be drawn up as part of each contract, specifying the frame-by-frame checking required and so on.

Microfilm reading machines

Manual and powered machines are available: in libraries that need more than one reading machine, the best advice in the writer's experience is to offer the users the choice. The selection of machines should depend partly on servicing contracts available. Microfilm reading machines must be serviced regularly, otherwise damage to the user copies of film can result, and microfilm as a medium will be unpopular with the users.

Conservation of the original

The qualities of modern newsprint have been mentioned above. The components of conservation of the original paper are deacidification, paper strengthening, and re-binding, combined with appropriate tests to determine pH and ink resistance.

Different methods of chemical deacidification have been tested and are in use in a number of major libraries, and they are quite appropriate to the needs of smaller collections facing the same problems of conserving valuable historical holdings or their deteriorating twentieth-century stocks. The British Library Newspaper Library uses a non-aqueous deacidification method, with an agent containing methyl magnesium carbonate which is sprayed on to the newsprint, depositing a buffer into the structure of the paper. Where paper is still embrittled after deacidification, lamination using a long-fibred neutral pH tissue with a weight of 8.5g.s.m., coated with an archivally-approved adhesive tissue and a rotary laminator are used. Extensive research is also in progress in several large libraries, principally aimed at establishing cheap methods for bulk treatment (see Bibliography). At present only two commercial services are available appropriate to the needs of smaller library collections. The provision of facilities in house for deacidification and lamination is probably more practical and cheaper than in-house microfilming.

Optical disc and CD-ROM

Some applications of CD-ROM and optical disc for newspaper preservation have already been made, and it is possible that CD will in future to some extent replace microfilm. Two alternative methods of storing newspaper-related material on optical disc systems are available, and have been used by different organizations.

The first method is to store the text content of the newspapers only. This text can be automatically indexed and rapid access provided via full-text information retrieval software. This method is being used by the *Northern Echo* newspaper and is similar to the method used by University Microfilms Inc. for the publication on CD-ROM of abstracts and indexes to seven American newspapers.

The second method is to store digitized facsimile images of the newspaper pages or parts of them. This has the advantage of reproducing the pages exactly as they appeared, showing size of headlines and all photographs and other graphic images. Its disadvantage is the greatly increased amount of storage space required (particularly for pages larger than A3 size), the need for sophisticated visual display screens and printing capabilities, and the need for indexing information to be created and input manually. Such systems are expensive and so far have only been used seriously for the storage of press cuttings collections, rather than for full page images.

One year of the *Toronto Globe and Mail* has been published on CD-ROM as a trial project.

A further limitation is the archival life of optical disc. No producer at present guarantees more than 25 years (although the life may prove longer) and this means that libraries are faced with replacement costs.

One encouraging development is that equipment has been developed by Meckel in the US which can read from microfilm to optical disc: it may thus be possible at some future date to transfer existing stocks of film to disc cheaply, so that the investment in microfilm will prove to have been a flexible and secure one.

IMPORTANT COLLECTIONS

The United Kingdom

No comprehensive union lists or guides to collections exist. The Standing Conference of National and University Libraries published a *World List of National Newspapers*, of which details are given in the Bibliography: it lists holdings of British and overseas national newspapers in the UK. The NEWSPLAN reports will in time provide location lists of UK local newspapers, region by region.

There is no special interest group of librarians concerned with newspapers, although in 1989 LINC, the Libraries and Information Co-operation Council (successor to the National Committee on Regional Library Co-ordination) formed a sub-committee on NEWSPLAN under the chairmanship of Dr Norman Higham, and the steering committees for the NEWSPLAN projects in the Regions have provided and should continue to provide stimulus and a focus for the exchange of experience and the discussion of shared problems.

The British Library Newspaper Library

The most important collection in the UK is that of the British Library

67

Newspaper Library, world famous for the riches of its holdings and for the degree of integration of its specialist services. The British Library is the only legal deposit library in the UK to acquire and retain all UK newspapers. The Newspaper Library, situated at Colindale in north-west London, holds all the UK newspapers, with some exceptions: London newspapers before 1800, which are held at present in the Great Russell Street building and will move to the St Pancras building; some (typically UK provincial newspapers from the years 1896–7 and 1911–13) which were destroyed in war-time bombing; some titles not claimed before 1844; some current, small-circulation local newspapers, particularly free newspapers, though efforts are now being made to secure deposit of all these as their existence is discovered; and newspapers in ethnic minority languages in non-Roman scripts, which are acquired on legal deposit but held by the Oriental Collections, at the time of writing in the Store Street and former India Office buildings, but also due to relocate to St Pancras. Newspapers are acquired from all countries of the world in Roman or Cyrillic scripts, though those in Oriental scripts are acquired and stored by Oriental Collections. The object is to acquire at least two titles from every country, including the 'newspaper of record', if there is one, and others to reflect the geographical and political range of the country. The collections include comprehensive collections of Irish newspapers, received on deposit by reciprocal agreement between the two countries, and UK periodicals that are published fortnightly or more frequently: this includes enthusiasts' and popular-interest magazines, trade journals and comics. The stock amounts to about 600 000 bound volumes and parcels and 230 000 reels of positive microfilm (excluding the stock of master negative).

The Newspaper Library has been on its present site since 1905, and has grown progressively, adding its own reading-room and bindery and microfilming unit, and developing an integrated service with responsibility for all aspects of newspaper work which would probably not have developed if the newspapers had remained in the main collections in the larger functional departments of the Library. It has reader seats for 100 readers, and is subject to constant heavy demand, frequently being full, particularly in the summer, which is the peak period of use. It is open to enquirers, free, on application: users who hold the main British Library pass are admitted without further formality, and a pass to use the Newspaper Library only can be issued there to anyone else on presentation of proof of identity, and provided the material required or the combination of material required cannot be obtained in another library that is reasonably accessible to the enquirer: for instance, London residents would not be expected to travel outside London to see newspapers that are held in other towns. Users under the age of 21 are admitted only by special arrangement. Over 26 000 reader visits are made each year, and over a third of the users are from overseas. The Newspaper Library provides reference and photocopying services, a postal and telephone enquiry service (though in-depth research cannot be done), and a back-up service for the provision of photocopies against inter-library loan forms. At present there is no lending of originals or microfilms. There are plans for a charged research service.

Microfilm has increasingly been the medium for preservation of and access to newspapers, and the Newspaper Library was one of the first institutions in the world to resort to large-scale microfilming as the solution to space and preservation problems: at present there is a microfilming unit of 27 cameras and over 60 staff, and a long-term programme of conservation work. The use of microfilm developed progressively after 1948, when the first cameras were acquired, and the Newspaper Library carried out extensive research into the technical aspects of filming and storage. Microfilm was first made to replace lost and damaged volumes after the war-time bombing, and then to replace the worst-deteriorated sections of the stock, particularly overseas newspapers (which from 1965 to 1975 were disposed of after microfilming: retention has since been resumed) and then the heavily-used UK national newspapers; microfilm was delivered to users to spare fragile originals from use. Later a policy was introduced of purchasing overseas newspapers on microfilm instead of the original, where possible, and of purchasing all conservation microfilm wherever film of good standard was commercially available or available from another library, instead of filming in-house. In the 1960s the Newspaper Library began to supply film to other libraries, particularly in the UK, filming from its own holdings. Finally in 1986 it adopted a policy of filming or buying film of all current UK newspapers, both local and national. The originals of national newspapers are still bound, and those of local newspapers are parcelled in acid-free paper and kept in good storage conditions, only being delivered to users if they have a special case for using the paper copy – for instance to provide good-quality copies of photographs, or to illustrate important changes in newspaper design and layout consequent on the introduction of new technology or the use of colour. Newspapers are not normally available for use until they have been either bound or replaced by film: delays in availability can be from 3 months to 2 years or more, depending mainly on speed of supply of purchased microfilm. Thirty-five mm. silver halide microfilm is used almost exclusively at the Newspaper Library, though fiche and 16 mm. film can be supplied to customers if wished, and some fiche is purchased. Only black-and-white film is used.

The Library is one of the largest suppliers of microfilm, and in 1988/9 supplied 8 750 reels of film, made to the best archival standards, to customers of whom about 80 per cent are public libraries in the UK. A catalogue of microfilm masters (see Bibliography) is published and available free from the Newspaper Library, Colindale Avenue, London NW9 5HE, tel. 071 323 7353; but any other titles held in the collections can be filmed on request, subject to copyright restrictions.

In 1986 the Newspaper Library launched the NEWSPLAN programme for the comprehensive preservation of UK local newspapers, with the British Library, other libraries, the library Regions of the UK and newspaper publishers acting in co-operation. It seeks to provide the basis for national planning of newspaper preservation and to take advantage of the opportunities for co-operation and cost sharing in microfilming. Its conception was in a research proposal from the South West Regional Library System, which the British Library (then Reference Division) funded in 1984-5, aimed to identify newspaper preservation needs in the Region and make recommendations. The research was carried out as a pilot study for planning on a national scale, and the programme was initiated after its very successful completion and further consultation.

NEWSPLAN is seen as consisting of two phases – research and implementation. The research phase in each of the library Regions of the UK has been managed through the library Regions and jointly funded by them and the British Library. Full-time researchers have visited, examined and listed all collections in their area, including those held outside the main stocks of libraries and archives, for instance in museums, private collections and newspapers' archives. All holdings have been examined to assess their physical condition, microfilming already done has been listed and the microfilm quality assessed, and recommendations have been developed, with priorities and a basis for costing, for a comprehensive programme of microfilming. Information about British Library holdings has been included as comprehensively as possible. The projects have been assisted by steering committees which have brought together newspaper experts from different collections in each Region, including representatives of newspapers' own libraries, which has had other benefits in providing a focus for the exchange of experience and information. Research projects have at the time of writing been completed (apart from the pilot project) in the East Midlands, the Northern Region, Yorkshire and Humberside, the West Midlands and the North West, and are in progress in Wales where a valuable foundation has been laid by the National Library, and in Ireland (both in the Republic of Ireland and in Northern Ireland, where much work on holdings lists has already been done). Proposals are being developed by LASER, the London and South East Library Region, and Scotland, where considerable progress has already been made by the Committee on Scottish Newspapers. The implementation phase, which is now in the early stages, involves the development of plans at local authority and Regional level, the British Library's commitment to microfilming those titles recommended to be filmed from its stock, and a concerted effort to build the whole into a national plan and seek the additional resources needed to fund it. An important step taken towards this goal was the formation of the LINC sub-committee in 1989.

The reports of the NEWSPLAN studies are being published by the British Library, and provide the basis for further development of holdings lists and bibliographies. They consist principally of lists of titles of the newspapers of a Region, but with general comments on the conditions of stock – sometimes dramatic – storage, microfilm quality and the individual titles. The information gathered by the project officers is also being kept up-to-date by the British Library and the Regions. The report of the pilot study carried out in the South West (see Bibliography) carries more general chapters on newspaper preservation and correct practice, and is an authoritative work of lasting value.

NEWSPLAN is a priority programme for the British Library and its corporate plan, and is well advanced towards becoming established nationwide. With its emphasis on co-operation, it has attracted interest all over the world.

The catalogue of the Newspaper Library as of 1970 was published in 1975 in eight volumes (see Bibliography) and is still in print, price £200.

The Newspaper Library welcomes enquiries from intending users and all concerned with the acquisition, handling and preservation of newspapers, and is happy to offer visits for interested groups of library professionals or students of librarianship. The initial contacts are:

Geoffrey Hamilton, Head, Newspaper Library 071 323 7362
(general enquiries about British Library policy and preservation planning)
John Westmancoat, Information Officer, 071 323 7357
(enquiries about holdings, newspaper history or visits, and reference requests)
Geoff Smith, Head of Public Services, 071 323 7354
(enquiries about supply of microfilm)
Kelvin Ithell, Head of the Microfilming Unit, 071 323 6360
(technical enquiries about microfilming or microfilm storage).

Some publications and papers concerning the Newspaper Library are listed in the bibliography.

The other copyright libraries

Five other libraries also have the right of legal deposit (often called copyright deposit) of UK newspapers – the National Libraries of Scotland and Wales, Bodleian Library, Oxford, Cambridge University Library, and Trinity College, Dublin. They are selective in what they acquire, and specialize in the relevant parts of the country. Their holdings of older newspapers are particularly important.

The holdings of the National Library of Scotland are virtually comprehensive up to 1800, but are incomplete for the period 1800 to 1974 (indeed there are 500 Scottish titles which survive only in the British Library). The Library's policy on acquiring Scottish newspapers broadened gradually in stages during the period 1932 to 1974, from which date the Library claims, via legal deposit, all Scottish newspapers. The Library makes particular efforts to acquire Scottish community newspapers – newspapers or journals often serving very local areas, often published infrequently, for instance only monthly, non-professionally produced, and in character something in between a newspaper and a parish magazine. The Library also tries to acquire all Scottish free newspapers.

The National Library of Scotland produced a *Directory of Scottish Newspapers* and established the Committee on Scottish Newspapers (a subcommittee of LISC Scotland) to prepare a plan for the preservation of Scottish newspapers (see Bibliography). At the request of government, it is currently promoting a fund-raising campaign to meet the costs of a Scottish microfilming unit devoted to newspaper needs, which would work in liaison with the British Library's microfilming unit at Colindale, and to its standards.

The National Library of Wales is similar in retaining the UK national press selectively, and newspapers of Welsh interest. As in Scotland, great emphasis is placed on acquiring community newspapers of which a considerable number are currently published in the Welsh language. Its holdings of originals, within these parameters, are complete after 1909 and a long-term programme to fill the gaps before the Library's foundation with microfilm made from newspaper publishers' files and other libraries' holdings has been making steady progress since 1971. Its holdings of Welsh-language *émigré* newspapers, from the USA and elsewhere, are of particular value.

The Bodleian Library does not have a specialist newspaper service or a single newspaper department. Of current UK newspapers it retains the major national newspapers of record together with a selection of major provincial papers. Where possible these are taken in microfilm, as are the Oxfordshire newspapers.

Cambridge University Library deals with all its newspapers in one department. It holds all the UK material national daily and Sunday newspapers and a good representative selection of those produced in East Anglia. All these newspapers are retained. Due to the size of the University Library, co-operation with other libraries in the region is limited to sharing the costs of any microfilming project.

Trinity College, Dublin, has a small but important historical collection, with substantial holdings of eighteenth- and nineteenth-century Dublin newspapers and currently acquires and retains five Irish daily papers and three London national daily papers.

Public libraries

Public libraries, including the larger collections in the county libraries, make an invaluable contribution through their holdings of local newspapers in their own areas and through their preservation efforts, and for the majority of users are the first port of call. The *Bibliography of British Newspapers* and the NEWSPLAN reports are listing their holdings and will serve to make their strengths and expertise more widely known – possibly a mixed blessing, as they are already heavily used and an increase in demand will need to be accompanied by investments in preservation, staffing and facilities.

The City Business Library, at present in temporary premises in Fenchurch Street, holds the largest range of current overseas newspapers (about 60 titles) of interest to the financial and business community in the City.

Academic and special libraries

In general, university and polytechnic libraries and the libraries of specialist research institutes within them have small but important resources. Most do not hold large collections of UK newspapers, though they will take the 'quality' press and some other national newspapers: they tend not to take local newspapers. Their holdings of overseas newspapers to support research in specialized areas are more important, for instance in area studies. There are no directories of holdings: the *World List of National Newspapers* (see bibliography) now out of date, is the best guide to what is available.

Embassies and consulates provide a useful back-up in taking the principal newspapers of their own country, but are not easily accessible for those outside London, and do not usually retain back files.

The newspaper industry

Both national and local newspapers support libraries, principally to provide their journalists with reference collections, fact-checking, access to other library sources, a library of photographs, and above all a press cuttings collection which typically covers other newspapers as well as the titles of the newspaper or newspaper group concerned. The national newspapers' libraries mostly clip and file all the other national newspaper titles: local newspapers may clip and file the competition and the national papers as a future source of reference. Cuttings collections are an expensive investment and increasingly a preservation problem (though some newspapers have resorted to microform and to CD-ROM as the solution to the preservation problems: CD-ROM is mentioned below).

In most cases they also hold a complete bound file of their own title or titles, sometimes in all editions. Their older files are not open to the public, though some newspapers will give access to enquirers, and will help with questions that can be answered from their cuttings collections in the absence of indexes. In many instances, though by no means always, the newspaper librarians are familiar with the holdings of the local library, and co-operate in microfilming and assisting enquirers, to mutual benefit. Microfilm replacement has been extensive and is continuing apace, as newspapers are subject to increasing economic pressures. These holdings are being investigated and listed by the NEWSPLAN projects.

There is an Association of UK Media Librarians, formed in 1986, of which the Secretary is Peter Chapman, librarian of the *Northern Echo* in Darlington. Membership is open to librarians handling text-based information in broadcasting or print news media.

Overseas libraries

Information about the main collections in other countries is difficult to assemble, and relatively little is published. The published proceedings of the First International Symposium on Newspaper Preservation and Access, organized by the IFLA Working Group on Newspapers (now the Round Table on Newspapers) in 1987 (see Bibliography) give more information about newspaper collections and the practices of libraries world-wide than any other source, and include the results of an earlier survey of national newspaper collections carried out by the Working Group. The information that follows is incomplete, and is based more on professional contacts than on published sources. Holdings lists that have been identified by the British Library have been included in the bibliography.

The UK is unusual in having a comprehensive collection of its newspapers in the national library. France in the Bibliothèque Nationale in Paris and the Scandinavian countries (the State and University Library in Århus, Denmark, the University of Oslo library and the Swedish Royal Library) have complete collections, based on legal deposit. South Africa in the South African Library in Capetown (not the State Library) has almost comprehensive collections, including those passed to it at the end of the

Colonial period by the Colonial Office, and in 1979 by the Parliament library. Current collection by legal deposit may be more comprehensive than historical holdings: 70 per cent of countries responding to the IFLA Working Group on Newspapers' questionnaire in 1981–83 claimed to be collecting all their countries' current newspapers.

But in general comprehensive collections are the exception, and the pattern of holdings and preservation is very variable. The USA and Canada have distributed responsibility for the collection, bibliographic control and preservation of newspapers. Newspapers are not subject to legal deposit in either the Library of Congress or the National Library of Canada, and responsibility for them rests with the State libraries in the USA and the provincial or territorial libraries in Canada. Preservation efforts in both countries (the US Newspaper Program and the National Library's Decentralised Program in Canada) are founded on the co-operation of libraries at the regional level to secure national coverage. Germany relies on legal deposit in the Länder, and the Deutsche Bibliothek in Frankfurt collects selectively and mainly on microfilm. The principal German collections are at the Institut für Presseforschung in Dortmund, the State and University Library in Bremen, the Bayerische Staatsbibliothek in Munich and the University Library in Munster. New Zealand's National Library in Wellington has important collections, including those passed to it by the Parliament Library, but the predominant pattern is local collection, and the National Library aims to build up a comprehensive retrospective collection of New Zealand papers on microfilm.

In the developing countries, the establishment of comprehensive collections in their relatively new national libraries is even more difficult. The former colonial powers for instance may hold newspapers that have simply not been collected in the country of origin, as was the case with India and Pakistan, where the deposit collections of the India Office Library and Records now form part of the British Library. Collections of their current newspapers in other major libraries of the world, such as those of the Library of Congress, Stanford University, the Centre for Research Libraries and the British Library, make an important contribution to the preservation of materials from those countries of the world where resources are scarce and problems are particularly acute.

BIBLIOGRAPHY

General

British Library Newspaper Library newsletter, 1– , 1981–   [Irregular].

Dewe, Michael (ed.) (1987), *Manual of Local Studies Librarianship*, Aldershot: Gower. ISBN. 0-566-03522-7, *passim*.

Gibb, Ian P. (1988), (in) *British Librarianship and Information Work 1981–1985*, ed. D. Bromley and Allott. London: Library Association Publishing Ltd., ISBN. 0-85365-538-3, pp. 36–43.

Gibson, Jeremy S.W. (1987), *Local Newspapers 1750–1920 England and Wales, Channel Islands and Isle of Man. A select location list*, Birmingham: Federation of Family History Societies, ISBN. 0-907099-46-7.

Guidelines for newspaper libraries, (1974–   ), written by members of the Newspaper Division of the Special Libraries Association, Reson, Va.: American Newspaper Publishers' Association.

Höfig, Willi, (1988), *Zeitungen sammeln: diskussionen und perspektiven*. Berlin: Deutches Bibliotheksinstitut (DBI-materialen 77).

Journal of Newspaper and Periodical History, (1984–   ), London, 2–6 Foscote Mews, London W9 2HH. 3 issues p.a.

Kurian, George Thomas, (1982), *Encyclopaedia of the World's Press*. 2 vols, London: Mansell, ISBN 0-7201-1646-5.

Linton, David and Boston, Ray, (1987), *The Newspaper Press in Britain: an Annotated Bibliography*, London and New York: Mansell, ISBN. 0-7201-1792-5.

McLaughlin, Eve, (1987), *Family History from Newspapers*, Birmingham: Federation of Family History Societies, ISBN. 0-907099-70-X.

Ubbens, Wilbert, (1986), *Zeitungen in bibliotheken*. Berlin: Deutsches Bibliotheksinstitut (DBI-materialen 49).

Upham, Lois N. (ed.) (1988), *Newspapers in the Library: New Approaches to Management and Reference Work*, London and New York: Haworth Press, ISBN. 0-86656-688-0.

Westmancoat, John, (1985), *Newspapers*, London: British Library, ISBN. 0-7123-0055-4.

Bibliography

Bergess, Winifred, Riddell, Barbara and Whyman, John (eds) (1982), *Bibliography of British Newspapers. Kent*, London: British Library, ISBN. 0-7123-0007-4.

Bluhm, Robin K. (1975), *Bibliography of British Newspapers. Wiltshire*. London: Library Association, Reference, Special and Information Section, ISBN. 0-85365-038-1.

Brook, Michael, (1987), *Bibliography of British Newspapers. Nottinghamshire*. London: British Library, ISBN. 0-7123-0061-9.

Manders, Frank, (1982), *Bibliography of British Newspapers. Durham and Northumberland*. London: British Library, ISBN. 0-7123-0008-2.

Mellors, Anne and Radford, Jean, (1987), *Bibliography of British Newspapers. Derbyshire*. London: British Library, ISBN. 0-7123-0124-0.

Cataloguing

Carter, Ruth C. (1986), 'The United States Newspaper Program: cataloging aspects', *Cataloguing and Classification Quarterly* **6** (4), (entire issue).

Guidelines for the Minimum Bibliographic and Holdings Description of Newspapers/Lignes directrices relatives à une description minimale des notices bibliographiques et des fonds de journaux, Ottawa: National Library of Canada, Decentralised Program for Canadian Newspapers, 1987.

International Guidelines for the Cataloguing of Newspapers. Prepared by Hana Komorous with the assistance of Robert Harriman, London: UBCIM Progamme (UBCIM Occasional papers 14), 1989, ISSN. 1012-327X.

Newspaper cataloguing manual, CONSER/USNP ed. Washington, DC: Library of Congress, Serial Record Division, 1984–　　.

Conservation and preservation

Grove, Pearce S. (1985), 'A revolution in newspaper access', (in) *Resource Sharing and Information Networks*, **3** (1), 1985, pp. 101–114.

Newspaper Preservation and Access, Proceedings of the Symposium held in London, August 12–15 1987. Ed. Ian P. Gibb. 2 vols. (IFLA publication 45, 46.) Munich, London, New York and Paris: K G Saur, 1988. ISBN. 3-598-21775-7, 3-598-21776-5.

Microfilm and microfilming policy

Bourke, Thomas A. (1986), 'The microfilming of newspapers: an overview', (in) *Microform Review*, **15** (3), 1986, pp. 154–156.

Griffiths, Penelope (1984), *Review of Microfilming Policy for Newspapers*, Wellington: National Library of New Zealand, (National Library bulletin no. 24). ISSN. 0110-6562.

Gunn, Michael J. (1985), *Manual of Document Microphotography*, London: Butterworth, ISBN. 0-240-51146-8.

Information Media and Technology. 2-M 1967–　　. CIMTECH (formerly National Research Centre for Documentation) Hatfield Polytechnic, College Lane, Hatfield, Herts. AL10 9AB, England. ISSN 0266 6960.

International Journal of Micrographics and Video Technology. Q. 1982–   . Elmsford: Pergamon Press Inc. ISSN. 0743 9639, *passim.*

Labarre, Albert, *Le plan de sauvegarde des collections de la Bibliothèque Nationale 1980–1985. Note établie en juin 1986.* Paris: Bibliothèque Nationale [unpublished].

Matheson, Ann (1987), 'Scottish newspapers', (in) *Library Review,* Autumn, pp. 179–85.

Microform Review. Q, 1972–   . Westport, Conn: Meckler Publishing Corp. ISSN 0002-6530 *passim.*

National Newspapers Colloquium, Nov. 12–13 1985. Report/Colloque national sur les journaux, compte rendu. Ottawa: National Library of Canada, 1986.

Newspaper Microfilming. Some Guidelines for Libraries and Newspapers, British Library Newspaper Library, (1988), free leaflet.

Preservation Microforms, British Library National Preservation Office (1988), ISBN. 0-7123-0171-2.

Scottish Newspapers. A Programme for Microfilming Scottish Newspapers, Report by the Committee on Scottish newspapers, Edinburgh: Committee on Scottish Newspapers, 1986.

Second survey of New Zealand Newspapers: final Report. Wellington: National Library of New Zealand, 1987. 2 vols, unpublished.

Microfilm standards

All the standards listed below are available from the British Standards Institution, 2 Park St., London W1A 2BS.

Glossary of terms for micrographics Part 1: 1981, General terms (ISO 6196/1).

Part 2: 1983, Image positions and methods of recording.

Part 3: 1984, Film processing (ISO 6196/3) BS 6054.

Guide to setting up and maintaining micrographics units, BS 6660: 1985.

Method for determining the resolution obtained in microcopying, BS 4657: 1970 (ISO. 3334).

Methods for determination of thiosulphate and other residual chemicals in processed photographic films, plates and papers: methylene blue photometric method and silver sulphide densitometric method, BS 5706 (ISO. 417): 1977.

Microform reader resolution test film, BS 4191C: 1976.

Processed photographic film for archival records, BS 5699.

Part 1: 1979. Specification for silver-gelatin type on cellulose ester base.

Part 2: 1979. Specification for silver-gelatin type on poly (ethylene terephthalate) base.

Recommendations for the preparation of copy for microcopying, BS 5444: 1977.

Recommendations for the processing and storage of silver-gelatin-type microfilm, BS 1153: 1975 (ISO. 2803).

Specification for 35 mm. and 16 mm. microfilms, spools and reels, BS 1371: 1973 (ISO. 1116).

Specification for 35 mm. microcopying of newspaper cuttings on A6 microfiche, BS 5513: 1977.

Specification for 35 mm. microcopying of newspapers for archival purposes, BS 5847: 1980, (ISO. 4087-1979).

Specification for density of silver-gelatin-type microforms, BS 5976: 1980 (ISO. 6200).

Specification for microform readers. BS 4191: 1976.

Directories of preservation microfilm

Microforms in Print, Irregular eds. and suppls., Westport, Conn.: Meckler Publishing Corp.

Microfilms of Newspapers and Journals for Sale 1985–86, British Library Newspaper Library. (1985 Covers UK and foreign and Commonwealth titles.)

Newspapers and Periodicals for Sale on Microfilm, Foreign and Commonwealth countries 1987–88, British Library Newspaper Library (1987).

Newspapers in Microform, 3 vols., Washington, DC: Library of Congress, 1984. ISSN. 0097-9627.

Periodicas brasileiros em microformas: catálogo coletivo, Rio de Janeiro: Biblioteca Nacional do Brasil, 1985. (Colecao Rodolfo Garcia, 18, serie B.).

Conservation of the original

Banik, Gerhard (1988), 'Problems of Mass Conservation of Newsprint in Libraries'. *Newspaper Preservation and Access*, Proceedings of the Symposium held in London, August 12–15 1987, ed. Ian P. Gibb, 2 vols. (IFLA publication 45, 46.), Munich, London, New York and Paris: K G Saur ISBN. 3-598-21775-7, 3-598-21776-5. 230, pp. 216–222.

Banks, Joyce M. (1985), *Note sur la désacidification de masses à la Bibliothèque Nationale du Canada*.

Clements, D.W.G. (in press), 'Emerging Technologies – Paper Strengthening', *Proceedings of the Conference on the Preservation of Library Materials, sponsored by the Conference of Directors of National Libraries, April 1986*, Vienna.

Cunha, G.M. (in press), 'Mass deacidification systems available to libraries', *Proceedings of New directions in paper conservation. 10th annual conference of the Institute of Paper Conservation*, Oxford.

'Désacidification à la Bibliothèque', *Nouvelles de la Bibliothèque Nationale* [du Canada], **14** (3/4), Mar./Apr. 1982.

Guidelines for the Treatment of Canadian Newspapers in Original Format, prepared by the Working Group on Canadian Newspapers in Original Format, Ottawa: National Library of Canada, 1988.

Kelly, G. (1987), 'Non-aqueous Deacidification of Books and Paper', *Conservation of Library and Archive Materials and the Graphic Arts*, ed. G. Petherbridge, London: Butterworth, p. 117.

Newsprint and its Preservation, Library of Congress Preservation Office (Preservation Leaflet no. 5), 1981.

Scott, Marianne (in press), 'Mass Deacidification at the National Library of Canada', *Proceedings of the Conference on the Preservation of Library Materials, sponsored by the Conference of Directors of National Libraries, Aporil 1986*, Vienna.

Smith, R.D. (1987), 'Mass Deacidification: the Wei [sic] to Understanding', *C & RL news*, January, p. 2.

'Non-aqueous Deacidification: its Philosophies, Origin and Status', *Proceedings of New directions in Paper Conservation. 10th annual conference of the Institute of Paper Conservation*. Oxford [in press].

Swartzburg, Susan (1980), *Preserving Library Materials: A Manual*, London: Scarecrow Press.

Wachter, Otto (1986), *Paper Strengthening: Mass Conservation of Unbound and Bound Newspapers*, Vienna: National Library of Austria, Institute for Conservation.

NEWSPLAN

Cowley, Ruth (forthcoming), *NEWSPLAN. Report of the NEWSPLAN Project in the North West*, London: British Library.

Gordon, Ruth (1989), *NEWSPLAN. Report of the NEWSPLAN Project in the East Midlands*, London: British Library, ISBN. 0-7123-0186-0.

Parkes, Andrew (forthcoming), *NEWSPLAN. Report of the NEWSPLAN Project in Yorkshire and Humberside*, London: British Library, ISBN. 0-7123-0218-2.

Parry, David (1989), *NEWSPLAN. Report of the NEWSPLAN Project in the Northern Region*, London: British Library, ISBN. 0-7123-0183-6.

Watkins, Tracey (forthcoming), *NEWSPLAN. Report of the NEWSPLAN Project in the West Midlands Region*, London: British Library.

Wells, Rosemary (1986), *NEWSPLAN. Report of the Pilot Project in the*

South West, London: British Library Research and Development Department, (LIR 38). ISBN. 0-7123-3057-7.

Important collections

Catalogue of the Newspaper Library, 8 vols., London: British Museum Publications for the British Library, 1975, ISBN. 0-7141-0352-7.

Green, Stephen P. (1984), 'The British Library's Newspaper Library in a New Era', *Journal of Newspaper and Periodical History*, **1** (i), pp. 4–11.

Johansson, Eve (1986), 'The British Library Newspaper Library: Looking Ahead', *Journal of Newspaper and Periodical History*, **2** (iii), pp. 34–7.

Whatmore, Geoffrey (1978), *The Modern News Library. Documentation of Current Affairs in Newspaper and Broadcasting Libraries*, London: Library Association, ISBN. 0-85365-530-8.

'News Libraries and Newspaper Collections', *British Librarianship and Information Work, 1976–1980*, ed. L.J. Taylor, London: Library Association, 1983. ISBN. 0-85365-825-0. pp. 37–43.

Union lists of newspapers

Directory of Scottish Newspapers, comp. Joan P.S. Ferguson, Edinburgh: National Library of Scotland, 1984. ISBN. 0-902220-40-3.

Gully, J.S. (1961), *A Union Catalogue of New Zealand Newspapers Preserved in Public Libraries, Newspaper Offices and Local Authority Offices*, 2 edn, Wellington: General Assembly Library.

Northern Ireland Newspapers... Checklist of microfilm held by Northern Ireland Libraries with Amendments to the [1979 edn], Belfast: Library Association, Northern Ireland Branch/Public Record Office of Northern Ireland Working Party on Resources for Local Studies, 1983.

Northern Ireland Newspapers... Checklist with Locations, ed. J.R.R. Adams, Belfast: Library Association, Northern Ireland Branch/Public Record Office of Northern Ireland Joint Committee, 1979.

Union List of Canadian Newspapers Held by Canadian Libraries/Liste collective des journaux canadiens disponibles dans les bibliothèques canadiennes, Ottawa: National Library of Canada, 1977.

Union List of New Zealand Newspapers before 1940 Preserved in Libraries, Newspaper Offices, Local Authority Offices and Museums in New Zealand, Wellington: National Library of New Zealand, 1985.

United States Newspaper Programme National Union List, 1985, microfiche.

Webber, Rosemary (1976), *World list of National Newspapers*, London: Butterworth, 1976, ISBN. 0-408-70817-4- (Supplement published as a special supplement to the *British Library Newspaper Library Newsletter*, 1985.)

4

Serials

ALBERT MULLIS

THE MATERIAL AND ITS PROBLEMS

A complaint often voiced by librarians and others concerned with serials is that there are too many of them, not only too many new titles being published each year but also too many titles currently available. On the surface this may seem a curious complaint when there are considerably more monographs published and in print. It has substance, however, when looked at in terms of cost. The average serial subscription is often considerably more costly than the average monograph. Unlike a monograph, it is a continuing commitment which may be almost indefinite. Furthermore, serials consume a higher proportion of the acquisitions budget in most academic and special libraries than other materials, and their continually spiralling costs in a period of declining financial resources shows them, in some libraries, taking up more than half (at times much more than half) of the total budget. As more and more is spent on serials so, inevitably, less and less is spent on other materials; although in some libraries, even in the best of economic times, serials have been, by the very nature of the library, the predominant consumer of the budget.

A serial is not only a potentially long term commitment in terms of purchasing cost but is also a long term commitment in terms of staff resources used in handling it and a continuing commitment in storage and preservation costs.

Generally there has been a slowing down in recent years in the amount of material in existing titles; but the number of new titles continues its seemingly inexorable march upwards. In the 1980s the growth in most fields, including sciences but not medicine, has slowed but in other fields, for example business, management and computing, there have been increases. Another factor which threatens to boost the number of new titles is desktop publishing.

For users of serials, accessibility is vital, and consideration needs to be given to the effect on users of library policies and procedures (see McBride, 1985). The many problems serials have in their management, and attempts to overcome them in the most efficient and effective way may obscure the problems faced by users. Satisfactory solutions to some of these difficulties are a matter of availability of adequate resources and of priorities. Too often, however, they could be solved simply by imagination on the part of the librarian or the ability to understand the user's needs, and to see problems and solutions from the user's point of view. Sometimes the librarian may be only too aware of the difficulties and the need to give better service but may be bogged down by the legacy of the past. Bryant (1988) indicates some of the challenges which face the British Library in just such a situation.

So far, what a serial is has been assumed. The international definition given in the International Standard Serial Number (ISSN) (ISO 3297-1986), also used by the International Standard Bibliographic Description for Serials (ISBD(S)) and followed, more or less, by the *Anglo-American Cataloguing Rules*, 2nd edn (AACR2) is:

A publication in printed form or not, issued in successive parts usually having numerical or chronological designations and intended to be continued indefinitely. Serials include periodicals, newspapers, annuals (reports, yearbooks, directories, etc.), the journals, memoirs, proceedings, transactions, etc. of societies and monographic series. This definition does not include works produced in parts for a period predetermined as finite. (*Anglo-American Cataloguing Rules*, 1988)

While newspapers are included within this definition they have been given separate treatment in this book. Although much of what follows will concentrate on periodicals, other kinds of serial, though often having much in common with monographs, will be covered when their problems are shared with those of periodicals.

The definition of periodical given in the *ISDS Manual* will be observed rather than that given in ISBD(S), that is:

A type of serial, normally published more frequently than annually, in which the issues are generally characterized by variety of contents and contributors, both within the issue and from one issue to another. (ISDS Manual, 1983)

Clear, unequivocal definitions are important in such functions as the assignment of ISSN and in cataloguing, especially for union catalogues where it is necessary to define clearly for all participants what kind of publications will be included.

Even such close definitions indicate a grey area between serials and monographs. Much report literature and grey literature is serial in nature, although of the monographic series type. It is arguable, for example, whether looseleaf amendment services, or at least some of them, are serials. Some librarians would not regard the proceedings of regularly held conferences as serials.

While what is or what is not a serial may be important in activities such as the assignment of ISSN, the assignment of bar codes, cataloguing and so on, it may have far less importance in activities such as acquisition. It may be best, however, to treat some monographic items, for practical purposes, as serials, such as multivolume works in progress. Osborn (1980) makes the following admirably pragmatic statement:

> In keeping with the times, then, a serial can be defined, for library purposes as any item which lends itself to serial treatment in a library . . . In doubtful cases one's judgement, based on the insights gained through years of handling serial publications, is all that is needed to decide on serial and nonserial treatment of an item. (A.D. Osborn, 1980)

Serials in libraries have problems from conception to death (if selection is regarded as the equivalent of conception). Death does not necessarily mean when the title stops publication or when the subscription or standing order has been cancelled. Serials kept in the collection after publication has stopped or after cancellation do not die until all volumes have been discarded. There is still life after apparent death, that is those titles retained will be stored, preserved and used.

It has already been said that a serial subscription or standing order, especially one for a periodical, represents a continuing expensive commitment. A monograph represents a single purchase, and usually once catalogued will, amendments to the catalogue record apart, be finished with. A monograph will, of course, represent a continuing commitment in terms of storage and preservation, but usually there is only one volume to store and preserve, whereas a serial by its nature will grow each year, thus multiplying the storage and preservation costs. Serials also represent a continuing cost in processing in terms of check-in of issues and claiming of issues not received. In some senses budget limitations impose greater selectivity for periodicals than they may do for monographs. Life cycle costing, a technique only just beginning to be applied in libraries, clearly shows that serial titles in the collection have greater continuing costs than those for monographs (see Enright, 1989 and Stephens, 1989). The cost of the subscription should not be the only cost factor taken into account when selecting a new title.

Acquisitions budgets for serials may be stretched further by resource sharing and co-operative purchasing arrangements between libraries. Such arrangements themselves have overhead costs, some not always immediately apparent. Not least in resource sharing arrangements may be the need to have a union catalogue of holdings, which in itself is a complex and costly undertaking.

Selection of serial titles is, perhaps, more difficult than that for monographs. There can be a greater reliance on reviews and approval collections in selecting monographs, although it must be admitted that reviews probably play a rather smaller part in the selection process than is generally assumed. New serial titles are much less likely to be reviewed, and where reviews exist, they are more likely than not to be based on the evidence of the first issue only. Decisions to select based on seeing a specimen issue or on a user recommendation are commonplace, although again decisions are being made on limited evidence. It is therefore important to keep serials subscriptions and standing orders under scrutiny even when not forced to do so by economic necessity.

There are a number of different means of acquisition. A title received by gift accrues no direct acquisition cost, but there are continuing costs of processing, storage and possibly preservation. Gifts, especially of unsolicited material, are often more trouble than they are worth. Material from Eastern Europe or the Third World may be acquired by exchange, although this, too, may present more problems than any apparent advantages and savings may indicate. All too often material received through gift and exchange continues to be passively received with little regard to its real value to the collection and the overhead costs that go with all titles, no matter how acquired. Acquisition from 'difficult' areas of the world may sometimes be simplified by using a specialist agent or a good local agent, if one exists. A choice must be made between using a single agent, or several, and performance also needs to be monitored to ensure best value for money. Purchasing direct from a publisher rather than through a subscription agent can be advantageous, and in some cases there is no choice.

The control process, that is the process of check-in of issues and the claiming of missing issues, is a particularly labour intensive activity which is more and more being assisted by automation. The latter presents problems of choosing the right system for a library's circumstances and needs and within its financial means.

Some may argue that cataloguing is a greater problem than control. Should the serial title be catalogued or not? To what level should it be catalogued? There are difficulties in cataloguing serials which, while all of them may not be peculiar to serials, are more serious for serials than they are for monographs. A serial is not finished with once the first issue received has been catalogued. When it stops publication, changes its title, or its subscription is cancelled, the catalogue record and its attendant holdings statement must be closed, and closure of an entry may take as long or longer than the original cataloguing. There are still, surprisingly, controversies about the cataloguing of serials in spite of the trends in standardization over the past twenty years or so. Should serials be classified? If so, should they be classified broadly or closely?

Following through the evolutionary process from life to death of a serial, therefore, there are the problems of accessibility of the collection to the user, the dissemination of information, circulation, and awareness. There are then the continuing problems of storage and preservation. Even when a serial dies or is deselected a good deal of activity is necessary to close the catalogue entry or delete it from the catalogue, to close the acquisition record and, where appropriate, to notify union catalogue editors.

Serials have problems in themselves. There are changes of title, of names of issuing bodies, of publisher, frequency, enumeration patterns, and format as well as the unexpected appearance of special issues, double issues, supplements and the like. There may also be interruptions and delays in publishing.

All the foregoing problems in serials and their handling have been those of serials published in the medium of print on paper. That medium will no doubt, in spite of rapid technological advances, remain the principal means of publication for some time. Most of the problems mentioned will, no doubt, remain as well. Increasingly, however, collection managers must learn to cope with serials in new media, and with information, now commonly found in print on paper, becoming more available by electronic means.

Although the serial has been the principal medium of scientific and technical communication for 300 years it has inherent drawbacks – delays in publication, restrictions on the length of papers, dispersion of information among a very large number of journals, and refereeing. Some remedies have been sought and found, such as microforms, separates, synopsis journals and selective dissemination of information, although these have brought only partial amelioration. Access is still not easy, there are for example, over 2000 abstracting and indexing services in science and technology. Currency problems have been alleviated, to some extent, by automation. Current contents publications and SDI online databases have become popular current awareness tools. There are also over 2500 online databases, many of which still need a librarian or information worker intermediary to be used to maximum advantage and cost-effectiveness. The future may lie to a degree with the development of expert systems and the concomitant growth of personalized information services, and with the ability to download citations from databases into personal computers. There may be further growth of the invisible college with electronic mailboxes, computer bulletin boards and computer conferencing, and an increase in full text databases. Probable too, is the advance of the tele-communications revolution with likely growth in personal possession of telefacsimile (fax) machines, with its associated impact on document delivery. Library functions in this future may be to train end users, to synthesize information and to control the storage of master copies of electronic media.

Some caution must be exercised in predicting the future. Undoubtedly changes will happen but probably not at the pace nor the scale that some forecasters suggest. The background and affiliation of forecasters should be noted. Often their predictions are commercially self-interested wish fulfilment. The pace of change will be tempered by economic circum-stances, the ability to deliver technology at the right scale at the right price, the ability of information intermediaries to cope with the change, the attitudes and wishes of end users, and the attitudes of existing information providers. Change will take place but it seems that the medium of print on paper will remain the principal medium well into the future.

The foregoing has highlighted many of the problems there are with serials as a form of publication and their management in the collection. Not all of the problems are unique to serials, but are more serious for them than they may be for other kinds of library material, particularly monographs. In what follows some of these problems will be looked at in greater depth.

ACQUISITION

Under this broad heading will be considered the functions of selection, budgeting, ordering, receipt (including the automation of serials control and acquisition), resource sharing (including the concept of union catalogues; actual examples are noted in the sections on 'Retrieval' and 'Notable collections'), deselection, and non-print media.

Selection

Finding a way through the maze of new titles and currently available titles is not easy. Not all titles selected are new in the sense that they are recently published. Some may be established titles which are being newly acquired by the library either as the result of a request, or from the results of a user survey within the library, or because of changed needs within the organization the library serves, such as changes in the curriculum or new directions in research and manufacture.

Knowing what is newly published may come from user demand and recommendation, publishers' announcements, solicited and unsolicited specimen issues, periodical directories and bibliographies, information provided by subscription agents, reviews, updating information from abstracting and indexing services, etc. Knowing what is available to build on an existing collection or to make provision for a new subject area means using directories and bibliographies having subject access, specialist bibliographies, survey articles (such as those appearing from time to time in *Serials Librarian* and *Serials Review*, though noting their North American bias) and so on.

As in the selection of any kind of library material there is a need for objectivity and consistency. Certain criteria need to be observed. A useful benchmark may be the number of interlibrary loan requests for a particular title, although care must be taken to ensure that the interest is going to be sustained. While use studies made in other libraries may be of interest they cannot do duty for local studies; but such studies need to be undertaken with particular care, may be very time consuming and their value will quickly date. Current use can only measure what you have not got. What would a prospective new title add to the collection which is not offered by titles already in it? What course or what research or other work being conducted in the library's parent organization would the title support? Is the title covered by one or more abstracting and indexing services? Does the library subscribe to all or any of these services? Coverage by such services is a useful indicator of value.

Keeping a record of rejected titles is a useful practice as it prevents going over the same ground twice. The reasons for rejecting a title a few years previously may still hold good, on the other hand circumstances may have changed. What may have been considered tangential to the organization's interests originally may now have become central.

No matter what objective measures are used to help determine whether or not to select a particular title, in the end the selector's experience and judgement will probably play the deciding role. Miller and Guilfoyle, at the University of Evansville, Indiana, have described a useful means of computer assisted selection (Miller and Guilfoyle, 1986).

There is considerable temptation to accept unsolicited items readily with little thought to the consequences. Unsolicited items may be one-off samples, ongoing gifts or odd items, some of which may have been received in error. They take time. A check must be made to ascertain whether the item was ordered or requested. If the check proves negative then a decision to discard or not needs to be made. It is useful to have guidelines so that acquisitions staff can filter out the more obvious candidates for the bin leaving the less obvious for selectors to determine whether a request for further issues is worth making. Decisions to discard need to be recorded to avoid going over the same ground every time an issue of an unwanted periodical arrives. In deciding to continue receiving a gift serial the continuing overheads should be taken into consideration.

Budgeting

Budgeting depends very much on planning and the careful collection of data, not only on the prices of existing subscriptions but on plotting prices over a period of time to predict possible increases. The effects of changes in exchange rates on subscriptions for foreign periodicals also need to be taken into account. Budgeting should be set in the context of collection development policies which should be drawn up for the whole collection as budgeting for serials cannot be done in isolation. A useful guide to trends in periodical prices is the Blackwell's periodicals prices index which is published regularly in *Serials: The Journal of the United Kingdom Serials Group* and *The Library Association Record*. There must be a clear understanding of the costs and limitations of forecasting and the construction of models which will most accurately reflect trends, that is have least error (see Emery, 1985).

The inflation of prices against the decline in acquisitions budgets in real terms points to the necessity for more information to control budgets, help determine what might be cancelled, and so on, especially if subject data is required, that is if costs are needed for different subject areas. More and more other data of relevance is being required in libraries, such as performance measurements and service costings to determine the real costs of performing various functions. While such data can be gathered, processed and analysed manually, if it can be computer assisted clearly not only is a lot of staff time saved but data and its processing and analysis can be made more sophisticated (although the temptation to gather and process information for its own sake must be resisted) (see James, 1985 and Shuster, 1989). More sophisticated systems in larger libraries should either provide such facilities as a matter of course or should be readily capable of enhancement to provide it.

Another useful survey, supplementing the Blackwell's index to some extent, is *Trends in Journal Subscriptions, 1982–1985*. This, the third survey of its kind (previous ones covered 1974–1978 and 1979–1981), covers members of the Publishers Association Serials Publishers Group and the Association of Learned and Professional Society Publishers.

Questioning the effectiveness, economy and efficiency of libraries has become more common. Librarians are being called upon to justify their actions and their expenditure. As an unnamed American academic has been quoted as saying, 'Statistics may be boring, but they are preferable to thumping the table.' A hope that occasional table thumping or lobbying may do the trick can no longer absolve librarians from gathering and keeping adequate data. In the UK the UGC/USR (now the Universities Funding Council (UFC)) figures are good for trends. SCONUL figures are best for comparisons (see Mann, 1989).

Thompson (1989), has shown the effects on serials and acquisitions budgets at the University of California. While experience in the United States is not necessarily mirrored in the UK there are probably sufficient points of similarity to take that experience as indicative. As the budget share for serials has increased less has been available for other materials. The ability of libraries to buy individual books, retrospective materials, microforms, reprints, non-book media, duplicate copies and rare books has been seriously eroded. This has an unbalancing effect on collection development. Disciplines which rely heavily on monographs and older materials, such as the humanities and social sciences, are seriously disadvantaged. The demands of current subscriptions and their inflationary price rises mean there is less for new subscriptions.

Ordering

There is the choice of ordering direct from the publisher or using a subscription agent. Though the latter may offer many advantages there are situations where direct ordering is preferable. An understanding of the publishing and distribution problems of serials leads to informed decisions. Serials can then be acquired more effectively and best use can be made of subscription agents' services.

Direct ordering is more time and resource consuming. An agent effectively removes much of the administrative work and hence its costs. Agents should have considerable expertise in dealing with publishers and extensive bibliographical sophistication which can be used in a variety of ways to the library's advantage. Inevitably the agent must cover costs by the imposition of a surcharge, the level of which may be negotiable. Publishers' discounts to agents have not been widespread in recent years and thus the subscription price can exceed the basic cost. Ultimately the quality of a subscription agent's service depends on the quality of service from publishers.

While an agency may be advisable, it is not always the most suitable means of acquisition. Potential difficulties in acquisition of each title need to be predicted. General problems are the country of publication, currency and the subscription cost. While by no means all foreign serials are hard to obtain, in general it may be said that Eastern Europe and the Third World present particular difficulties. Currency problems may be circumvented by using an agent who specializes in these difficult areas. In the Third World all sorts of social, political and economic disruptions may conspire to make serial publishing difficult. The publishing trade in these countries may also be poorly organized and in such cases direct ordering is unlikely to be any more successful than using an agent.

Agents may find themselves at a financial loss with non-commercial serials. Where titles are part of an institutional membership package the best approach may be direct. The less formal the organization the probability is that the more difficult it will be to acquire its publications. Records control in such organizations tends to be rudimentary because personnel are likely to be voluntary and subject to rapid changes. Mailing lists are lost or misplaced and re-establishing contact becomes difficult. Agents are bound by commercial realities. Librarians are, perhaps, more able to use their professional expertise in such cases. If agents have a disproportionate amount of this material cluttering their systems it may have a negative effect on their services to everyone's disadvantage.

Primary and secondary serials marketed nationally and internationally by commercial publishers (including learned societies and the like) should cause no problems to agents. Ultimately the library's administrative systems should not be allowed to dictate policy on the best sources through which to acquire materials.

In selecting an agent the choice is much more limited than it is in choosing library suppliers to provide books (see Merriman, 1988). Changing an agent who is giving poor or inadequate service may be an upheaval unless the library's acquisitions and order records are automated when block changes (with a good automated system) are relatively straightforward. There is, however, a general lack of understanding by librarians on how serial publishers and agencies work. Each library has its own set of procedures, priorities and problems and a good agent will make an effort to appreciate these and accommodate them to their systems. There is some obligation, however, on the library to accommodate itself within reason to the agent's system.

An agent must provide timely response to orders and claims, accurate invoicing and prompt replies to problems and queries. Additionally the agent should provide internal library accounting information on invoices, arrangements for various billing and shipping addresses, management reports and intercession with difficult publishers. There may also be services which the librarian does not want, or does not know he wants, and those the librarian may want but which it may be unreasonable to expect. The librarian, then, must separate genuine needs from desires.

Another matter which librarians will concern themselves with in selecting an agent is discounts. Nowadays agents get little in the way of discounts from publishers and there should be some wariness about the offer of discounts. It is not unusual, however, for agents to offer modest discounts on large orders and to offer discounts if subscriptions are renewed by a particular date.

The librarian must also ask the question: Is this company right for me? It is a matter which is unquantifiable. While one library may get very good service from a particular agent and hold him or her in high regard, it does not necessarily follow that the circumstances and working practices of another library will fit equally well.

Should a library centralize on one agent? If the agent gives efficient, effective service and the library feels comfortable with that agency then there seems no good reason why all or most subscriptions should not go to one agent providing, of course, there are no local rules about spreading spending. The more recent unfortunate tendency for parent organizations to demand going out to tender for everything may well, in the end, have adverse effects in compelling agencies and suppliers to cut corners.

Some factors which may mitigate against centralizing on one agent are, first, some agents may not accept standing orders, for example for annual publications, monographic series and so on, and it may then be best to order periodicals through an agent and other serials through a bookseller; second, some materials can only be ordered direct or may best be ordered direct; third, it may be considered best to use a domestic agent for home publications and otherwise use overseas agents; fourth, for some parts of the world the use of a specialized agency may be advisable. Perhaps the one course that should not be taken is to use a bookseller who may handle serials as a favour or as a loss leader.

There are many variables in service from agents and librarians have not given sufficient study to these. Some work has been done on evaluating services, but much more needs doing (see Bonk, 1985 and 1986).

Receipt

In spite of the advance of automation in recent years many libraries, and not only small libraries, still use manual methods to record receipt of serial issues, invoice and payment details and claims. The commonplace systems are Kardex, Roneodex and Kalamazoo, all well known proprietary ledger systems. Perhaps for a modest number of titles handled in a well managed acquisitions section this is still an efficient method of recording.

Manual records do need to be well and clearly set out and the quality of recording needs to be very good in terms of consistency and clarity. Too often acquisitions sections' staff tend to disregard the fact that staff other than themselves will need to use the record. Among disadvantages of manual methods there are the relative slowness of input and recording, the lack of different access points unless elaborate indexes are compiled, the inability of other users to consult the files other than in person or over the telephone, the relative slowness and inefficiency with which they enable claiming to be done, their high labour-intensity, and so on. Automation will overcome most of these problems and perform more efficiently. It will enable acquisitions staff to control budgets, provide management information much more effectively and it will allow effective monitoring of supplier performance. Most libraries now should be able to buy a system off the shelf to suit their needs. There are few libraries in the United Kingdom of such size and complexity that would not have all or most of their needs satisfied by one or other of the available systems.

Claiming missing issues is often seen as an unattractive process with manual systems, although a system of different coloured record cards for different frequencies and the use of moveable markers should obviate some of the disadvantages. The need to claim promptly, and certainly within an agent's or publisher's claim period, means that at times issues are missed because they have gone out of print. Some librarians allege that claims can be satisfactorily picked up as issues are received and the receipt of the previous issue has not been recorded. That may be so, up to a point, but it does not allow for failure in supply when non-receipt may not come to notice for some time and it may also mean that the claim period has elapsed. Automated systems can generate claims automatically. Recently a representative of an American subscription agency has written that the widespread use of automated claiming systems in the United States has led to such a rise in the volume of claiming that it has caused a decline in the quality and accuracy in the claiming process. The quality control which existed in manual systems has been reduced by this dependence on automated systems. He also alleges that many suppliers are now tending to disregard first claims. These assertions obviously need investigating. Algorithms can be used to tailor claiming to the needs of different kinds of material. There is no reason why quality control should not still be applied with automated systems. There is no reason why the claiming mechanism cannot be optional, that is, where appropriate it can be overridden or claims can be referred to a manager before action is taken.

The various systems available are documented by Leeves (1989). There is a wealth of articles in the professional press about systems and individual libraries' experience although these tend to be predominantly American. Limited British experience is documented in *Serials* and *VINE*. Boss (1986), has produced a very useful check list to help evaluate systems and the James E. Rush Associates series *Library Systems Evaluation Guides* is equally useful.

Resource sharing

No library, not even the largest and most comprehensive, can fulfil all its users needs and resort must be made even in such libraries to interlibrary lending or referral to a holding library. Strangely, relatively little work has been done on the cost effectiveness and cost benefits of resource sharing. It is certainly not a panacea to cure the ills of inadequate budgetary provision which fails to meet reasonable demand. One of the objects of resource sharing is to enable the co-operating libraries to save money and to make their budgets go further, and at the same time maintain or improve the level of service. Sometimes, regrettably, the term becomes a euphemism for rationalization.

There is a need for accurate information about co-operative activity so that sound management decisions can be made from a position of fact rather than from supposition. Factors which need to be studied are document supply, access and reciprocity, co-operative acquisition and storage, transport infrastructure, and the impact of new technology.

Will co-operation allow something to be done which is needed but which is not being done or not being done well? Will co-operation provide the same level of service to as many users as now or will it do better? Will it allow savings without deterioration in service or with better service? If not, is it cost effective? Does co-operation have the financial, technical and staff resources to achieve its objectives in the most efficient manner? Does it take adequate account of new technology? All these questions need investigation and answers before co-operation can be undertaken to the clear benefit of all the participating libraries (see MacDougall, 1989).

Although a proportion of requests made to the British Library Document Supply Centre (BLDSC) could be satisfied in local co-operatives what would be the cost implications? Local co-operatives require a transport system, staff to process requests and loans, and the overhead of a union list. In local co-operatives dependence on other libraries may lead to a fall in the services of the depending library.

The complexities of compiling and keeping up to date a union catalogue and the resources required to do so should not be underestimated, no matter how limited its coverage. Unesco and IFLA have produced useful guidelines which repay close attention before a union catalogue is launched or an existing one revitalized. Whiffin's (1983) guidelines are somewhat more detailed.

A useful methodology, originating in the United States within the Research Libraries Group and being developed in the United Kingdom by the British Library for British and European purposes, is Conspectus (see Stam, 1986). This methodology enables a library to describe the quality of its collections in a codified and standardized way. The resulting description provides a basis for rationalization and co-operation for collection development and it also has applications in many other areas. Further information is available from the Conspectus Officer at the British Library, Humanities and Social Sciences.

Deselection

Weeding the collection is a function which is carried out too little. It improves the efficiency and vitality of a collection in the same way that unnecessary items weaken it. A core collection of journals will usually satisfy a very high percentage of demand and needs to be identified. Space, often at a premium, may be saved not only by discarding but by substituting microform (and, in time, CD-ROM and other disc media) for hardcopy.

Librarians want balance, wide subject coverage and quality in their collections. Part of the way to achieve these as well as handling the problem of cancellations enforced by economic necessity is to draw up objective criteria for de-acquisition. Such criteria may include, among others, decisions to discard titles which are not indexed in indexing and abstracting services held by the library, those which have stopped publication and do not have cumulative indexes, incomplete sets, or early volumes of long runs.

There are discouraging factors; among them, the numbers game, that is the attitude that the more volumes there are in the library the more important it is. There are work pressures, because it cannot be denied that weeding and cancellation exercises are very time consuming. There are the inevitable emotional and intellectual blocks, not only of staff (with, perhaps, some feeling about the sacredness of the collection) but also of users. Richard De Gennaro, in a 1977 article in *American Libraries*, remarked upon the weakness that librarians have for numbered series of any kind (the desire to have a run from volume 1, number 1 or a complete set of a series). Users have similar weaknesses, especially if the threatened journal is one in which they are wont to publish. Publishers have weaknesses for journals and numbered series because their publication tends to create captive markets.

Libraries are spending more to buy less. Librarians must, therefore, become more skilful in identifying the little used and be ruthless in weeding. The core collection, once identified, must be maintained. Care must be taken not to assume too readily that interlibrary lending and resource sharing will fill the gaps. If we all throw away our copies then clearly we won't be able to borrow. There must be a mechanism within co-operative ventures to ensure that last copies are not discarded without agreement.

Criteria for measuring the worth of journals to the collection need to be devised. Usage is obviously an important criterion of value, if it can be properly and reliably measured. Indications of usage are if the journal is circulated (although here there may be inertia on the part of the recipients – some may really not want to see it or may not need to see it but continue to receive it on circulation), in-house usage, including photocopying, ILL requests and citation analyses.

Subjective measures may be used to determine intrinsic value. This means using the professional judgement and opinion not only of collection managers but also subject experts among users. Matters such as physical quality, length of the library's run, indexing coverage, ownership by a prestige library having a 'model' collection, presence in reliable lists of 'essential' titles, intellectual level, appropriateness for anticipated user groups, and so on all need to be taken into account.

If discarded or cancelled will the journal be available from elsewhere? What will be the cost and convenience of obtaining articles if the journal is no longer in the collection? Will users have access to runs in other neighbouring libraries?

To determine the desirability of discarding or keeping a title a good deal of data and analysis is needed. Gathering and analysing the data may be costly. Full-scale usage studies can be costly and where the cost cannot be justified or met then estimates based on judgement and past experience have to be used. If usage studies are used to help make decisions in weeding and cancellation exercises then they must be locally based. Such studies will have a limited life because of changes in policy, funding and curriculum or changes in direction of research, policy, marketing and so on in the parent institution. Each library is unique. It has its own group of users, purpose and set of physical facilities (material may be under-used, not because it is not wanted, but because access requires too much fuss and delay).

In dividing up a limited budget (making allowance for the need to acquire new titles), the cost of obvious core items needs to be deducted. The remaining titles may then be ranked by a scoring mechanism applying a weighting to each of the criteria being used to determine the value of a title. Cancellation exercises are often disappointing in their outcome. The University of California at Berkeley Biology Library found that of 845

97

current titles with no recorded use 651 were gifts. Thus cancelling low use journals may not always yield hope for savings. Yet 'free' publications may cause many processing problems and their processing and retention is not free.

The more useful articles out of the many available on deselection and usage studies are noted in the Bibliography.

Non-print media

Microforms have a number of advantages and must also be considered as an essential preservation medium. They take significantly less space than hardcopy. A microform run is more likely to be intact. They cost considerably less than purchasing a hardcopy reprint or second-hand run. For rare, out of print and certain other kinds of material they may be the alternative to not having the material at all. However, they are not suitable for all materials, especially where illustrations, particularly coloured illustrations are important, such as art journals. There is understandable user resistance to them. They cannot be presented as superior to hardcopy but more positive marketing and presentation might lead to greater, if reluctant acceptance. All too often microform readers are inadequately serviced and poorly placed in the library. If users are given good, adequately serviced and sited readers and if they are made fully aware that if it was not for microform the material would not be in the library at all then, perhaps, they might be used and accepted more.

So much that is written about new media is by technical people and those representing manufacturers. Technical people have a tendency to deal with the possible and not necessarily the desirable and the marketable. The new disc media offer many advantages. They may be convenient for storing and acquiring back runs. They may make it possible to have individual/ departmental prices for larger journals. In some instances they could remove the need for print on paper journals. They may be convenient for document delivery. They are, especially CD-ROM, attractive and exploitable technologies. They allow the storage and retrieval of relatively large amounts of information at a reasonable price. The growth in numbers of personal computers could lead to a demand from users for readier access.

On the other hand, there are also disadvantages in the new disc media. At present, in a dynamic market, there are few standards. The technologies are oriented to the single user workstation. They cannot yet be attached to a mainframe or minicomputer for concurrent access by a number of users. The immaturity of several competing technologies (video disc, optical digital disk, CD-ROM) means there are a number of economic and investment considerations to be made by manufacturers and publishers. The extent of market impact and acceptance by users is still not yet clear. The displacement of some serials by electronic media will be through a gradual evolutionary process rather than a dramatic and immediate one.

Brindley (1988), has explored the rival merits of hardcopy, online and CD-ROM. Though incrementally taking up more space each year and cumbersome and time-consuming to search, comprehensive back runs of major abstracting and indexing services are assets not easily replaced. Arguably as shelf space becomes more valuable and more back runs become available on CD-ROM then there might be a phasing out of print. However, print is relatively easy to use. It can be browsed and used simultaneously with other material, and although it requires laborious copying of citations, simultaneous multiple use is easy.

Online has the benefit of centralized access, comprehensive backfiles, easy multi-file searching and is more up to date than CD-ROM. It is the most sophisticated medium to support complex queries; but users generally need an intermediary especially as time-related charges can significantly penalize an inexperienced user.

With CD-ROM backfile coverage is patchy at present. As files increase in size there is the penalty of loading and re-loading discs for multi-year searching. CD-ROM is not as fast as online. It entails the purchase of equipment which cannot support multi-user access at present. On the other hand, it is oriented to end users and is popular with them, it requires no intermediaries, is relatively easy to use and there are no time-related charges.

The balance of advantage between the various media will vary from library to library depending on their clientele and the emphasis given to supporting different activities. It seems that libraries will continue to support a mix with each co-existing. The ability to provide easily and cheaply networked access to CD-ROMs would greatly facilitate the shift from paper to CD-ROM. Too often publishers are not mindful of budgetary constraints when packaging their increasingly integrated product lines.

The literature on CD-ROM and other new media is considerable, with whole journals and conference proceedings devoted to them. Some of the more accessible material is noted in the Bibliography.

CATALOGUING

A monograph, unless it is a work in progress with an open entry in the catalogue, is bibliographically complete and once catalogued, corrections to the record apart, it is finished with. A serial, however, does not have this stability. What may happen to it in its lifetime is entirely unpredictable. Titles change, are merged, split, and resurrected. Frequencies, publishers and places of publication change. Some journals have regular supplements and inserts which are effectively separate journals.

The common practice, for economy's sake, is to have an open entry in the catalogue which will not be closed until the title ceases or the library cancels its subscription. Added complications are introduced when a library may have a limited retention period for a serial. For example, it is not unusual to keep only the current and the previous issue of an annual or directory or at best to keep a very short run or to keep only short runs of certain periodicals. A catalogue entry for a currently held title represents the serial as it was when the first issue was published or as it was for the first issue received in the library (which may not be quite the same as the first issue). The entry is, as it were, a snapshot taken at a particular moment in the serial's life. The entry for a live serial does not represent the entire run held.

When a title ceases or the subscription has been cancelled then the entry will need to be closed. Necessary notes will need to be made about changes of frequency during the serial's life, minor title variants and so on, and where appropriate linking notes such as 'Continues...', 'Continued by...', 'Absorbed by...', 'Merged with...to form...', and 'Split into...' will be put into the record. The enumeration, coverage and publication dates and number of volumes will have to be closed or entered. The holdings statement will have to be completed with gaps in holdings appropriately indicated. The amount of work required to close a catalogue entry for a serial may be at least as much as that used to create the original entry.

The way a serial is recorded in the catalogue may not match the way it is recorded in the acquisitions record. In some libraries the two are tied together. The acquisitions record will often be the only reliable source of data on holdings for a live serial. The catalogue entry will not indicate gaps in holdings until it is closed. It would be useful, therefore, to link automated catalogues to automated acquisitions records.

The principal controversies which exist and which excite most debate are over successive versus earliest or latest entry, entry under title or corporate body (especially of generic titles) and over identification versus bibliographic description. Those controversies are adequately covered elsewhere (see Mullis, forthcoming article).

Whatever the arguments, there can be no doubt that standardization of cataloguing rules and the progressive adoption of automation have resolved or, at least, stilled them. Beginning with the Paris Principles in 1961, leading to the publication of the first edition of AACR in 1967, there has been a continuing development of standardization in cataloguing. The development of the International Serials Data System (ISDS) from 1971, with the publication of its *Guidelines* in 1973, and ten years later the publication of the *ISDS Manual*, has been paralleled by the activities of the IFLA programme for Universal Bibliographic Control (UBC) and the publication of the international standard bibliographic descriptions, notably, in this context, by the publication of ISBD(S) in 1974, substantially revised and made compatible with ISDS rules and published in 1988.

The development of machine-readable cataloguing and of the MARC formats has had a profound effect on cataloguing standards and the need for them. Inevitably, records available from the principal national libraries, in whatever physical form, are compiled according to the prescriptions of AACR2. The growth of bibliographic utilities, often with the opportunity to share catalogue records, similarly imposes the need for standardization. Shared cataloguing and derived or copy cataloguing all call for common standards if the benefits of sharing, deriving or copying are to have maximum effect. Participation in union catalogues also imposes adherence to common standards.

Some librarians argue that there are kinds of serial which are sufficiently different from the general run to warrant special treatment. The kinds which tend to be singled out as not adequately dealt with by AACR2 are mono-graphic series, report series, sub-series, conference proceedings, legal materials, and newspapers. Putting aside the last (which are treated elsewhere in this work) it seems that those who argue for this special treatment confuse the bibliographic condition of 'serial', of which the foregoing are just types (and not necessarily mutually exclusive types) with particular problems which may exist over availability, acquisition, preservation and the like. They are all serials and all can be adequately recorded bibliographically using AACR2.

What to catalogue and what not to catalogue and to what level of detail to catalogue is a problem which is not peculiar to serials. Some libraries may be content to use the acquisition record as the catalogue (which is fine if it is generally available). Some may catalogue non-periodical serials and periodicals which are to be permanently retained; those which are to be kept for short periods only may then be separately and briefly listed, and such practice seems a disservice to the user. Different kinds of serial may be accorded different kinds of treatment depending on the volume of material received, its importance within the collection and the availability of other bibliographic finding tools. It seems quite evident, in spite of any con-troversies, that the cataloguing standard which should be used is AACR2.

CLASSIFICATION

Whether serials are classified must depend on the circumstances of individual libraries. Arguments about whether serials are worth classifying and whether classification has any real meaning in so far as serials are concerned apply, usually, only to periodicals. It is usual to classify annuals, directories and the like; sometimes such publications are shelved separately, especially collections of directories, and, occasionally, classifications other than the general one used in the library are applied. Collections of report literature may be kept in report series and then in number order within each series. Serials which form parts of other collections, such as Parliamentary Papers, UN documents and United States Government Printing Office publications may be kept with those collections in their document number order, retrieval being effected by reliance on the published indexes for the material.

The main problem is periodical literature. Some will argue that if permanently held journals are adequately covered by abstracting and indexing services subscribed to by the library then that is sufficient. That argument may hold for journals in science and technology; although there is a probability that not all titles held by the library are covered. It is less likely to hold for the social sciences and even less so for the humanities.

While most demand for journals will be for specific articles, nevertheless there is a need for browsing and for relating material in a particular subject field together, whether it is monographic or serial. Indeed, proponents of the classification of periodicals on shelves may claim that the first and most important basic advantage of classification is that all material on a subject may be brought together. Classification may be broad either as a matter of policy or because of the nature of the material. Opponents of classification may argue that a number of journals are multidisciplinary in coverage and can go at only one place on the shelves. The subject or classified catalogue can compensate for this by multi-access points under all appropriate subjects.

Bringing material together on the shelves by subject may allow the browser to come upon new or unfamiliar titles within his or her field of interest. Browsing in an unclassified collection, especially in one of some size, leaves much to chance and may lead to uneconomic underuse of some titles. The browsing argument may apply much more to the humanities and, to some extent, to the social sciences than it does to science and technology.

It is sometimes argued that periodicals are generally too broad in their subject coverage to give their classification much meaning or value, but there has been a tendency over the last twenty years or so for more and more serials to be published with narrower subject coverage. It is also argued that periodicals tend to change or vary subject coverage over time and that may lead to the chore of reclassification, especially if close classification is used. However, such changes are not especially frequent and if classification is reasonably broad then the need to reclassify will occur only very occasionally.

Classifying periodicals, as well as subject indexing them, should draw attention to their purpose and coverage and bring them together with monographs so that the whole collection can be used comparatively, effectively and in depth. Making the most economic use of space may militate against bringing together periodicals and other materials on shelves. In small libraries, or in those where the collection is small, and in smaller, specialist libraries there may be no need to classify periodicals. It may be sufficient, for example, to class ten journals on different aspects of economics at a general number in a smaller, general library, whereas in a larger or more specialist library more exact classification may be useful to its clientele.

Whether to classify at all and whether to classify broadly or narrowly must depend on the size of the collection and how it is used. Each library must decide, depending on its circumstances, what it can best afford and what best serves its users.

RETRIEVAL

Cataloguing and classification of periodicals and their representation in subject catalogues are part of the general topic of retrieval. This section will concern itself, however, with the retrieval of information *about* serial titles not in the collections, that is, bibliographic information and location of holdings of particular titles, for example in union listings and the catalogues of individual libraries; and with information about particular articles in journals, whether in the collection or not, that is, with abstracting and indexing services.

The material available may be divided into three groups. The first is that which will be most useful for bibliographic information, whether for the purposes of cataloguing or acquisition. The second group may be used for locating particular serials in libraries, that is to say the catalogues of individual libraries and union catalogues. This group will also be useful for bibliographic information. The third group comprises indexing and abstracting services, and concerns itself with specific article citations. This last group will also be useful for bibliographic information. Space does not permit more than a small number of examples indicative of what is available. More general guides and directories and bibliographies of bibliographies should be consulted for more detailed pictures for particular purposes.

The most generally useful of sources for information on currently available serials is *Ulrich's International Periodicals Directory* published by Bowker. This now includes *Irregular Serials and Annuals*, previously published separately. It includes file names for about 1300 publications available online and information on some 200 serials in CD-ROM format. *Ulrich's Quarterly* comes as part of the purchase price and provides updating information between the annual issues. The *Ulrich's* database is also available online via DIALOG, BRS and ESA/IRS Dialtech and is updated every six weeks. There is also a CD-ROM version, *Ulrich's Plus*.

Until now, *Ulrich's* has been without a rival. However, *The Serials Directory* from EBSCO Publishing may well become that rival. Among its various claims to provide more than *Ulrich's* is that the latest edition has 123 000 titles compared to 111 600 in *Ulrich*. There is also a CD-ROM version of *The Serials Directory*.

Other useful general sources of information are subscription agents' catalogues. They vary considerably in coverage, arrangement and information included. All give subscription prices and that information is usually more current than *Ulrich*. All are rather shy when it comes to including information on handling charges. All could be made easier to use.

Current British Journals, 5th edn, 1989 is a subject guide to periodicals published jointly by BLDSC and the United Kingdom Serials Group and includes over 9000 titles. A slightly earlier select list is *Walford's Guide to Current British Periodicals in the Humanities and Social Sciences* (Library Association Publishing).

While the availability of products in CD-ROM and online is noted in *Ulrich* and *Current British Journals*, for instance, there are also specialized sources. *The CD-ROM Directory* (TFPL) covers about 200 products and the *International Directory of Information Products on CD-ROM* (Alan Armstrong and Associates) covers abstracting and indexing services and bibliographies as well as other products. *Books and Periodicals Online: A Guide to Publication Contents of Business and Legal Databases* (Learned Information) covers more than 6800 serials included in databases.

Union catalogues and the serials catalogues of individual libraries will not only be of use in locating particular serials but will also be of value bibliographically. While not a catalogue or union catalogue the *ISDS Register* on microfiche includes records for all titles which have had ISSN assigned. It contains about 450 000 records. *New Serial Titles*, compiled and published by the Library of Congress, has bibliographic and holdings information for about 520 libraries in the United States.

The world's major list of serial titles is the CONSER file (formerly the CONversion of SERials Project, now the Cooperative Online Serials Program). It is a project which aims to catalogue all possible serials acquired by the Library of Congress, the National Library of Canada and most major collections in North America. The programme is a co-operative association of libraries that upgrade and maintain serial records in the OCLC database (which is now accessible online in this country through BLAISE-RECORDS). There are about 750 000 records in the file. Authenticated records are available through USMARC and CANMARC tape distribution services, NST and a COM fiche version available from NLC, as well as through OCLC.

Other foreign files of general utility, all of which are available in COM fiche, are the *National Union Catalogue of Serials held in Australian Libraries* (NUCOS), the Scandinavian union list, NOSP, the French national union catalogue, the *Catalogue collectif national informatise des publications en serie* (CCN), and the German serials database, *Zeitschriften-Datenbank* (ZDB); the latter two catalogues are particularly extensive. All of these files are international in scope and include current and retrospective information. They have, of course, particular strengths for the material of their country of origin.

There is no up-to-date file of general utility for the United Kingdom since the demise of the *British Union-Catalogue of Periodicals* (BUCOP) and *BUCOP. New Periodical Titles*. BUCOP was published in four substantial volumes in 1955–58 followed by a supplement up to 1960. The main work contains more than 140 000 titles with holdings reported from 440 libraries. It was a considerable enterprise for its time given that it was manually compiled and produced by conventional printing methods. In 1972 it was estimated that by then only 70 per cent of holdings and locations were accurate and their accuracy would, of course, be even less now. Nevertheless it remains a useful source of information. BUCOP was continued by *BUCOP. New Periodical Titles* (BUCOP.NPT) with its subset *The World List of Scientific Periodicals*. The last separate edition of the latter, the fourth, was published in three volumes, 1963–65. The number of libraries reporting their holdings to BUCOP.NPT steadily dwindled over the years and the number of new titles the very small editorial team could cope with was limited. The quarterly issues were cumulated annually and there are two larger cumulations covering 1960–68 and 1969–73. Thereafter, only the annual cumulations are available until its closure with the 1980 volume.

The British Library, which had assumed editorial responsibility for BUCOP.NPT in 1974, replaced it by *Serials in the British Library*. It was intended that SBL, a quarterly printed listing with a rolling annual cumulation on microfiche, should include not only all serial titles newly acquired by all departments of the British Library but also those newly acquired by 20 other major libraries, including the other copyright libraries in the United Kingdom and Ireland. Continuing downward pressures on resources within the Library eroded that intention. By 1987 coverage was restricted to those titles acquired by the London-based collections of the Library, with three quarterly printed issues and an annual printed cumulation. This revamped version of SBL has keyword subject access. A microfiche cumulation, *Serials in the British Library, 1976–1986*, comprising records of over 57 000 titles acquired by the London collections in those years, is now available.

The holdings of the Yorkshire-based part of the British Library, the Document Supply Centre, are well covered by the annual *Current Serials Received* which lists 72 000 titles currently received by BLDSC and the Science Reference and Information Service (SRIS), the *Index of Conference Proceedings Received* (monthly, with annual cumulations), which adds about 18 000 items each year (it is also accessible through BLAISE-LINE as *Conference Proceedings Index*), and the *Keyword Index to Serial Titles* (KIST) which is published quarterly and annually on microfiche. KIST provides access to over 335 000 serial titles held by the British Library, Science Museum Library and Cambridge University Library. There is a CD-ROM version, *Boston Spa Serials*. SRIS publishes from time to time useful listings of particular kinds of serials held in its collections, such as abstracting and indexing periodicals, trade directory information on serials, house journals, periodicals on agriculture, and so on.

Examples of listings covering specialized fields are the *Register of UN Serial Publications*, which includes approximately 4 000 titles from 38 organizations and is produced by ACCIS (Advisory Committee for the Coordination of Information Systems), the *Union List of Art Periodicals* from ARLIS, a fourth edition of which, covering about 10 000 titles, is due in 1990, and *The British Union Catalogue of Music Periodicals* (Library Association/International Association of Music Libraries (UK), 1985) which includes about 3000 titles in 280 libraries in the UK and Ireland.

There is a plethora of abstracting and indexing services, with science and technology better represented than the humanities and social sciences. A useful guide is *The Index and Abstract Directory: An International Guide to Services and Serials Coverage* (Birmingham, AL: EBSCO Publishing). This includes about 950 abstracting and indexing services which cover the titles in EBSCO's database of about 123 000. The rival merits of hardcopy, online and CD-ROM have already been explored earlier under 'Non-print media'. There would be little value in giving examples of the numerous services available except, perhaps, to mention the products of the Institute for Scientific Information (ISI), such as *Journal Citation Reports*, *Science Citations Index*, *Current Contents*, *Social Sciences Citation Index*, and the *Arts and Humanities Citation Index*. On a much more modest scale there are Library Association Publishing's *Applied Social Sciences*

Index and Abstracts (ASSIA), the *British Humanities Index*, *Current Technology Index*, and *Library and Information Science Abstracts* (LISA).

ACCESSIBILITY AND USE

It was said earlier that problems of collection management may obscure problems which readers may have in using and accessing serials. Too often the librarian's concerns with bibliographic control, preservation and security of the collection tend to come before the reader's needs and it is often forgotten that the collection exists for the reader's use. For example, the user may not be aware that the publication he seeks *is* a serial, or fine divisions within the term 'serial' which librarians may have, such as that 'Advances in...' type of material is kept in one part of the library while conference proceedings are kept elsewhere. The user's citation may not match the catalogue entry; the title, for that matter, may not even be catalogued. If the title is found in the catalogue the entry, if it is an open entry, will not tell the user whether the issue wanted is held. Even if it does show that it is held, it will not show that the issue is at binding or on circulation. It may, of course, be misfiled, lost or damaged. It may be in a remote store. It may have been received but still be in process. It may not have been received but not yet claimed, or it may have been claimed but to no effect. If it can be loaned it may be for a very short, non-renewable, period. Photocopying facilities may not be available for the user's own use and there may otherwise be delays in photocopying.

Some help to the user may be given, where appropriate, by circulating current issues. Unless multiple copies can be provided, or at least a circulation copy, then other users will be denied use of that issue until it has been returned from circulation. Alternatively, a current awareness service may be provided, perhaps in the form of a current contents bulletin backed up by the provision of photocopies of articles on request.

In some libraries loans of journals are not permitted, or at least they may not be lent if less than *x* years old. In others overnight loan of bound volumes and single issues may be allowed. Longer loan periods deny others access when the borrower may simply need to refer to one article in a bound volume. Access to stacks for browsing should be allowed if it does not present a security problem. A common practice is to display current issues, and a useful kind of display shelving is that which allows unseen but accessible storage of other more recent issues. While, inevitably, permanently retained journals will be bound, binding should be organized to ensure that journals are away at binders for a minimum period of time. If possible binding, at least for high demand journals, should be carried out in the least busy times of the year, such as the summer vacation. There should also be adequate photocopying facilities for users, with satisfactory safeguards for preservation and copyright purposes. Librarians must find the right balance between good public service and the preservation and security of the collection. The latter should not cause the collections to be needlessly underused.

PRESERVATION

Preservation policies must form an integral part of collection management policies. They should have regard for the range and scope of the collection, the needs of users, the use of the collection and the realities imposed by the availability of resources. Whether a serial is to be preserved, and how it is to be preserved, as with any other item in the collection, will be based partly on the value of the item to the collection.

Full binding in buckram may not always be the most appropriate method of preservation. Less expensive binding, such as cloth, or partbinding for well-used material, will be more appropriate in some cases. In other cases boxing and wrapping (in acid-free containers or wrappers) may be adequate. Another solution will be either microfilming or purchasing an already available microform. Use surveys may help to determine the mode and level of preservation. Little used materials should have least preservation. Heavily used materials should be protected early. In determining policy and guidelines staff responsible for selection should be involved just as they and cataloguers (if they are not one and the same) should be responsible for determining what should go on the spines of bound volumes (see Chapman, 1987).

Bound volumes, of course, take less space. They are less likely to go missing or be misplaced than unbound issues. They are easier to refer to and handle than a large unbound file. Saving money by having bound volumes which are too thick and heavy may be counterproductive as large, heavy volumes are more difficult to photocopy and are more likely to incur damage in handling. Volumes must be sufficiently flexibly bound so that they can be opened for photocopying without the binding being damaged (see Milkovic, 1986). In-house binding may be an inexpensive method for lesser used, low value material (see Root, 1989).

Automated acquisitions and serials control systems may be of assistance in the binding process. Some systems may have binding alert built into them; regular reports are produced which highlight volumes of journals now ready for binding, that is all issues of a binding volume and, where applicable, the title page and index, have been received. The system may also be programmed to generate picking lists in classified or other shelf mark order so that binding staff can go round shelves picking off unbound volumes.

Microforms are increasingly used for preservation, apart from their value in space saving. The future of microform is clouded by the potential storage capabilities of the new disc technologies. Even if microform is overtaken by other technologies libraries will still have them in their collections. The location of microform masters in British libraries is now much more readily known through the Register of Preservation Microforms compiled by the British Library. This is accessible through BLAISE-LINE and will also be available shortly on microfiche.

Useful listings of microforms available for purchase are *International Microforms in Print, Guide to Microforms in Print* (Meckler Publishing), and the Chadwyck-Healey *Micropublishers' Trade List Annual*.

Useful practical manuals for planning microfilming projects and evaluating microforms are, *Preservation Microfilming: A Guide for Librarians and Archivists* (ALA), *Microforms in Libraries: A Manual for Evaluation and Management* (ALA), and *Preservation Microforms*. The last is a particularly easy to follow guide on British practice for those new to the subject.

NOTABLE COLLECTIONS

Unlike other materials covered in this volume, such as maps, printed music, sound recordings and so on, it is not to be expected that there are notable collections of periodicals or, indeed, of serials generally held in quite the same way as those materials. There are, nonetheless, notable collections, often identifiable from the published catalogues of particular libraries or, less accessibly, through union catalogues. It is to be expected that certain specialist libraries will have notable collections within their fields of interest, such as architecture and building at the British Architectural Library (RIBA), fine and applied arts at the National Art Library (Victoria and Albert Museum), botany at the Royal Botanic Gardens, Kew, and natural history at the Natural History Museum. The copyright libraries will, of course, have extensive collections in many fields, and one would expect the National Library of Wales to have notable collections concerning Wales, Welsh language and culture and Celtic studies generally. The copyright libraries will also hold collections of material which by its popular and ephemeral nature other libraries would not normally collect and keep.

Among more general collections that of the colleges and institutions which make up the University of London is significant. The *University of London*

Union List of Serials, available on COM microfiche, includes about 80 000 titles with 120 000 holdings. The single most significant part of the 'collection' is at the Senate House library. The British Library of Political and Economic Science at the London School of Economics has particular strengths in the social sciences and is especially strong in labour history, economics, politics and official statistics. The University of Cambridge's *List of Serials*, available on microfiche with six-monthly updates, covers not only the University Library, which is one of the six copyright libraries, but also the one hundred or so libraries within the University.

Specialist union lists are sometimes useful indicators of notable collections. The UK Marine and Freshwater Sciences Libraries Group's *Union List of Serial Holdings* has about 6000 titles. The *Union List of American Studies Periodicals in UK Libraries* covers about 2500 titles.

The most significant collections in the UK, by far, are of course held at the British Library. There are actually a number of collections presently scattered among various buildings in London and the collections at BLDSC. The Library is estimated to have holdings of over 520 000 titles, of which about 182 000 are current. There is some overlap between the London and Yorkshire collections, especially in copyright material, but even when that overlap is taken into account there is still, by any standard, a considerable collection. There is, however, no single listing or database of the Library's holdings. The disparate organizations which were brought together in 1972 and later to form the British Library have catalogues compiled according to different bibliographic conventions over a widely varying number of years. Many serial titles are held in general files which include both monographs and serials, such as the *British Library Catalogue* (BLC) (essentially the *General Catalogue* of the former Department of Printed Books of the British Museum Library), its successor, the current catalogue of the Humanities and Social Sciences division, the current catalogue of SRIS, and BNBMARC. These are available in microfiche and online and in the case of the BLC the printed catalogue is now being converted to machine-readable form, will eventually be available online and is becoming available on CD-ROM. BNBMARC is also available in CD-ROM. Catalogues and lists which contain serials only, such as KIST and SBL, have been covered above under 'Retrieval'. The catalogue of the Newspaper Library (available at present in print only) covers over 40 000 titles not all of which are newspapers in the conventionally accepted sense. Periodicals published more frequently than monthly and received through copyright deposit are, by and large, kept at Colindale and included in the catalogue. The most useful general sources on the British Library serials collections are those by Ede and Mullis (1984) and Phillips (1989).

110

BIBLIOGRAPHY

General

Acquisitions Librarian, vol. 1– , no. 1– . New York: Haworth Press, 1989–   , ISSN 0896-3576.

Advances in Serials Management: A Research Annual, Vol. 1– Greenwich, Conn., London: JAI Press, 1986–

Bourne, R. (ed.), (1980), *Serials Librarianship*, London: Library Association, (Handbooks on library practice).

Collection Building: Studies in the Development and Effective Use of Library Resources, vol. 1– , no. 1– . Syracuse, NY: Gaylord Professional Publications, 1978–   , ISSN 0160-4953.

'Collection Management in Sci-Tech Libraries', Ellis Mount, ed. *Science & Technology Libraries*, 1989, **9**(3).

Gorman, G.E. and Howes, B.R. (1989), *Collection Development for Libraries*, London: Bowker-Saur, (Topics in library and information studies).

Graham, M.E. and Buettel, F. (eds), (forthcoming), *Serials Management: A Handbook*, London: Aslib in association with the United Kingdom Serials Group.

Library Acquisitions: Practice and Theory. vol. 1– , no. 1– , New York, Oxford: Pergamon Press, 1977–   . ISSN 0364-6408.

National Acquisitions Group, *Conference, 1986–*   [Proceedings].

Osborn, A.D. (1980), *Serial Publications: Their Place and Treatment in Libraries*, 3rd edn, Chicago: American Library Association.

Serials: the Journal of the United Kingdom Serials Group. Vol. 1– , no. 1– , [Witney]: UK Serials Group, 1988–   . ISSN 0953-0460, continues: *United Kingdom Serials Group Newsletter*.

Serials Librarian, vol. 1– , no. 1– , New York: Haworth Press, 1976–   . ISSN 0361-526X.

Serials review, vol. 1– , no. 1– , Ann Arbor, Mich.: Pierian Press, 1975–   , ISSN 0098-7913.

United Kingdom Serials Group, *Conference*. [Proceedings. 1975–1987], ISSN 0141-1810, (*Note* 1975 and 1977 were 1st and 2nd Blackwells Periodicals Conference).

United Kingdom Serials Group Newsletter. no. 1–vol. 9, no. 2, November 1978–December 1987, ISSN 0141-545X, continued by: *Serials: the Journal of the United Kingdom Serials Group*.

Wortman, W.A. (1989), *Collection Management: Background and Principles*, Chicago: American Library Association.

Selection, budgeting and ordering

Bonk, S.C. (1985), 'Toward a methodology of evaluating serials vendors', *Library Acquisitions: Practice and Theory*, **9**, (51–60).

Bonk, S.C. (1986), 'Variables in vendor service', *United Kingdom Serials Group Newsletter*, **8**(1), 22–4.

Emery, C.D. (1985), 'Forecasting models and the prediction of periodical subscription costs', *Serials Librarian*, **9**(4), 5–22.

Enright, B., Hellinga, Lotte, Leigh, Beryl (1989), *Selection for Survival: A Review of Acquisition and Retention Policies*, London: British Library.

'The impact of rising costs of serials and monographs on library services and programs', Sul H Lee, (ed.) *Journal of Library Administration*, 1989, **10**(1).

James, P.V. (1985), 'Low cost serials budgetary control', *United Kingdom Serials Group Newsletter*, **7**(2), 32–34.

'Libraries and subscription agencies: interactions and innovations', Peter Gellatly, (ed.) *Serials Librarian*, 1988, **14**(3/4).

Mann, P.H. (1989), 'Periodicals and the academic library budget', *Serials*, **2**(2), 27–33.

Merriman, J.B. (1988), 'The work of the periodicals agent', *Serials Librarian*, **14**(3/4), 17–36.

Miller, R.H. and Guilfoyle, M.C. (1986), 'Computer assisted periodicals selection: structuring the subjective', *Serials Librarian*, **10**(3), 9–22.

Prichard, R.J. (1988), 'Serials acquisitions: the relation between serials librarian and subscription agent', *Serials Librarian*, **14**(3/4), 5–10.

Shuster, H.M. (1989), 'Fiscal control of serials using dBase III+', *Serials Review*, **15**(1), 7–20.

Stephens, A. (1989), 'Life cycle costing', *British Journal of Academic Librarianship*, **3**(2), 82–88.

Thompson, J.C. (1989), 'Confronting the serials cost problem', *Serials Review*, **15**(1), 41–47.

Serials control

Boss, R.W. (1986), 'Developing requirements for automated serials control systems', *Serials Librarian*, **11**(3/4), 37–70.

James E. Rush Associates, Inc. (1984), *Acquisitions*, Powell, Ohio: James E. Rush Associates, (Library systems evaluation guide; vol. 4).

James E. Rush Associates, Inc. (1983), *Serials control*, Powell, Ohio: James E. Rush Associates, (Library systems evaluation guide; vol. 1).

Leeves, J. (1989), *Library Systems: A Buyer's Guide*. 2nd edn, London: Gower Press, 1989.

Vine, no. 1– . London: Library and Information Technology Centre, 1971–   .

Resource sharing

MacDougall, A. (1989), 'Academic library co-operation in the East Midlands of England', *Serials*, **2**(1), 21–25.

Stam, D.H. (1986), 'Collaborative collection development: progress, problems, and potential', *IFLA Journal*, **12**(1), 9–19.

Unesco and International Federation of Library Associations and Institutions, (1982), *Guidelines for the Compilation of Union Catalogues of Serials*, Paris: Unesco, (PGI-83/WS/1).

Whiffin, J. (1983), 'Union catalogues of serials: guidelines for creation and maintenance, with recommended standards for bibliographic and holdings control', *Serials Librarian*, **8**(1).

Deselection

Bostic, M.J. (1985), 'Serials deselection', *Serials Librarian*, **9**(3), 85–101.

Gennaro, H. de (1977), *'Escalating Journal Prices: Time to Fight Back'*, *American Librarian*, **28**(2), February, 69–74.

Oldroyd, R.E. (1986), 'Managing deselection to ease the financial straitjacket', *Serials*, 88–103.

Palmer, J. and Sill, L. (1988), 'Keeping track: the development of an ongoing journal usage survey', *Serials*, **1**(2), 30–33.

Tallman, K.D. and Leach, J.T. (1989), 'Serials review and the three-year cancellation project at the University of Arizona Library', *Serials Review*, **15**(3), 51–60.

Wallace, D.P. and Boyce, B.R. (1989), 'Holdings as a measure of journal value', *Library and Information Science Research*, **11**(1), 59–71.

Westbrook, L. (1986), 'Weeding reference serials', *Serials Librarian*, **10**(4), 81–100.

Non-print media

Bowers, R.A. (1986), 'The future of the distribution of serials on optical media', *Serials Review*, **12**(2/3), 11–17.

Brindley, L. (1988), 'Online versus print versus CD-ROM', *Serials*, **1**(2), 21–24.

Butler, B. (1986), 'Scholarly journals, electronic publishing, and library networks: from 1986 to 2000', *Serials Review*, **12**(2/3), 47–52.

'CD-ROM Conference, York, September 1989', [Proceedings], *Serials*, 1989, **2**(3), 32–62; 1990, **3**(1), 26–45.

Collins, A. (1989), 'Managing CD-ROM in an academic library', *Serials*, **2**(2), 35–39.

Mitchell, J. (1989), 'CD versus online', *Serials*, **2**(3), 45–48.

Summit, R. and Lee, A. (1988), 'Will full-text online files become "electronic periodicals"?', *Serials Review*, **14**(3), 7–10.

Cataloguing

Anglo-American Cataloguing Rules; prepared under the direction of the Joint Steering Committee for the Revision of AACR. 2nd edn, 1988 revision. Ottawa: Canadian Library Association; London: Library Association Publishing; Chicago: American Library Association.

Bryant, P. (1988), 'Bibliographic access to serials: a study for the British Library', *Serials*, **1**(3), 41–46.

Bryant, P. (1989), '"What is that hyphen doing, anyway?" – Cataloguing and classification of serials and the new technologies', *International Cataloguing and Bibliographic Control*, **18**(2), 27–29.

International Federation of Library Associations and Institutions, *ISBD(S): International Standard Bibliographic Description for Serials*, rev. edn 1988, London: IFLA UBCIM Programme.

ISDS International Centre, *ISDS Manual*, ed. A.A. Mullis, (1983), Paris: ISDS International Centre.

Mullis, A.A. (forthcoming), 'Cataloguing and classification', *Serials Management: a Handbook*, London: Aslib.

Retrieval and accessibility

'Directory of union lists of serials', 2nd edn, *Serials Review*, 1988, **14**(1/2), 115–159.

Galloway, C. (1988), 'Subscription agents catalogues: goldmine or minefield?', *Serials*, **1**(1), 59–61.

Hanson, E. and Serebnick, J. (1986), 'Evaluation of the public service functions of serial file systems', *College and Research Libraries*, **47**(6), 575–586.

Harrington, S. (1989), 'The central periodicals/microforms room: one way to ease user frustration', *Serials Librarian*, **16**(1/2), 1–15.

McBride, B. (1985), 'Accessibility of serials', *Serials Librarian*, **10**(1/2), 149–160.

Murfin, M.E. (1980), 'The myth of accessibility: frustration and failure in retrieving periodicals', *Journal of Academic Librarianship*, **6**(1), 16–19.

Varley, G. (1989), 'The serials policy of ARLIS', *Serials*, **2**(3), 24–26.

Preservation

Chapman, P. (1987), 'Preserving knowledge for the future', *Serials '87*, 88–96.

Gwinn, N.E. (ed.) (1987), *Preservation Microfilming: A Guide for Librarians and Archivists*, Chicago: American Library Association.

Milkovic, M. (1986), 'The binding of periodicals: basic concepts and procedures', *Serials Librarian*, **11**(2), 93–118.

Preservation Microforms, (1989), London: Kodak/National Preservation Office.

Root, T.A. (1989), 'Inhouse binding in academic libraries', *Serials Review*, **15**(3), 31–40.

Spreitzer, F. (ed.) (1985), *Microforms in Libraries: a Manual for Evaluation and Management*, Chicago: American Library Association.

Notable collections

Ede, S. and Mullis, A. (1984), 'British Library serials databases', *Serials '84*, 23–33.

Phillips, A.B. (1989), 'Bibliographic developments: United Kingdom – Serials databases and networks', in 'Symposium on Managing the Preservation of Serial Literature', Washington, D.C. [*Proceedings*], London: IFLA.

5

Cartographic materials

ANDREW TATHAM

CARTOGRAPHY – THE SUBJECT BACKGROUND

It would not be unjust to suggest that cartography is taken for granted. It is almost impossible to open a newspaper, to travel, or to undertake many normal tasks without often unwittingly encountering maps, the product of cartography. It is perhaps a truism that all information has a spatial component, that it relates not only to a particular time, and to a particular subject, but also to a particular location. It is a truism, however, which provides the basis for cartography.

Cartography has recently been defined as 'The discipline dealing with the conception, production, dissemination and study of maps' (ICA, 1991). The 'conception, production, dissemination and study' will be considered below, but in order to make very much of this definition, it is necessary to define the object of the activity, the map. The Working Group on Definitions in Cartography of the International Cartographic Association which produced the above definition, has defined 'map' as 'A conventionalised image representing selected features or characteristics of geographical reality designed for use when spatial relationships are of primary relevance.' (ibid.) There are other ways of defining the word 'map', but this definition includes a number of essential elements which are relevant to library practice.

First, a map is a conventionalized image. This has a direct bearing on library practice, since many users are not aware of the conventions and a map librarian* may spend a significant amount of time in providing

---

* The terms 'map librarian' and 'map library' have been used throughout this chapter, although readers will be familiar with synonyms such as 'map curator' or 'map keeper' and 'map room' or 'map collection'. Sadly there is no single English equivalent for the French terms *cartothèque* and *cartothècaire* (see Hodgkiss and Tatham, 1986).

informal map-reading training. By contrast, a general librarian rarely has to teach people to read!

Second, a map represents 'selected features or characteristics of geographical reality'. Some selections are made consciously – a map of power transmission lines is unlikely to show nature reserves. Other selections are made subconsciously – an administrative map of the whole of Europe is unlikely to show small areas like civil parishes. The map librarian has to be able to guide users to appropriate sources. In passing, it may be noted that 'geographical reality' can be extended to 'imagined geographical reality', thus permitting Tolkien's map of Middle Earth to be included (Tolkien, 1968), but cannot be extended to 'spatial reality', thus permitting diagrams of atomic structure to be excluded.

The final element which is relevant to library practice is that a map is 'designed for use when spatial relationships are of primary relevance'. Maps provide representations of the spatial component of information either in isolation or in relation to the spatial components of other data sets. The value of this ability to relate data sets through their spatial components is demonstrated in Figure 5.1. The distribution pattern of Figure 5.1(a) shows certain concentrations of data points, but is otherwise of somewhat limited value. By comparison, relating the same data to a second data set, as in Figure 5.1(b), allows a much more interesting interpretation of the original data. It could, for example, be posited that the two data sets were causally related and some further investigations could be undertaken to test this thesis. A more complex analysis might be demonstrated by the case of a town centre which required a bypass. A number of routes are suggested. By relating the road network data set to other sets of data, including terrain, high quality agricultural land, and historical monuments, it would be possible to make judgements about the cost effectiveness and practicality of each proposed route. These two examples, from archaeology and planning, give some idea of the breadth of studies to which maps can make a contribution, providing the spatial element in the body of know-ledge, not just as a pair of co-ordinates in a list, but in relationship to other relevant data. Even the less specialist applications of cartography, the maps found in newspapers or on television weather forecasts, are performing a similar function of relating spatial data with each other and with the set of spatial knowledge held by the reader or being given to the reader in the accompanying verbal report.

Just as a variety of verbal reports and listings of numerical data is essential for presenting certain aspects of data sets to the best advantage, so a variety of cartographic materials is essential for presenting the spatial aspects of these data sets. In terms of library provision it is important to note that there is indeed a variety of cartographic materials, most notably in their

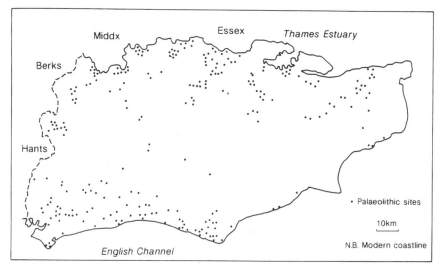

(*a*) Palaeolithic sites in South East England

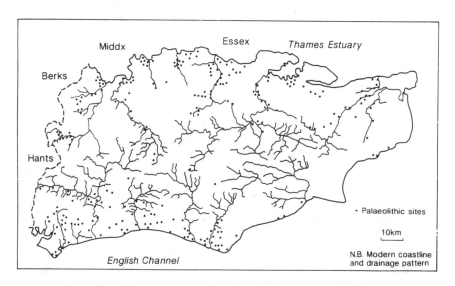

(*b*) Palaeolithic sites and drainage pattern in South East England

**Figure 5.1 Spatial relationships clarified by correlation of two
data sets**
Source: Drewett, P., Rudling, D. and Gardiner, M. (1988),
The South East to AD 1000, London: Longman, p. 3

118

format, from microfiche, through slides, overhead transparencies, atlases and folded maps to flat sheet maps. In addition, many map libraries will be responsible for wall-maps, relief models, globes, remotely sensed imagery (whether from airborne or satellite platforms, or in the visible or non-visible parts of the spectrum) and data held in digital form for use in geographical information systems or other manipulative computer packages.

The map library is involved in each of the processes within cartography mentioned by the definition. Indeed, since the definition is using the four named processes in their broadest senses, the map library is even more involved. Perhaps the best method of illustrating this involvement is to follow the process of creating a new map. The first step is the recognition of the need for a map, perhaps to illustrate an article or a report, or to fill a perceived gap in the market. This is followed by thinking out the elements to be mapped and then researching source material, both statistical and cartographical, and hence using the map library. Following selection of the best sources, draughting can begin the production process, again using the resources of the map library. Once the production is completed, a copy of the map may be held in, or bought by, the map library, thus extending the dissemination of the map and making it available for study.

A number of parts of the subject have an active research community, and it will be helpful to conclude this opening section of the chapter by mentioning some of these, as the rest of the chapter will deal almost exclusively with cartographic materials rather than cartography itself. Cartography is a practical subject and, as with any practical subject, there is in addition to the cartographic materials *per se*, a considerable body of literature connected with developments in design and production. Such literature is frequently accompanied by examples which are themselves of interest to researchers (Ordnance Survey, 1991).

Over the last 25 years, cartographic communication has been a continuing research interest covering the interface between cartography and psychology (see Board, 1976). In recent years, attempts have been made to link the theory to practical design improvements, and recent work in this field tends to be classified as cartographic design. Computer-aided production techniques have also been well covered in the literature, and in particular by the proceedings of the Auto-Carto series of conferences (ACSM, 1977–   ).

In many libraries, cartography will be closely linked to geographical information systems (GIS), which frequently use cartographic forms of output. There is a certain overlap here, although most cartographers would regard GIS as another link in a production chain which may or may not result in cartographic output.

119

Finally, since cartographic artefacts are extant from at least 6200 BC, there is a considerable body of research interest in the history of cartography (not to be confused with historical cartography which is the modern mapping of data at a point in historical time, for example, a map of Roman London published in 1983 (London, 1983)). The history of cartography has its own specialist journal (Imago Mundi, 1935–   ) and research directory (Clutton, 1989).

USER GROUPS

Although several libraries undertake user surveys either regularly or as an occasional exercise, the results are rarely published. Different collections are particularly popular with certain categories of user, but a common feature is the wide variety of user groups. Naturally, they do not all require similar material, and this section will attempt to identify the typical requirements of the main user groups.

General recreational

Except in a few larger research map libraries, such as the British Library, which discourage general recreational users, or those specialist collections, such as County Record Offices, which have little to offer them, this group of users will often be one of the most numerous, if not the most numerous. There are several components of the group. Walkers will usually have their own maps of familiar areas, but may well use a library's maps for preparatory work on a new area. A larger component is formed of self-drive and short-break tourists. Their requirements are for maps to explore tourist areas and to accompany guide books. Thus, for example, the *Michelin Green Guides* of France and other European countries (for example Michelin, 1986) give direct references to the Michelin map series (for example France, 1990), while the *Landranger Guides* of British tourist areas (Ordnance Survey, 1985–   ) refer to the Ordnance Survey's 1:50 000 map series (Great Britain, 1974–   ). It is thus important for the map librarian to be familiar with the guide books available for different areas, particularly those held in the library. A further common requirement of this group is for street plans, particularly of tourist centres. Another component of the general recreational user group is the follower of current affairs who finds the sketch maps in newspaper or television reports insufficient.

Litigation and planning

As anyone who has purchased a house will know, cartographic materials are part of the legal process. This link is even closer in countries where legal ownership of property is related to a cadastre, a land and property survey published in cartographic form, to which all later boundary disputes and agreements are related. However, maps are related to many other aspects of litigation, and the court rolls from the medieval period onwards are an important source of early manuscript mapping (Skelton and Harvey, 1986). Early editions of large scale mapping are also called into play in property disputes while, similarly, work on international or intranational boundaries often requires the evidence of older maps. In one recent dispute, (De Vorsey, 1982), both parties retained historians of cartography as expert witnesses, and the evidence of early maps was a crucial part of both cases.

Turning from cases involving older maps to future plans, the presentation of any new development is likely to involve cartographic materials, both as part of the statutory planning process, and as part of the debate over the desirability or otherwise, of the development. Maps, and especially national or regional atlases, will also provide many of the tools for strategic planning.

The extent to which the map library will be able to provide for this group of users will depend usually on how closely the existing holdings correlate with their requirements. For instance, it is unlikely that a map library that is not already strong in large scale topographic mapping of the area will be able to consider serving property disputants, since the purchase of the necessary stock would be prohibitively expensive.

School projects

Use by pupils and students undertaking educational projects is a feature particularly of the larger urban local library. These libraries may well find it necessary to provide special facilities in terms of staff or services and some will find it cost-effective to prepare educational materials in co-operation with local schools or educational authorities. When providing a service for this intensive but irregular use, there is always a conflict between wanting to encourage the use of cartographic materials and the ability to do so with existing staff or space availability and without causing too much interference to other users.

Genealogists

For many county libraries and record offices, genealogists form the largest proportion of users of the map collection. Since their most usual interest is to trace the addresses found in registers of births, marriages and deaths, their normal requirement is for street plans at scales in the region of

121

1:10 000.* The period of their interest stretches backwards from the early part of the present century. At the level of detail required for genealogical research, most map libraries will only be able to cater for enquiries concerning the local area, with a range of plans showing the nineteenth century developments of towns as well as the pre-urbanization settlements. Local names and street names are of considerable interest, and some map librarians have found the compilation of a gazeteer, with dates of construction and demolition of houses or streets which no longer exist as well as dates of re-namings, to be a worthwhile effort.

Local historians

The cartographic materials used by some local historians are very similar to those used by genealogists. However, although the subject is so broad that it is hazardous to generalize, a much wider range of dates and scales (as small as 1:100 000) will usually be required. The relationship between maps and local history is, indeed, so close that in some libraries the map library falls within the domain of the local history librarian. A type of map of particular interest to this user group is the estate map, especially if it is related to textual material. A similar range of information, that is, field names and their sizes, owners and tenants, houses, their owners and occupiers, is also given for whole parishes by tithe maps and enclosure maps. Unfortunately, none of these classes of maps covered the whole country, and there are cetainly areas that were almost wholly devoid of any detailed survey prior to the work of the Ordnance Survey which covered the whole of England and Wales in 1801–73 (see Figure 5.2).

Historians of cartography

The third group with an historical interest in cartographic materials consists of historians of cartography. Until about twenty years ago, the primary interest of this group was in manuscript cartography and hence the number of map libraries involved in their research remained small. However, this has changed and in the United Kingdom, for example, members of the Charles Close Society specialize in the history of the Ordnance Survey and publish a quarterly bulletin (Sheetlines, 1981–   ). This new emphasis has resulted in a significant increase in the number of map libraries

* Scale is the mathematical relationship between features on the ground and the representation of those features on the map and is expressed verbally (e.g. one inch to one mile) or as a representative fraction (e.g. 1/10000) or as a natural scale (e.g. 1:50 000). This last, for example, means that one unit (e.g. one millimetre) on the map is equivalent to 50 000 units on the ground (e.g. 50 000 millimetres = 0.5 kilometres).

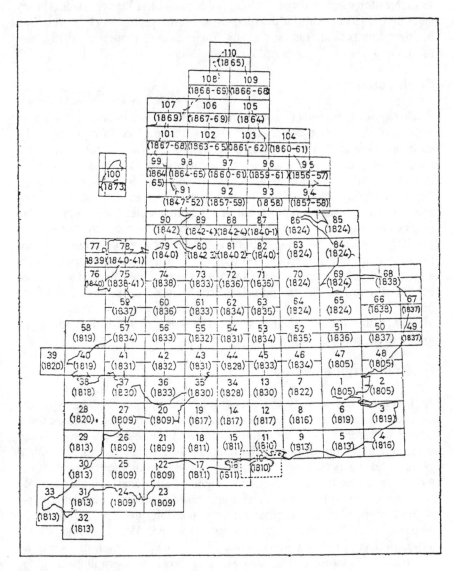

Figure 5.2 Ordnance Survey mapping of England and Wales, 1801–73

Source: Not known

involved in research since many of the variants or 'states' of Ordnance Survey mapping are not to be found in the Copyright Libraries or in the major map collections.* Indeed, a recent work cited 28 different libraries as sources for specific states of Ordnance Survey First Edition maps (Harley and Oliver, 1991). Similar detailed carto-bibliographic work is occurring in other countries including Canada (for example, Dubreuil, 1989), and the United States (for example, Stark, 1989).

Earth scientists

While the foregoing user groups are likely to be met in any map library, the rest of this section covers user groups that are more frequently to be encountered in academic or specialist map libraries. The central requirement for earth scientists is for geological information, but the term is also used to include soil science, hydrology, geomorphology and related subjects. Again, it is almost impossible to generalize about so diverse a group of users, but a frequent requirement is for both thematic and topographic maps of the same area. Topographic maps show the 'skeleton' of an area – relief, drainage, communications and buildings, while thematic maps isolate one or more subjects for portrayal. It is usual therefore, for a library to hold earth science mapping for a specified area of interest or at a specified degree of detail which can be related to the topographic holdings of the library. The few specialist earth science map libraries, by contrast, hold a much fuller range of earth science mapping and a rather restricted topographic stock.

Environmental scientists

Although earth scientists are concerned with the physical basis of the environment, the term environmental scientist is used here to include those whose research is into the effects of human activity on the physical environment. This group will thus include, for example, applied geomorphologists, soil scientists, hydrologists or climatologists studying the effects of pollution in the land, water or air. One may also include here archaeologists studying the environment of past eras. The requirements of this group, if such a generalization is possible, are for such thematic mapping as is available, (for example, Europe, 1991; Poland, 1991) although many may be collecting the data from which such maps will be constructed. Because of this interest, large scale topographic mapping,

---

* The terms 'state', 'series', and 'edition' are somewhat confused in their usage. However, 'state' usually means a reprint which involves some change to the mapped detail.

enabling site location, is a common requirement, as are small scale base maps for the preparation of results for publication.

Social scientists

Although geographers as a body are a large user group, they have not been treated as a single user group in this chapter since their requirements will vary considerably. Some will use maps as earth scientists, others as environmental scientists, and yet others as social scientists. Most 'human geographers' come within this last group which has a particular interest in the ways that society organizes itself and operates. The spatial components of society, that is the parts of the subject that can be portrayed cartographically, are generally measured in relation to administrative units. Cartography provides a valuable key to the interpretation of variations in each social statistic in a way that simple tabulation cannot. A library which serves social scientists needs to hold not only examples of their work, often found in national or regional atlases (for example, Smidt, 1984–1990; Scott, 1989), but also maps of administrative and other statistically important divisions (for example, Germany, 1991; Europe, 1990).

PATTERNS OF USE

It will be readily understood that with such a variety of users, patterns of use are also enormously varied. There are some important external influences, which affect nearly all map libraries, but there are also more local considerations. The nature of users' enquiries also affects the pattern of use, both directly and indirectly.

External influences

Without doubt, the largest external influence on map library use comes from the education sector. Teachers, at every stage from primary to university, from compulsory education to adult education, set projects which intentionally or not, result in a surge of map library users. Because of the structure of the academic year, these surges generally occur between September and May rather than during the summer examination and holiday periods. A similar, albeit generally smaller and more random surge effect is generated by the planning process of major projects noted above. There are also, without doubt, surges in demand caused by media exposures, either of current affairs (or, indeed, by those affairs themselves) or of stories of interest (notably historical anniversaries). Although the latter may be predicted, the former clearly cannot. Rather more predictable is the holiday use of map libraries, which although it occurs throughout the year, rises to a peak in the late spring and summer.

Local considerations

Map libraries can create an interest or capitalize on a latent interest, by publicity. Setting up a special exhibition, for example, can bring people into the map library who later return with their own enquiries. Even if this is not possible, it will be found that in many libraries, maps are among the most attractive of possible display items, and a relatively high profile may be achieved as a part of a general publicity effort. It has to be recognized however, that as with any publicity, it is not often possible to relate any changes in patronage directly to the publicity exercise.

Two further factors which have a much clearer influence on patterns of use are the location and staffing of the map library. An ideal location might be characterized as being close to the central enquiry point within the library, adjacent to the materials likely to be used in conjunction with the maps (guide books, statistical works, geological memoirs) and close to the library's exhibition area. Such ideals are rarely achieved and many map libraries are physically separate from their parent bodies, with minimal facilities. This inevitably has a deleterious effect on patterns of map use.

Staffing also affects map use directly. As has already been mentioned, map use requires a much higher ratio of staff time to reader's enquiry than most book use. This staff time must, furthermore, be provided by informed staff. Since informed staff time is like all staff time, in short supply, it follows that many map libraries can only offer a less than full or ideal service. There is a very real fear amongst many map librarians that because the service is less than full, patronage is less than it might be, and that in the light of this a further reduction of service may be imposed, starting a downward and self perpetuating spiral.

The nature of users' enquiries

As may be understood from the foregoing sections, users of map libraries have a very great variety of requests, ranging from the highly specific to the delightfully vague. At the unspecific end of this continuum are the requests characterized by map librarians as 'I want a map'. Users arriving with this request have to be patiently and politely questioned until a rather more specific requirement emerges. What is almost certain however, is that the distinguishing factors that produce this greater specificity will be the area to be covered and the purpose for which the map is required.

This information allows the map librarian to review, usually mentally, the library's holdings and select the map or maps with the most suitable subjects, dates and scales. It will be noted that there is no mention of an 'author', nor of a 'title'. Although these are the two most direct entry points in a book catalogue, they are, as will be discussed below, irrelevant to most user requests in the map library.

One group of requests which seems to contradict that assertion may be characterized as 'I want an Ordnance Survey map' or 'I want a Michelin map'. The use of a corporate author in the request does not, however, imply that this is an 'author search'. It is much more likely to be either a tautology, or a euphemism for a 'good' map, or the brand name is being used as a synonym for a particular feature of the desired map such as 'topographic' or 'suitable for motoring'. That these usages do occur is demonstrated in the subsequent questioning of the user who enlarges the original request in areal or scalar impossibilities such as 'a Michelin map of South Australia' or 'an Ordnance Survey map of Africa'. It may be noted in passing that the names of such corporate authors can change relatively frequently, so that the Swedish national mapping agency, for example, has had three names in ten years; few users manage to keep up with these changes.

STOCK MANAGEMENT

In any particular map library, the management of the stock will rely on the librarian's perception of the user groups, their requirements, and the pattern of use which these generate. In this respect, the map library differs little from the general library. There are, however, three aspects of cartographic materials which require an entirely different approach to stock management. These are format, the concept of a map series, and the value of chronological sequences. This section of the chapter will discuss each of these in turn.

Format

As mentioned in the introductory section of the chapter, cartographic materials occur in many formats all of which impose special and different conditions on stock management practice. By far the largest number, however, are flat sheets of varying dimensions. Flat sheets must be kept as flat as possible. Folding map sheets may appear to offer the advantage of easier storage, but against this must be counted the cost of increased damage to the stock caused by folding. Furthermore, folding affects the dimensional stability of the map sheet, which reduces their value to users requiring to take linear or areal measurements from the map. Secondly, the flat sheet format discourages browsing. Even if the sheets are kept in folders of twenty of so, it is very difficult to browse through a drawer containing two hundred or more map sheets. Considerable care has to be exercised in extracting a map from its location and in replacing it, since a single sheet of paper is prone to tearing. Furthermore, as will be seen below, the predominance of map series in most map libraries means that it is unlikely that browsing would be successful search strategy, even if it were a practical one.

Map series

About 90 per cent of all cartographic materials are maps forming parts of map series. This is a concept specific to cartographic materials, and is defined as:

> a number of related but physically separate and bibliographically distinct cartographic units intended by the producer(s) or issuing body(ies) to form a single group. For bibliographic treatment, the group is collectively identified by any commonly occurring unifying characteristic or combination of characteristics including a common designation (e.g. collective title, number or a combination of both); sheet identification system (including successive or chronological numbering systems); scale; publisher; cartographic specifications; uniform format; etc. (Stibbe, 1982, p. 230)

Stibbe then describes three types of map series. These are contiguous area map series, special or thematic map series, and chronological map series. The contiguous area map series is the most common, including most topographic mapping and a good proportion of thematic mapping. As implied by the name, such a series covers a single contiguous area such as a country or a continent. Some are thus very numerous, with several thousand sheets. Usually, although by no means invariably, the series will have a common scale, a single publisher and a common specification. Most national topographic mapping is found in contiguous map series.

Much less common are chronological map series which are individual maps that are revised regularly, retaining their characteristics. Perhaps the best examples of chronological map series are the State or Provincial Highway Maps published by many of the state and province governments in North America.

Between these two groups of map series, at least in terms of frequency of occurrence, are special or thematic map series. This is a rather miscellaneous group, including maps of the same area covering different themes (for example Africa, 1974–   ), maps of different areas covering the same theme (for example Great Britain, 1974–   ), or maps which are regarded as a series by the producer (also known as 'producers' series') and provided either with a common title (for example World, 1970–   ) or with a common numbering system (for example Antarctica, 1964–   ). There is often a rather hazy dividing line between this last sub-group and a thematic atlas issued in a number of parts. However, the publication plan of the latter is usually established prior to any of the parts being produced as a contents page, whereas the former does not usually have a precise pre-determined programme.

Chronological sequences

Although maps have been described as a palimpsest (Hoskins, 1985), each one has a *terminus post quem*, the date of printing. Even if some changes in the landscape occurring before that date may be omitted in error or because of their minor nature, it is clear that no changes occurring after that date can be included. Thus if a map bears a printing date of 1860, for example, and yet shows a railway known to have been built in 1876, then the printing date is clearly inaccurate and has probably been left unchanged from an earlier state through an oversight. Works such as Harley and Oliver (op. cit.) are able to order states of a map sheet relatively by considering internal evidence: external evidence from railway construction dates and so on permits an absolute chronology to be applied.

In addition to this requirement in cartochronology, there is also the requirement of the wider communities of historically interested researchers who are, as noted above, an important constituent of most map library user populations. Their requirement too, is for chronological sequences within a map series. This profoundly affects stock management as it is normal practice to store each series together. Since for the purposes of map revision, each sheet in a series is regarded as a separate entity, it follows that in a long-lived series, there may be several different editions and states of each sheet (see Table 5.1 and Figure 5.3). Because of the value of chronological sequences, many map libraries will retain at least one copy of each of these different editions and states, at least for the local region. These parts of the holdings will consequently be continuously expanding, although the rate naturally varies according to the revision policy of, and economic restraints on, the production agency. This provides a sharp distinction with most library practice, which is to relegate or dispose of superceded editions, maintaining only the latest edition in stock and hence having, in this aspect of the collection, a steady state or zero growth management policy.

Table 5.1: Great Britain, 1:50 000 mapping – series, editions and states of sheets 123–34

Sheet No.	Series : LR/M726	LR	SECOND	FIRST/M726	FIRST
123	A 1984;				A/* 1976; A 1974.
124	A 1984;			A/*/* 1982	A/* 1979; A 1974.
125	A 1984 #;				A/*1980; A 1974.
126	A2 1989 +; A/* 1987; A 1985;				A/*1979; A 1974.
127	B 1990: A/*/*/*/* 1988; A/*/*/* 1986; A/*/* 1984; A/*/* 1982;		A/* 1980; A 1977;		A 1974.
128	A/*/*/*/* 1987; A/*/*/* 1985; A/*/*/* 1983; A/*/* 1981;		A/* 1979; A 1977;		A 1974.
129	A5 1989; A/*/*/* 1987; A/*/*/* 1985; A/*/* 1984; A/* 1982;		A 1979;		A/* 1976; A 1974.
130	A2 1990; A//* 1985; ? ;	A 1980;			A 1974.
131	A4 1988; A/*/*/* 1987; A/*/* 1984; A/* 1982;		A 1979;		A 1974.
132	A/*/* 1987; A/* 1984; #		A 1979		A/* 1978; A 1974.
133	A2 1989; A/* 1985;	A 1980;			A 1974.
134	A3 1989; A/*/* 1987; A/* 1984;	A 1980;			A 1974.

Notes

Series Although divided into five series in the table, it could be argued that some of these do not require separate treatment, or if they do, the different treatment is purely in cartobibliographic terms. In use, and often for storage purposes too, the whole set may be treated as one. The major points of difference are as follows:

First Series – photographically enlarged from predecessor at 1:63 360 on new sheetlines;

Second Series – redrawn to new specifications on same sheetlines;

LR = Landranger Series – change in marginal and cover information only;

M726 – military grid and imprint added to standard product.

Changes have also occurred during the period 1974–91 in cover style, contour interval and colour specification. These changes occurred randomly in respect of the above table.

\# These two sheets were printed with integral covers. Following unfavourable reaction, card covers were reinstated.

+ The Ordnance Survey's scheme of notation for revision within a series was:

letter = edition (i.e. major revision)

/* = state (i.e. minor revision)

/ = reprint (i.e. no revision).

However, as can be seen from the examples in the table, the notation scheme could get out of hand and it was replaced during 1988 by:

letter = edition (i.e. major revision)

number = state (i.e. minor revision)

(Ordnance Survey, 19)

The military notations for revision found on M726 series sheets is a simple number for each revision, so that for sheet 126, for example, the military notations (with Ordnance Survey notations in brackets) are: 3 (A2); 2 (A-*); 1 (A).

? There may be another notation (A/) here.

130

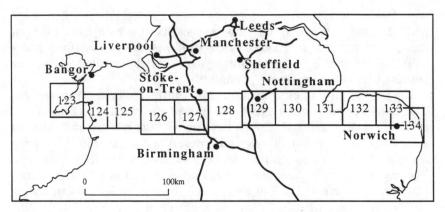

Figure 5.3   Ordnance Survey sheets 123–34, 1:50 000 series
Source: Ordnance Survey, (1986), *Discover Britain with Ordnance Survey Landranger Maps*, 1:1 000 000, Southampton: Ordnance Survey.

SPECIAL CLASSIFICATIONS

Because of the great variation in map libraries, in their users and holdings, it is not surprising that many different classification schemes have been used. Some of these reflect the realities of map library stock management in practical or theoretical terms, while others reflect more general archival or library practice. Since it is as mentioned above, fairly difficult to browse through a map collection, the scheme of classification is much more often a guide to location than a necessary expression of intellectual order and control. Consequently, it is not surprising that many locally developed schemes are idiosyncratic. As may be expected from the earlier discussion, most systems are based on area as the primary classifier; however, there are instances of other primary classifiers, such as size, provenance, date or subject.

Size is most often used in map libraries where a good proportion of the stock is in single sheets, and where the space available is severely limited. It has been claimed (Ehrenberg, 1973) that this method uses space 30 per cent more effectively than folding. For some map libraries it is worthy of consideration on this claim alone. In the very limited form of a locationally qualifying prefix, size classification is familiar to the many librarians who have separate folio and outsize sequences. In map libraries, this is paralleled by separate sequences for folded maps, atlases and rolled maps. To some extent, this is a classification by form rather than size, but within the latter

131

two classes, pure size may be adopted as the principal classifier, since both are found in widely disparate sizes. Because both these types of cartographic material are handled as single entities, using size as the primary classifier and relating other features of the material through the catalogue entries, becomes a workable possibility.

The second form of classification to be considered here is provenance. This is an archival concept, and hence is most often used in records offices or archives. In essence it regards the origin of the records as their most significant feature for classification purposes. A primary division in a county record office might thus separate court records from administrative records. The latter might be divided by orginating department – engineers', planning, recreation. Each of these could be subdivided by originating section – strategic planning, planning applications, appeals. Cartographic materials could occur in the files that make up any of these subdivisions. Intellectually the records are maintained in the same relationship that they were given by the office that created them. This relationship is represented by the list which is the chief finding aid. However, it should be noted that maps are often stored separately from the records of which they are a part for conservation reasons. Both in the list and in the files themselves, a note is inserted giving the details of the cartographic item and a call-number or shelf-mark so that it can be identified and studied in parallel with the textual records.

A third form of primary classification could be date. This might be appropriate to a small collection which included very few areas or subjects, maps of a single town, for example. It would rapidly become unusable as a primary classifier in a larger or more varied collection, not only because of the number of items involved, but also because of the frequent difficulty in providing a map with a single date. Any map will have, working backwards in time, a date of accession into the map collection, a date of printing, a copyright date, a date of last revision, and a date of original survey. Many will be much more complicated, with different revision dates in different parts of the map. As demonstrated above, latest revision dates are often, and more helpfully, used as a subordinate classifier, distinguishing between different states of a map.

The final form of classification to be considered before turning to area-based systems is subject. As with date, few map libraries have holdings that are small enough and yet diverse enough to make this a practical primary classifier. Once again there is the added difficulty that maps are usually multi-thematic. Even the simplest maps, (see, for example, Figure 5.4), can be used in more than one way. Many, apparently mono-thematic maps are, in fact, published on a topgraphic base which could be used independently of the thematic data, while topographic maps themselves are really multi-thematic maps with a vengeance. Administrative areas, hydrology, relief, communications, settlement patterns and land-use are just some of the subjects carried on topographic mapping, and no map librarian would want to classify topographic maps under any one of these headings.

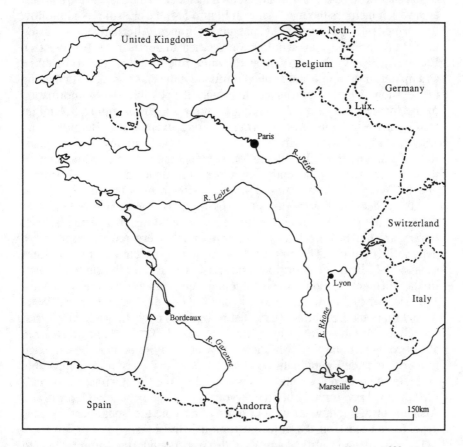

Figure 5.4   Simple map of France, showing some adjacent Western European countries
Source: Ormeling, F.J. (ed.), (1976), *De Grote Bosatlas*, Groningen Wolters–Noordhoff, pp. 42–3

The use of area reflects, as has been discussed, the realities of user requirements. It also reflects, as will be demonstrated below, the practicalities of map librarianship. However, an area-based classification does

133

have its difficulties. These are, principally, in the method of dividing the world into areas and in the method of assigning maps to these areas. Of these, the former is inevitably affected by the holdings of the map library, while the latter has a more general application, independent of the Library's holdings. Stated in its simplest terms, the question is whether the classification should be based on the largest area included in the map or the smallest area which includes the map. Thus in Figure 5.4, the classifier could follow the former rule and classify the map under France. Alternatively, by using the latter rule, the map would be classified under Europe (or Western Europe). Clearly, the decision as to which rule to follow has to be taken as a matter of principle and applied throughout the classification. In making the decision, the map librarian has to balance the possible loss of information of the former rule (a map covering the area shown in Figure 5.4 might also be a useful source of information for Luxembourg, Belgium, and Andorra, as well as for parts of the Netherlands, Germany, Switzerland, Italy, Spain and the United Kingdom) against the possible redundancy of information from the second, where a search under the class 'Europe', or even 'Western Europe', would produce many maps of little or no interest.

Having decided how to assign maps to areas, the next problem is to define the areas. Here, although the users and holdings of a particular map library are much more likely to be influential, there remain some more general difficulties. The first of these is how to define descriptive areas such as 'the Middle East' or 'the South-Eastern states' (of the United States). In the former example, the problem is confounded by the westward extension of the area, in common usage, since the Second World War. At that time, the Levantine coast, that is modern Israel, Lebanon and Syria, as well as Jordan, were termed 'the Near East'. This area has now been absorbed by an enlarging 'Middle East' which may sometimes be extended further to include Egypt in the south and Turkey in the north. A comparable problem of core and periphery is provided by the 'South-Eastern states'. Florida must presumably be in everyone's list, and probably Georgia and Alabama also, but how far west or north of the core the 'south-east' extends depends not least on the adjacent regional divisions.

The use of geo-political units, with fixed boundaries, might seem to overcome the difficulties of defining descriptive areas. However, one difficulty is merely replaced by another, as boundaries do change. A map of Poland dated 1760 would cover a very different area from one dated 1860 or 1960 (Figure 5.5). Not only do boundaries change, but whole administrative systems can be superceded. The 15 *Bezirke* of the German Democratic Republic were the basis for several map series, but as can be seen from Figure 5.6, the six *Lände* that replaced them following the reunification of Germany in 1989 are not simply amalgamations of the former areas, but their creation has involved several significant changes of boundary.

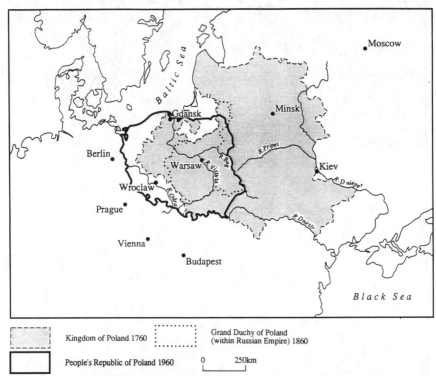

| | Kingdom of Poland 1760 | | Grand Duchy of Poland (within Russian Empire) 1860 |

People's Republic of Poland 1960   0   250km

Figure 5.5 Map showing successive political boundaries of Poland, 1760–1960
Source: Westermann, (1963), *Westermanns Atlas zur Weltgeschichte*, Brunswick: Westermann, pp. 116, 126, 160.

In creating a classification, there is clearly a balance to be struck between flexibility and precision. Each map library has specific needs to be served by its classification, and if adopting an existing method does not provide a satisfactory solution, then an adaptation may well be necessary.

Of the more widely used existing systems, the following may be regarded as representative. The Library of Congress classification scheme is widely known throughout the library world and needs little general introduction. However, the part of schedule G which deals with cartographic materials is unlikely to be well known to many non-specialists, and will be outlined here (Library of Congress, 1976).

There is a primary division of form, so that Atlases are G1000.3–G3122, globes are G3160–G3182, and maps are G3190–G9980. In each

135

Figure 5.6   Map showing Bezirke of GDR (pre-1989) and later division into Lände
Source: Cartactual, (1990), 'New Federal States', *Cartactual*, 145, Map CA145/2–90

division, numbers are allocated by area, thus G1000 is for atlases of the moon and planets, G1001–G1061 are world atlases, and G1100–G3122 are atlases of regions or countries. Within the division for maps, the final digit of each number indicates a type of mapping and controls the subsequent parts of the classification. Where permitted, an alpha-numeric code called a Cutter follows the four digit area number to provide specified divisions of the area number, for example, individual counties or cities. The Cutter number can be followed by subdivisions of parish or ward. The area number and its dependent Cutter number can be followed, except in the case of general maps, by a subject code. The next element in the classification is the year, defined as the year of the situation, although as noted above, there may well be different situation dates in different parts of the map, and even where there is but one, it may not be readily ascertainable. For series mapping, the date is replaced by a code indicating the scale. The final element is another Cutter number, this time indicating the authority responsible for the map (see Table 5.2). As with any geopolitically-based classification, there is a need for periodic revision of the main area numbers, and occasionally there are also major overhauls of parts of the scheme. Map librarians who are unfamiliar with Library of Congress classification will probably find the Cutter number system somewhat clumsy, and some libraries prefer to use the first three letters of the area or authority name.

Another classification scheme used widely in general libraries is the UDC (Universal Decimal Classification) (UDC, 1985). It has been adapted for use with cartographic materials, firstly by the International Geographical Union (IGU, 1964), whose recommendations were incorporated in the English text (UDC, op. cit.) and more recently in proposals made by the Dutch organization CCK (Riesthuis et al., 1988). UDC is a hierarchical system and cartographical materials are defined within the general heading 'geography, biography and history', 9, as 'non-textual representations of a country', 912. This is followed by codes for form, including scale, area and subject. These can be presented in the order regarded as most suitable for the library concerned. In a map library, this would typically be area, subject, form. The IGU tables for area were based on physiographic regions (see Table 5.3), but CCK's proposal is for a revision of the UDC's 1985 system which is regarded as flawed (Riesthuis, op. cit.). The CCK revision retains classes based on administrative divisions, with features that extend beyond one class, being classed in the next higher division of the hierarchy. The proposal extends to second order administrative divisions, using the local forms of names (transliterated where necessary). Further detail can be provided by subject headings, either in the form of place names or postcodes (see Table 5.4).

Table 5.2   Library of Congress area table
Source: Library of Congress, 1976

G3190–G3199 Universe
G3200–G3272 World
G3290–G3292 Americas
G3300–G4374 North America
G4390–G5184 Caribbean & Central America
G5200–G5668 South America
G5670–G5696 Eurasia
G5700–G6966 Europe
    G5750 England general
    G5751   thematic
    G5752   regional
    G5753   county
      .S8   Surrey
        :3M6   Mole Valley District
          C5   Geology
            s10   scale
              .G7   Great Britain Geological Survey
    G5754 England city
      .L4   Leatherhead
        C5   Geology
          1988   date
            .L4   Leatherhead & District Historical Society
G7000–G7342 USSR
G7400–G8198 Asia
G8200–G8903 Africa
G8950–G9082 Australasia
G9095–G9794 Oceans
G9800–G9803 Antarctica
G9900–G9980 Unlocalized maps

The third classification scheme will be unfamiliar to general librarians as it was designed specifically for map library use. This is the scheme used by the British Ministry of Defence, usually known by its publication number, GSGS 5307 (Ministry of Defence), or by the name of the author of the first version of the system, Captain Parsons (Parsons, 1946). It too is a geopolitically arranged system, allotting a letter to each of fourteen major geographical divisions, administrative divisions, or towns (see Table 5.5). Scales and subjects are treated by separate cross-referenced indices.

Table 5.3 Physiographic area tables
Source: Left – (IGU, 1964); Right – (UDC, 1985)

	(1-922) Arctic
	(1-923) Antarctic
(4) Europe	(1-924) Europe
(4-9.1) Fennoscandia	(1-924.1) Northern Europe
(4-9.2) British Isles & Atlantic France	(1-924.2) Western Europe
(4-9.3) North Central Europe	(1-924.3) North Central Europe
	(1-924.4) Alps
(4-9.4) SE Central Europe	(1-924.5) SE Central Europe
(4-9.40) Carpathian Mts	(1-924.51) W. Carpathians
	(1-924.52) E. Carpathians
	(1-924.53) S. Carpathians
	(1-924.54) Transylvanian Mts
(4-9.41) Pannonian Basin	(1-924.55) Pannonian Basin
(4-9.42) N. Carpathian foreland	
(4-9.43) E. Carpathian foreland	
(4-9.44) Dinaric & N. Balkan Mts	
(4-9.45) Bulgaria–Thracia	
(4-9.450) Dobruja	(1-924.56) Dobruja
(4-9.451) Danubian Plateau	
(4-9.452) Balkan Ranges	(1-924.57) Balkan Ranges
(4-9.5) Iberian Peninsula	(1-924.6) Mediterranean Europe
(4-9.6) Central Mediterranean	
	(1-924.7) Crimea & Caucasus
(4-9.7) Greece and Islands	
(4-9.8) E. European Plains	(1-924.8) E. European Plains
(4-9.9) Urals	(1-924.9) Urals
(5) Asia	(1-925) Asia
(6) Africa	(1-926) Africa
(7) N. & Central America	(1-927) N. & Central America
(8) S. America	(1-928) S. America
(9) Oceania & Poles	(1-929) Australasia & Oceania

Two final points must be noted. The first is that record sharing, which has become possible with automation and better communications tends to provide an impetus towards standardized classifications as these are already available in the shared record. The second, which works in the opposite direction, is that automation renders the idea of classification by area less essential. Most automated systems include the capturing of co-ordinate data and most can search the database to produce, for example, all maps

139

Table 5.4 UDC area tables

Source: Left – (UDC, 1985)
Right – (Riesthuis et al., 1988)

(1) Place and Space in General	⟨0⟩ Imaginary world
(2) Physiographic designations	⟨1⟩ Outer space
(3) Places of Ancient World	⟨2⟩ Earth
Countries & Places of modern world	⟨3⟩ Oceans & Seas
(4) Europe	⟨4⟩ Europe
(41) British Isles	⟨4.000⟩ Northern Europe
(410) United Kingdom	⟨4.200⟩ Western Europe
(410.1) England	⟨4.240⟩ United Kingdom
(410.11) South East Region	⟨4.240.360⟩ Surrey
(410.128) Surrey	⟨4.240.360*KT22⟩ Leatherhead
(43) Central Europe	⟨4.400] Central Europe
(44) France	
(45) Italy	
(46) Iberian countries	⟨4.600⟩ Southwestern Europe
(47) European Russia	
(48) Scandinavia	
(49) Rest of Europe	
(491) Iceland	
(492) Netherlands	
(493) Belgium	
(494) Switzerland	
(495) Greece	⟨4.8000⟩ Southeastern Europe
(496.1) Turkey in Europe	
(496.5) Albania	⟨4.810⟩ Romania
(497) Balkans	⟨4.830⟩ Jugoslavija
(497.1) Yugoslavia	⟨4.850⟩ Balgarija
(497.2) Bulgaria	⟨4.870⟩ Shqiperi
(498) Rumania	⟨4.890⟩ 'Ellas
(5) Asia	⟨5⟩ Asia
(6) Africa	⟨6⟩ Africa
(7) North & Central America	⟨7⟩ America
(8) South America	⟨8⟩ Oceania
(9) Oceania & Polar Regions	⟨9⟩ Antarctica

which include the co-ordinates 'x' and 'y'. Indeed, rather more usefully, the database can be searched for all maps including 'x' and 'y' at a scale of z and dating from a to b and on the theme of z. In other words, 'area'

Table 5.5 GSGS area table
Source: Ministry of Defence, 1978

A   Universe
B   World
C   Europe
C1:1   Northern Europe
C1:5   Central Europe
C1:6   Western Europe
C1:8   South Eastern Europe
C6   Albania
C7   Bulgaria
C8   Greece
C9   Romania
C10 Yugoslavia
C16 United Kingdom + Irish Republic
C17   England
C17:8   Southeast
C17:57   Surrey
C17:70   towns
D   Asia
E   Africa
F   North America
G   Central America & West Indies
H   South America
I   Australasia
J   Pacific Ocean
K   Atlantic Ocean
L   Indian Ocean
M   Arctic Regions
N   Antarctica

---

is superceded by 'place' as the search criterion, although this statement must be immediately qualified by the acceptance that 'place' can have an areal extent which varies from a few square metres to a continent or more.

RETRIEVAL

Reference has already been made to the unsuitability of the librarian's traditional approaches to retrieval, that is, author and title. Before

141

considering the practicalities of retrieval in map libraries, it is worth outlining the reasons for this unsuitability.

Except in the case of antiquarian mapping mentioned below, the vast majority of maps are the products of corporate authors. Many of these are very long lived, albeit with changes of name which may or may not affect the products; and many have been responsible for not only a very large number of maps, but also of a very large number of different series of different areas. Ordnance Survey International, for example, in its earlier manifestation as the Directorate of Overseas Surveys was responsible for the production of mapping in Commonwealth countries and overseas Territories throughout the world for over forty years. An author-based retrieval system would have to enter all the mapping produced by the Directorate amounting to many thousands of items under 'Great Britain, Directorate of Overseas Surveys', whether the mapping being catalogued was of Nigeria or Fiji, the Antarctic or The Gambia. Even if the catalogue only provided series level entries, the corporate author heading 'Great Britain, Directorate of Overseas Surveys' could have considerably more than a hundred series records. This example is by no means unique, and clearly demonstrates the unsuitability of this approach, even without considering the nature of users' enquiries noted in an earlier section.

Titles are equally unsuitable, once again because of the lack of specificity provided by many titles. As an example, one may cite the title *Carte géologique*. Although in some cases, this may be qualified by *de France* or *de Québec*, there are examples of the unqualified title in many countries as disparate as New Caledonia and Poland. Once again, the difficulty is not confined to this example, nor to single sheet maps. Series mapping inevitably complicates the matter since not only is there a title for the series as a whole, but each sheet has an identifying name and/or number as a sheet title. As with author, title is a useful part of the description of a cartographic item, but is entirely unsuited to the task of catalogue main entry or retrieval.

Turning now to the practicalities of retrieval, as hinted at the end of the last section, computer aided cataloguing and retrieval systems are being introduced in map libraries. However, before considering some of these, it is as well to discuss their predecessors.

In the majority of map libraries the primary retrieval aid was, and for many still is, a card index. The contents of each card vary depending on the details of the cataloguing system, but rarely include full bibliographic details. The cards operate at different cataloguing levels. First, there are cards for single sheet maps. Such maps are equivalent to monographs in a general library, and can be dealt with in a fairly full and detailed fashion. Many antiquarian maps fall into this category. Complications concern the amount of detail to be included on the card (how much of the often lengthy titles, for example) and the attribution of cartographer and area. In antiquarian mapping, unlike most modern mapping, the 'authors' are often important, and the term in this context can include designer, draughtsman, engraver, and in some cases, printer, map-seller and dedicatee. Map Libraries with a significant amount of antiquarian mapping may well keep an author file in addition, for retrieval by personal name.

An extension of the single sheet map is the multi-sheet map. This format occurs when the whole map is too large to fit on one sheet. It is usually identifiable by having but a single border and a single legend panel, so that all the sheets are to be used together. The single index card will record the appearance of the map as 'one map in six (for example) sheets'.

A number of such single sheet maps include insets or subordinate maps. These may be enlargements of complex parts of the main map, or entirely separate maps at different scales and themes. Insets or subordinate maps can be a very useful data source, but in many map libraries they are not given treatment which is as full as that afforded to single sheet maps, and are included only as a 'note' on the card of the parent map.

To some extent, atlases can be considered to be an extension of the notion of subordinate maps. Atlases can certainly be handled as monographs and hence have a single index card. However the individual plates of each atlas have a cartobibliographic history of their own, often being revised and transferred to another atlas from the same publisher. Potentially therefore, every plate and inset should have a separate entry, but this can only be an unobtainable ideal for most map libraries.

Clearly, if series mapping were to receive the same treatment as single sheet maps, many libraries would be facing a major problem in map retrieval, not least because of the difficulties, already mentioned, of assigning individual sheets within a series to their 'correct' area classes. A different method has thus been developed particularly for contiguous area map series. This is the index-sheet or graphic index. A diagram showing the layout of the sheets, sometimes on a highly simplified topographic base, is prepared. Those sheets held by the map library can then be marked. Careful marking systems can show variants, parallel series, different editions and the numerical strength of holding of each sheet (see Figure 5.7). It should be noted however that if the graphic indices are intended to be used by map library users, as well as map library staff, it is a virtue to err on the side of simplicity in their construction.

It will be clear that while graphic indices are an economical way of retrieving maps from series, they have a number of disadvantages. First, each index is normally only capable of showing one series, or perhaps two if they share the same sheetlines. Thus, for those countries which the

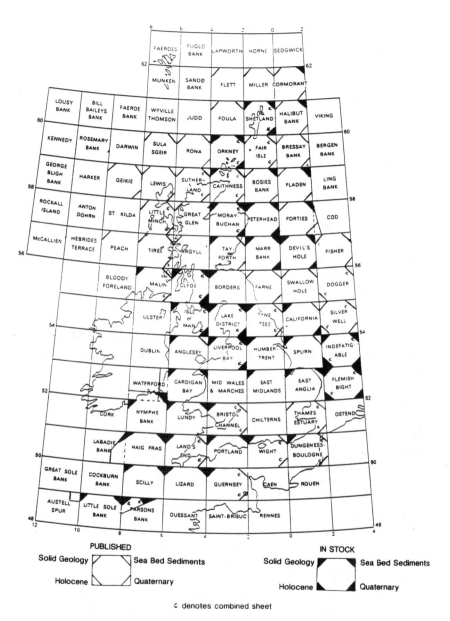

PUBLISHED

Solid Geology ▢ Sea Bed Sediments

Holocene ▢ Quaternary

IN STOCK

Solid Geology ◣ Sea Bed Sediments

Holocene ◣ Quaternary

⊂ denotes combined sheet

Figure 5.7   Graphic index sheets for a geological map series of England and Wales

Source: British Geological Society, (1991), Catalogue of Printed Maps, Keyworth, pp. 6–7

144

map library covers intensively, there will be several indices to be consulted for each enquiry. Second, although series are often long-lived, they are not immortal, and eventually will be superceded by a new series which quite frequently, will be on different sheetlines. Even where the sheetlines remain, there will be difficulties in using the same index because of the need for clarity in marking it up. Third, while graphic indices do indeed provide an economical retrieval system for series mapping, they are not able to combine that economy with a similar ease of retrieving non-series mapping. For many map librarians, the dichotomy between series mapping and non-series mapping causes concern, not least because it is not relevant to the general user who wants a map of x, and is entirely indifferent to the cartobibliographic niceties of series mapping or single-sheet mapping.

In an environment where the users' needs are seen as the driving force of any retrieval system, it is clear that computer-aided systems have a considerable potential. The user could specify a desired location, and could qualify that by date, or scale, or subject, or a combination of these, and the database would be searched for items fulfilling the desired parameters. By contrast, in a manual system, the limitations of the index card/graphic index system mean that the solution of a complex enquiry too often relies on the skill and knowledge of the map librarian.

Although computer-aided map cataloguing systems have been under development for a number of years (see Shepherd and Chilton, 1980, for an early example), they have yet to reach their full potential as cataloguing and retrieval systems, rather than simply as cataloguing systems. The distinction is important, separating those systems designed to use the computer to provide the greatest possible assistance to every user request, from those which use the computer to automate the existing cataloguing practice. Amongst the former may be cited several systems originally developed for book libraries, and subsequently expanded to include cartographic materials (for example, Blaise (Blaise, 1981–) or Libertas (Tatham, forthcoming)). Cartonet (Morris, 1987) and its derivatives (for example, MODMAP) (Millea, 1991) have by contrast attempted to start with the user's requirements and marry them to the cartobibliographic data for each map. Here the system connects a relational database, Oracle, into which are entered standard MARC cataloguing fields, with a purpose-built on-screen graphic searching facility. The user selects an area of interest, windowing in to greater detail on the graphic on the screen if required, and adding other search parameters such as data or scale of subject.

Standing between these two approaches are those systems which, while developed independently of book cataloguing are nevertheless, princi-pally cataloguing tools. Amongst these, the best developed is Opaline (Duchemin, forthcoming) which has been used for all map cataloguing at the Bibliothèque Nationale since 1987. Unlike Cartonet, Opaline does not have a graphic searching facility, but attempts to overcome this by indexing places down to commune level for France, and similar order administrative divisions in other countries, and by extensive authority files for superceded administrative divisions. The work is as yet incomplete, and it is not yet possible to decide whether a text search system like Opaline works better, or is preferred by a wider proportion of users, than a graphic search system like Cartonet. It may be that even if such a comparison were made, it would not stand the test of time, since computer literacy and facility in keyboard skills are increasing rapidly, especially amongst the map library users of the future.

IMPORTANT COLLECTIONS

National map libraries

Although collections in military control may be larger and have more accessions each year, they are, naturally, not generally accessible. Without doubt therefore, the most important collection in each country is that of the national map library. These national collections usually have two functions that are of particular importance in the present discussion.

First, they are copyright, or legal deposit, libraries. That is to say that in order to register copyright, a publisher must deposit a copy of the map in the library. This should mean that one copy of every map published in a country is deposited, and therefore that the depository forms a complete publication history of mapping in the country concerned. In practice there are, of course, difficulties. A publisher may not copyright every minor revision of a map and hence some states may be missing from the copyright library. A publisher may even omit to deposit a copy at all. If the work is somewhat obscure, the depository may not learn of its existence and hence may fail to obtain the legal deposit copy. The copyright library is not usually under a legal obligation to retain every item deposited, and may operate a selective retention policy. Finally, the position of mapping within the body of the copyright law has been variously interpreted in different countries at different periods of history, and it has not always been accepted that cartographic materials are required to be deposited in the same way as monographs. This is an area of increasing interest as publishers move away from traditional forms of paper product to electronic publishing. For all these reasons it has to be accepted, therefore, that a copyright depository does not hold a complete publication history for the country concerned. However, most national libraries do retain that, or something like it, as an aim.

146

Acquisition policies for national map libraries have tended to develop from the notion of attempting to hold a complete cartographic publication history of a country. Mapping of the country produced elsewhere is often acquired. Maps of the United States, or of the area which later became the United States, that were made in France or Spain for example, are of interest to the Library of Congress. Further, maps of other countries produced by nationals of the country concerned may also be acquired. The collections of the National Library of Scotland include under this heading mapping undertaken by Scots the whole world over as they travelled as merchants, missionaries, administrators, soldiers or explorers (Webster, 1991). National map libraries may in addition collect material that reflects the historical activity of the nation, including its former extent, colonial interests, or military involvement, even if such mapping may be of an area which is now a foreign country, produced by a foreign national. Thus, for example, British mapping of French activity in the Batavian Republic, the modern Netherlands, during the Napoleonic Wars might well be of interest to the Bibliothèque Nationale in Paris.

In addition to the function of the national collection in reflecting its centrality in the consciousness of a nation, a national map library is also a repository of knowledge *per se*. Knowledge of those characteristics of the world that are portrayed cartographically is as important as that in the form of words or music or pictures, and most national libraries will attempt to acquire to some extent both the current expression of such cartographic knowledge (that is, modern topographic and thematic mapping) and the means by which that body of knowledge has been formed (that is, historical mapping).

Commercial map libraries

The map libraries of commercial organizations are primarily intended to assist in the work of that organization, whether it be map production, or an entirely different field such as hydrocarbon exploration or production, public transport, or distribution, to give but three examples. Each commercial map library will reflect the nature of the business carried out by its parent body. Thus for example, in the case of a transport system, the map library may contain simply the maps and plans necessary for the current operation of the system. Alternatively, cartographic materials generated over many years may be retained, giving a valuable insight into the origins and growth of the system. As the cartographic materials in a commercial map library are held to assist the work of that organization, it will often be found that casual enquiries are discouraged, while more serious enquiries may be charged a search fee and may also be permitted

147

to consult only a limited set of mapping which is felt by the commercial organization not to present a risk to its business interests.

Academic map libraries

Most universities and similar institutions have a map library. This may be part of the central library, or it may come under the control of a teaching department, usually geography or geology. Even in the second case, access is not normally confined to members of the department, and in both cases there are usually arrangements to permit consultation by members of the general public. The details of such arrangements vary enormously, as do restrictions on physical access and opening hours. It is a common sense precaution against a wasted journey, as well as a courtesy, to telephone in advance of making a visit. Map libraries in academic institutions probably have the most ideosyncratic acquisitions policies of any type of map library and this is an additional reason for a prior appointment, as the actual existence in that collection of the desired material can be ascertained.

The acquisitions policies of academic map libraries are indeed ideosyncratic, not least because of the dual role of the parent institutions in research and teaching. The demands of individual research workers on a map library change and develop over time, and the staff themselves change too, bringing new interests and research areas to prominence. Most academic map libraries will contain at least the remnants of earlier research projects, pockets of mapping scattered across the globe and lying outside the library's acquisition policy. In doing so, they may well offer useful additional dimensions to one facet of the library's role in support of teaching, that is the provision of examples of different cartographic contents and styles. Another common teaching requirement, although one which in England at least has been less important in recent years, is for multiple copies of the same map. These class-sets or teaching-sets can provide, *inter alia*, examples of significant features, or a comparative study of particular features or areas, or practice at some appropriate interpretational skill. A third aspect of teaching that is supported by map libraries is individual student project work. This shades into the research category discussed above, but also, because each project is less substantial, and because there are many more of them, support for student projects also shades into a more general reference role. Any academic map library will have, to a greater or lesser extent, a general reference function. It may well be true to say that this has a greater importance in those map libraries that are part of the central library provision rather than part of a teaching department, but whatever the institutional framework in which the map library is found, this function will exist.

148

Related to the academic map library is a small group of map libraries belonging to learned societies, principally those in geography or geology. The origins of the societies vary, from the promotion of exploration to the promotion of scientific rationalism. Consequently the holdings vary; some, like that of the American Geographical Society for example, being major collections of national importance. So too do their present circumstances vary, some having their own premises and library facilities (for example, the Royal Geographical Society), others being housed within the national library (for example, the Société de Géographie), or within an academic library (the Geological Society of London). Consequently, access varies, but is often restricted to members of the society.

Public map libraries

In the public map library, the last-mentioned element of an academic map library's work, that is, providing a general reference service, becomes the major element. The level to which a public map library can achieve an aim of providing a general reference service will depend entirely on the importance attached, or which the map librarian can cause to be attached, to the map library as opposed to other parts of the library. This is true for any map library that is part of a larger institution, but it seems particularly apposite in the public sector, where marginalizing the map library into an arm of the local history library, or the planning department, seems all too easy. Despite this, there are some very important public map libraries, for example those of the City of London (the Guildhall Library) or of New York (New York Public Library).

Another part of the public, that is local government, provision of cartographic materials is supplied by archives and record offices. As remarked earlier, medieval and later court proceedings are an important source of historical cartographic material. In so far as these proceedings were held by local, rather than national courts, their records will usually be found in local archives. With the growth of responsibilities of local government, these local archives have grown to include many other sources of cartographic materials. Furthermore, many local archives have had added to them the records of local commercial organizations and other institutions, especially religious bodies, all of which are potential sources for cartographic materials, and particularly for cartographic materials of historic interest.

Directories

Because in any one country, or in any part of a country, the number of map libraries or of institutions holding cartographic materials may be quite large, and because of the diversity of holdings of and access to these map libraries, a number of directories have been produced. These are guides, both for the professional map librarian wanting to advise a user on further resources, and for the user wanting to commence or extend a research project. Typically, such directories give a short summary of holdings including special collections, as well as details of access, facilities, and contact information (Carrington and Stephenson, 1985; Chibnall, forthcoming; Wolter et al., 1986). The information is usually collected by questionnaire and is updated by new editions from time to time.

BIBLIOGRAPHY

This bibliography contains both those works cited in the text and also the more important works in the literature which deal with cartographic materials in libraries. These are marked *. Entries marked † have useful bibliographies for further reading.

ACSM, 1977– , *Proceedings of the International Conference on Computer-Assisted Cartography, Auto-Carto*, Falls Church VA: American Congress on Surveying and Mapping.

Africa, 1974– , *Afrika-Kartenwerk*, 1:1 000 000, Bonn: Deutsche Forschungsgemeinschaft.

Antarctica, 1964– , *Antarctic Map Folio Series*, New York: American Geographical Society.

Blaise, 1981– , *BLAISE-LINE User Manual, Section 23 – Cartographic Materials*, London: British Library National Bibliographic Service, BLAISE Information Services.

Board, C. (1976), *Bibliography of Works on Cartographic Communication*, London: International Cartographic Association – Commission V – Communication in Cartography.

Bulletin of the Association of Canadian Map Libraries and Archives, Ottawa.

Bulletin of the Special Libraries Association Geography and Maps Division, 1947– , Bethesda MD.

Carrington, D.K. and Stephenson, R.W. (1985), *Map Collections in the United States: A Directory*, New York: Special Libraries Association Geography and Maps Division.

Cartographiti, 19 – , Newsletter of the Map Curators' Group of the British Cartographic Society, Brighton.

Chibnall, J. (forthcoming), *A Directory of United Kingdom Map Collections*, London: British Cartographic Society.

Clutton, A.E. (1989), *International Directory of Current Research in the*

History of Cartography and in Cartobibliography, Tring: Map Collector Publications.

De Vorsey, L. (1982), 'Historical Maps before the United States Supreme Court', *The Map Collector*, 19, pp. 24–31.

Dubreuil, L. (1989), *Sectional maps of Western Canada 1871–1955, An early Canadian Topographic Map Series*, Occasional Paper No. 2, Ottawa: Association of Canadian Map Libraries and Archives.

Duchemin, P.Y. (forthcoming), *Opaline*, in Smits, J. (forthcoming), *Proceedings of the 7th Conference of Groupe des Cartothècaires de LIBER*.

Ehrenberg, R.E. (1973), 'Non-Geographic Methods of Map Arrangement and Classification', *Drexel Library Quarterly*, **9** (4), 49–60.

Europe, 1990, *Tabula Regionum Europae sub Auspiciis Concilii A.R.E.*, 1:6 000 000, Budapest: Cartographia.

Europe, 1991, *Corinair Emission Maps*, 1:10 000 000, Brussels: Commission of the European Communities, DGXI, Programme Corinair.

*Farrell, B. and Desbarats, A. (1984), *Guide for a Small Map Collection*, Ottawa: Assocation of Canadian Map Libraries and Archives.

France, 1990, *sh. 235, Midi-Pyrénées*, 1:2000 000, Clermont Ferrand: Michelin et Cie.

Germany, 1991, *Bundesrepublik Deutschland Ausgabe mit Verwaltungs-grenzen*, 1:1 000 000, Frankfurt am Main: Institut für Angewandte Geödäsie.

Great Britain, 1974– , *Landranger Series (previously First Series, Second Series)*, 1:50 000, Southampton: Ordnance Survey.

Great Britain, 1980– , *Mountain Map Series*, 1:40 000, Doune Harvey Map Services.

Harley, J.B. and Oliver, R.R. (1991), *The Old Series Ordnance Survey Maps of England and Wales*, Vol. VIII, Northern England and the Isle of Man, Lympne Castle: H. Margary.

*[†]Hodgkiss, A.G. and Tatham, A.F. (1986), *Keyguide to Information Sources in Cartography*, London: Mansell.

Hoskins, W.G. (1985), *The Making of the English Landscape*, Harmondsworth: Penguin.

ICA, 1991, *Report of the Working Group on Cartographic Definitions*, London: International Cartographic Association.

IGU, 1964, *Final Report on the Classification of Geographical Books and Maps*, London: International Geographical Union, Commission on the Classification of Geographical Books and Maps.

Imago Mundi, 1935– , *The Journal of the International Society for the History of Cartography*, London.

Information Bulletin of the Western Association of Map Libraries,

1968– , Santa Cruz CA.

*†Larsgaard, M.L. (1987), *Map Librarianship*, Littleton CO: Libraries Unlimited.

Library of Congress, 1976, *Classification Class G, Geography, Maps, Anthropology, Recreation*, Washington: Library of Congress.

London, 1983, *Londinium – A Descriptive Map and Guide to Roman London*, 1:2500, Southampton: Ordnance Survey.

Meridian, 1989– , Bulletin of the Maps and Geography Round Table of the American Library Association, Lawrence KS.

*Merrett, C.E. (1976), *Map Cataloguing and Classification: A Comparison in Approaches*, Occasional Publications No. 7, Sheffield: University of Sheffield Postgraduate School of Librarianship and Information Science.

Michelin, 1986, *Guide de Tourisme Michelin: Gorges du Tarn*, Clermont Ferrand: Michelin et Cie.

Millea, N. (1991), Report of the Map Curators' Group Pre-Symposium Meeting, Southampton, 5 September, 1991, *Cartographiti*, No. 28.

Ministry of Defence, 1978, *GSGS5307 Manual of Map Library Classification and Cataloguing*, London: Ministry of Defence Chief of General Staff.

Morris, B.A. (1987), *CARTO-NET; A Cartographic Information Retrieval System*, Research Paper No. 33, London: British Library Research and Development Department.

*Nichols, H. (1982), *Map Librarianship*, London: Bingley.

Ordnance Survey, 1985, *Landranger Guides to . . .* (various titles), Southampton: Ordnance Survey.

Ordnance Survey, 1988, *Edition Letters, Symbols and Copyright Dates for Small Scale Maps*, Information Paper 5/1988, Southampton: Ordnance Survey.

Ordnance Survey, 1991, *OS Routemaster Map Series – A New Direction*, Information Paper 9/1991, Southampton: Ordnance Survey.

Parsons, E.J.S. (1946), *Manual of Map Classification and Cataloguing*, London: War Office.

*†Perkins, C.R. and Parry, R.B. (1990), *Information Sources in Cartography*, London: Bowker-Saur, (especially Part 4 – Map Librarianship).

Poland, 1991, *Air Pollution in Southern Poland*, 1:500 000; insets at 1:1 000 000, Plate 1.1-PL1, in Jordan, P. (ed.), 1989– , *Atlas Ost- und Südosteuropa*, Vienna: Osterreichisches Ost- und Südosteuropa-Institut.

*Post, J.B. (ed.) (1983), 'Map Librarianship', *Drexel Library Quarterly*, **9**, (4).

Riesthuis, G.J.A., van der Waal, E.H. and Zandstra, J.G. (1988), *New UDC Auxiliary Tables for Cartographic Materials and Geographic Information*, Utrecht: CCK.

Scott, J.W. (1989), *Washington: a Centennial Atlas*, Bellingham WA: Center for Pacific North West Studies, Western Washington University.

Sheetlines, 1981– , The publication of the Charles Close Society for the study of Ordnance Survey Maps, Exeter.

Shepherd, I. and Chilton, S. (1980), 'MAPLIB: an automated map enquiry system', *SUC Bulletin*, **14**(2), pp. 1–23.

Skelton, R.A. and Harvey, P.D.A. (1986), *Local Maps and Plans from Mediaeval England*, Oxford: The University Press.

Smidt, M. de, 1984–1990, *Atlas van Nederland*, 's-Gravenhage: Staatsuitgeverij, 20 parts.

Stark, P.L. (1980), *A Cartobibliography of Separately Published United States Geological Survey Special Maps and River Surveys*, Occasional Paper No. 12, Santa Cruz CA: Western Association of Map Libraries.

*Stibbe, L.P. (ed.) (1982), *Cartographic Materials: A Manual of Interpretation for AACR2*, Chicago: American Library Association.

Tatham, A.F. (forthcoming), '*Cartographic Materials and LIBERTAS*' in Smits, J. (forthcoming), *Proceedings of the 7th Conference of Groupe des Cartothècaires de LIBER*.

Tolkien, J.R.R. (1968), *Lord of the Rings*, London: Allen and Unwin.

UDC (1985), *Universal Decimal Classification*, International Medium Edition, English Text, Part 1, Systematic Tables, London: British Standards Institution.

Webster, D.C.F. (1991), 'The Ubiquitous Scot', *The Map Collector* 56, pp. 31–37.

Wolter, J.A., Grim, R.E. and Carrington, D.K. (1986), *World Directory of Map Collections*, Munich: K G Saur.

World, 1970– , *World Travel Map Series*, various scales, Edinburgh: Bartholomew.

6

Sets

STUART WAUMSLEY

THE MATERIAL

A substantial body of literature has been produced over the years on innumerable aspects of music librarianship but little attention seems to have been directed towards the special problems of handling sets of music and the related area of collections of play sets. One of the reasons for this may well be the uneven distribution of material in libraries, which ranges in scope from vast to non-existent. Consequently many librarians have never needed to address themselves to the problems of managing sets as a regular routine, although they could have been faced with the task of trying to obtain such material from elsewhere. This chapter considers those areas which are peculiar to the administration of sets of music and plays and illustrates both common and divergent features which arise from the handling of such material.

From a librarian's point of view the one feature which links both music and drama is the fact that they are both performing arts, for which sets of copies are an indispensible requirement for groups of people who wish to produce live music or theatre. A musical score in itself is little more than an inert set of coded instructions, but it is also an absolutely crucial link in the chain between a composer's creative impulse and the performers' re-creation of that initial inspiration. Similarly, a play text, although not abstract in its language, contains the latent potential for realizing the many facets of the medium in which the author has chosen to communicate. Consequently music and drama collections in libraries are often combined into a single administrative unit but the apparent logic of this arrangement needs to be set against the fact that the problems of handling the material itself and the needs of the user are not necessarily identical. What is beyond

154

dispute, however, is that multicopy collections stimulate performance and the librarian has a key role to play in this process.

FORMS

The material itself takes a variety of forms, each of which creates its own individual problems. Plays are perhaps the easiest items to control for they are mostly required in English and fall into the category of 'normal' printed material which can be located in standard sources of information such as BNB or BBIP. They also invariably have ISBNs and are blessed with a uniformity of format which contrasts markedly with the multitude of versions in which a single piece of music may appear. Music, being by definition an abstract and consequently, an international language, has a publishing field of some complexity. A quite unpretentious collection could easily include scores from America, Britain, Czechoslavakia, France, Germany, Hungary, Italy, Poland and Russia and one could double the list of countries without any difficulty to achieve even a modestly comprehensive coverage of the repertoire. Consequently national systems of control such as the *British Catalogue of Music* or the Music Publishers' Association's *Catalogue of Printed Music on Microfiche*, although useful in themselves, are inevitably only partial in their coverage and therefore of limited use in the wider context. Music is rarely published with an ISBN although work currently being undertaken by the International Association of Music Libraries is making the possibility of an international numbering system for music somewhat less remote than hitherto. Furthermore, the music trade seems to be in a constant state of flux with agencies for foreign publications changing frequently, long-established publishing houses merging into larger units whilst, ironically, one-man or small-scale publishing enterprises are springing up whose output sometimes slips through the net of bibliographic control and whose publicity cannot compete with the big names. Only a comprehensive and regularly updated collection of publishers' catalogues can begin to make sense of this confused state of affairs and this is a point we shall need to underline in a slightly different context in due course. In addition, suppliers' lists, such as those produced by Cramer Music or Blackwell's Music Shop, can be of invaluable help in collating the output of such wide-ranging sources.

The one type of score likely to be handled more frequently than any other when dealing with sets is the vocal score. This normally includes all the vocal parts (both chorus and solo) of a choral or operatic work together with a keyboard accompaniment which, where relevant, is a reduction of the orchestral material. If the work is intended to be sung unaccompanied a keyboard part is sometimes included to assist the voices during rehearsals only. Even though the terminology for differing types of music score is usually quite unambiguous, both users and publishers sometimes interchange the terms 'vocal score' and 'piano score'. In the context of multiple copies, the needs of a borrower requesting thirty copies of the piano score of *Oklahoma* should be clear, even if a request from an individual requiring a piano score of the same title might be treated with a certain amount of suspicion and referred back to source. Similarly, borrowers sometimes use the term 'full score' when they mean the vocal score of a complete work which is otherwise available in some kind of abridged version, and the librarian will need to interpret the data accordingly. As far as operatic works are concerned, the vocal score and the libretto are of equal significance, for provided the work is to be staged and not sung as a concert version, each is complementary to the other. Normally a vocal score will contain no spoken dialogue, and this will be found in the libretto together with the words of all the sung material, stage directions and sometimes other information useful to the producer. There are a few exceptions to these general principles, especially in school operas, where both words and music are sometimes included in the same volume; or with a musical such as *Jesus Christ Superstar*, which is only available for sale as a single volume that contains the complete libretto and musical excerpts.

An alternative to the vocal score, which will rarely be encountered except where multiple copies are involved, is the chorus or choral score. This, as its name suggests, contains the individual parts sung by the chorus but excludes both solo parts and accompaniment. Occasionally the parts for each voice will be published individually or as separate copies for male and female voices. They may offer a cheaper alternative to purchasing quantities of vocal scores, or they may only be available in this form leaving one no choice in the matter. Although they offer a tempting prospect, especially in times of economic restraint, it should be noted that they are almost universally disliked by choral and operatic societies, whose members find it difficult to follow the progress of a work when faced with nothing more than an indication of a specific, and often considerable, number of bars rest.

Orchestral musicians, however, are constantly faced with the same problem and have to make the best of it as it is impractical to treat an orchestral work in any other way than as a collection of individual parts. Sets of instrumental parts, both orchestral and chamber, are potentially the most troublesome category of material a librarian is likely to handle, as they contain varying quantities of unique copies which must be present in their entirety if the set is to remain usable. Whether a set of parts is required for an instrumental, choral or operatic work it should include, wherever possible, a full score for the conductor's use. Full or miniature scores for personal study should be purchased and displayed separately, in order that the performing material will not be deficient when required for use. Sometimes a set will only be published with a piano conductor or other form of short score but these rather skeletal productions are of little use as study material.

The only other type of set a library may need to consider having in stock would comprise multiple copies of miniature scores to be used for study purposes in school, college or evening class. As this is not performing material its potential use is unlikely to be as great as sets of instrumental or vocal parts and, even in educational institutions, will probably not be regarded as a matter of the highest priority.

ACQUISITION

It hardly needs to be mentioned that the cost of stock acquisition is of overwhelming significance in the maintenance of a collection of plays and music, and this factor is unquestionably a major stumbling block in establishing a new service. In order to satisfy the needs of even a small choral or operatic society it is unlikely that fewer than 20 copies of a single title would be required and considerably more where larger forces are involved. In addition an operatic society will usually need a set of libretti as well as a set of vocal scores, and a choral or operatic group may also require a corresponding set of orchestral parts where such material is available. As far as dramatic societies are concerned, a performing set, comprising the number of characters in the cast plus three or four additional texts for production purposes, should be regarded as the level of provision below which a service should not fall. Using this formula a play set will average around ten copies but whether that level should ideally be raised to cater for the demand for class sets of twenty or more copies is a matter which must inevitably be related to the level of funding available. Although there are a few standard musicals currently retailing in this country at between £25 and £35 per copy – and others up to £55 each – this is mercifully not the norm and the average price for a choral or operatic vocal score is likely to be between £6 and £7 per copy (1991 prices) assuming that there is no substantial spending at either end of the price spectrum. One should not be deluded, however, into thinking that small-scale choral pieces (such as anthems, motets, madrigals, partsongs and individual choruses from cantatas, musicals, operas or oratorios) which have not been included in the calculation above, are substantially less expensive to provide for, although the unit cost can be expected to be in the region of £1.25, it is more than likely that a choir will need between ten and twenty items in order to put together a programme of reasonable length. An average vocal set for both large and small-scale works is likely to be around 25 copies but local circumstances, such as the existence of one or more large societies and virtually no small ones, could radically alter the level of demand. Just as the general lending library may need to purchase several copies of a book if it is in heavy demand, so a large music and drama library will sometimes find it necessary to purchase several sets of those items which are perennially popular. As far as plays are concerned, which retail at an average price of around £5 per copy for a full-length and £2 for a one-act text, the problem is unlikely to be great enough to require more than a few multiples of ten copies, but demands for music scores may make it sometimes necessary to hold several hundred copies of a single work. Orchestral parts average between £2 and £3 each and, even with a modest quantity of string parts (such as 65432) together with a single set of wind parts and a full score, a classical or early romantic symphony can hover above the £100 mark with a substantial late romantic work increasing to two or three times that amount. Some libraries buy considerably larger quantities of string parts than this, and a few even buy a double set of wind parts to act as an insurance against the loss of what would otherwise be unique copies in a set. However, two moderately endowed sets of the same work does allow a much greater flexibility, in that both sets can be issued, either to two different groups simultaneously or to a single source when larger quantities are needed. As a long term investment, £100 is quite a small initial outlay for a package that can be used by thirty or forty performers an indefinite number of times. Having said that, it is on the other hand, a sobering exercise to estimate that the country's largest collections of music sets represent an investment in stock at current prices of something in the order of £1 million. Admittedly they have been built up over some considerable time, and although many library systems could not justify an operation on this scale, the discrepancy between these centres of excellence and other parts of the country where such material is non-existent indicates a serious deficiency in the British library system and a root cause of many of the problems of supply.

AVAILABILITY

From this situation stems the first problem of availability, which is simply locating items that are not available locally. As far as single copies are concerned, there is an extremely good chance that if the desired score is not in the local library, the request will be satisfied from either within the regional library system or from the British Library Document Supply Centre (BLDSC). As far as sets are concerned the situation is not so straightforward because the British Library does not hold sets of plays or music (with the exception of chamber music) and the depth of coverage throughout the country, as we have already noted, is quite erratic. It has not been uncommon for requests to circulate around the land for weeks, if not months at a time and still be circulating after the performance was supposed to have taken place.

A major step forward in the control of this inefficiency was the publication in 1982 of the *British Union Catalogue of Orchestral Sets* (BUCOS) at the instigation of the United Kingdom branch of the International Association of Music Libraries. Although not comprehensive in its coverage, it represents the single most important step so far in the supply of music sets. A second and considerably enlarged edition appeared in 1989. If the user has been the principal beneficiary, that is as it should be, but one also hopes that music librarians' reputations will have risen because of an improved level of service.

A parallel approach to the coverage of vocal sets subsequently foundered because of the sheer volume of material involved and the burden of responsibility fell on the regional library systems to produce union catalogues of their own members' stocks. Although they were initially slow to respond, there is now the prospect of most regions or major regional collections being represented by a printed catalogue in the forseeable future. A British union catalogue of vocal sets in a form which could be regularly updated (online or microfiche) would be an ideal solution to the problem but that seems a remote possibility at the present time. As far as plays are concerned, there is nothing even to compare with this except a few published catalogues of individual libraries' holdings. This is almost inevitable as there are comparatively few specialist drama librarians operating in the field and there is no professional group in which mutual problems can be aired. The demand for plays is not generally at the same level as that for music and the cost of buying play sets is comparatively modest which, at least in theory, gives a greater chance of the demand being satisfied locally. This is partly borne out by the fact that, in my own experience at least, virtually all requests received from outside one's area are from music societies rather than drama groups. Such approaches, which take place on a daily basis, must be indicative of a failure at local level, either because the library has not delivered the goods or because the user has no confidence they will get what they want.

The second problem of availability concerns access to material which can only be obtained from sources outside the library system. This is particularly acute in the field of orchestral parts where large numbers of works still in copyright are not, and in many cases never have been for sale. These can only be obtained on hire from the publisher on payment of a (sometimes considerable) fee. The process has accelerated rapidly over recent years so that a large body of material which used to be for sale has now been transferred to the hire catalogue or may not even be available at all. The situation applies equally to light as well as classical pieces and is not solely confined to copyright works, for many publishers' lists which cover the standard classical repertoire are now only a shadow of what they used to be. Similarly, many sets of orchestral parts for choral works are only available on hire, even though the publisher has vocal scores available for sale. The only significant reversal of this trend is to be found in the catalogue of E.F. Kalmus which includes a vast repertoire of instrumental parts for orchestral, choral and operatic works. The principal drawback with them is that as they are virtually all facsimile editions of out-of-copyright material and as the source is never acknowledged, one is never quite sure what one is getting, although it is sometimes possible to recognize a particular publisher's house style. The situation is even more confused for musicals as there are a number of examples of well-known works, as well as many less popular titles, where the vocal score is for sale but the libretto is only available on hire, and even the odd instance where the reverse is true. Added to this is the further complication that the publisher of the vocal score and the publisher of the libretto of a particular musical are sometimes different so that the source of the orchestral material, which is invariably on hire, is not immediately obvious. There have also been occasions when a publisher has not been willing to supply libraries with material, even though it has been available for sale to groups.

A direct consequence of this state of affairs is that libraries receive requests for sets of music they cannot supply. If we are to avoid the unnecessary and unprofessional practice of requests circulating around the country with little or no chance of them ever being satisfied, it is absolutely essential that librarians regard their role as suppliers of information with the same degree of seriousness that they apply to delivering the material itself. The two elements are simply two sides of the same coin. It is less than satisfactory for a library to supply a set of vocal scores of *Oliver*, for example, but leave the borrower completely in the dark about the libretti it is unable to supply. He needs to be told not only that the libretti are not for sale and never have been, but also the exact source from which they can be hired (which in this instance is *not* the publisher of the score). Unfortunately no single source collates this kind of information and it is essential to gather as comprehensive a collection of publishers' catalogues as is humanly possible, amongst which the hire catalogues should be regarded as being of equal importance as those listing material for sale.

As few publishers operate a mailing list, the stock should be replenished annually as part of the library's regular routine. Occasionally a publisher will levy a charge for a catalogue, and although it may well go against the grain to have to pay for promotional material, it should be regarded as an essential part of a library's reference collection and purchased if there is no alternative. A reasonably comprehensive collection of catalogues should occupy more shelf space than the *New Grove* and, in its own way, constitutes a reference tool of comparable significance. There is a case for including in the library's catalogue, details of the most regularly recurring works which are only available on hire, so that when less experienced members of staff are checking for what, on the face of it, are perfectly plausible requests, the catalogue will provide them with an instant answer to the query.

As far as plays are concerned this kind of problem is virtually non-existent for a play will either be in print or out of print, and this can normally be established quite easily. One may be asked quite frequently if a play has been released for amateur use and the answer can often be found in a publisher's catalogue or in the pages of *Amateur Stage*. If in doubt the enquirer should be referred to the publisher (or owner of the performing rights where the two differ) because newly published plays and musicals as well as older titles are frequently not available for amateur use whilst professional productions are running. A surprising number of amateur productions have to be abandoned when rehearsals have reached an advanced stage because a society has not previously established that the work has been withdrawn.

Establishing and building a collection of sets is an enterprise which requires a certain amount of judgement. The acquisition process needs to be subject to a much tighter critical scrutiny than would be applied to the development of a collection of single copies, especially in a public library where the terms of reference are not as closely defined as in a library serving a single institution. It is not simply a matter of economics, although finite resources inevitably have a major influence on the decisions that have to be made, but also of the long-term value of the works under consideration. It should be emphasized that long-term value is not necessarily synonymous with artistic quality. In a public library if not elsewhere, a collection that reflects only what are generally regarded as the masterpieces of Western culture is only partially comprehensive, for the demands of the world at large encompass the entire spectrum of taste, of which the varying hues are not necessarily mutually exclusive. It would be easy enough to compile a list of core works of the repertoire that any self-respecting library should not be without, and this would undoubtedly have some validity for a collection of single copies in almost any context.

As a formula for a collection of sets it would be impossible to apply universally, as local needs will vary dramatically from place to place. There would be little point in housing a set of vocal scores of Verdi's *Requiem* if no large choral society operates in the area, or a set of parts of a Tchaikovsky symphony if the local orchestra is only of Mozartian proportions. On the other hand, large-scale works do not automatically demand large resources so that Bach's *Mass in B minor* may well be performed by a small chamber group specializing in authentic interpretations of early music. In such a case the choir is likely to demand an authoritative text such as the one published by Bärenreiter rather than the ubiquitous Novello edition. There will however, be many occasions when the most 'correct' edition is not the one that will be required. With such a perennially popular work as *Messiah* for example, the widespread image of what constitutes Handel's masterpiece is enshrined in the Novello score edited by Ebenezer Prout; whilst ironically, the same publisher's version edited by Watkins Shaw is closer to Handel in both spirit and letter, even though one would not normally supply it to a society unless specifically asked to do so.

DEMAND

The possible permutations of demands a library may need to consider are almost infinite. The technical ability may range from elementary to professional, the style from pop to Palestrina, the period from medieval to modern, the mood from frivolous to tragic, the scale from miniature to epic and the ensemble from intimate to immense. Potential users will include dramatic societies, play reading groups, operatic societies (producing classical works as well as musicals), mixed-voice choral societies ladies' choirs, male voice choirs (some of which may be church choirs, senior citizen's choirs or concert parties), orchestras (including string ensembles), chamber groups, brass bands, wind bands (including jazz ensembles) and *ad hoc* groups whose composition will constitute anything but a standard combination of instruments. In addition, the needs of the educational world encompass an even wider range of material than is needed elsewhere when one takes into account the growing body of material which has been specially written or arranged for use by young people.

Consequently a collection of sets is likely to include a sizeable proportion of items which would not even merit a passing comment in a history of music or literature and not only the young will require technically or even emotionally undemanding material. Stainer's *Crucifixion* and Maunder's *Olivet to Calvary* still figure in the top twenty list of requests received, together with what appears to be their late twentieth-century equivalents in the form of the religious cantatas of Roger Jones and John Peterson among others. It is all too easy to adopt a superior attitude towards them but, whatever one's personal response may be, they fulfil a need and a library service must satisfy that need. At the best of times the measurement of artistic quality is a notoriously elusive pursuit, and when faced with the situation that what one half of the population finds trivial the other half finds uplifting, a public service cannot afford the luxury of passing judgement. If the numerous pop cantatas published during the last two decades have been forgotten by the end of the next twenty years, the intense use to which they have been subjected will have more than justified their existence on the library shelves. In the same way a large proportion of plays produced by amateur societies do not have any literary pretensions, and the fact that many of them are only remembered by their titles rather than their authors tends to underline the fact. In the field of school music where an anthology of short pieces is so devised that they may be performed by almost any combination of instruments available, practicalities take precedence over artistic considerations. Similarly, a well-known piece from the classical repertoire, which has been simplified or arranged so that it can be played by the less technically proficient or by non-standard ensembles, has a significant role to play whether or not it may offend the purist.

Although the librarian must respond to the needs of the users of the service, this response will need to be tempered by considering all requests in the context of the collection as a whole. The smaller the collection, the more critically they have to be examined in order to preserve some sort of balance within the existing terms of reference. Should societies who borrow *Carols for Choirs* and *Messiah* year after year really buy their own copies, or does the library have an obligation to carry on supplying this kind of need *ad infinitum* simply because that need exists? There is no single answer to the question, given that there is no such thing as unlimited resources. The scope of the collection, the size of the bookfund and the general philosophy of the library service will all have an influence on the final decision. One factor which should not be overlooked, however, is that in the close-knit world of amateur dramatics and music making, performances quite often stimulate other performances of the same work, so that a library's positive response to a request for a title not in stock will trigger a chain reaction of demand for the same item from neighbouring societies on a surprising number of occasions. In broader terms there is no doubt that the best services not only readily respond to user needs in this way but also act as a catalyst in stimulating further activity, by placing before the potential borrower attractive and useful material that they might not have encountered hitherto.

Ironically it is not necessarily in the less familiar areas of the repertoire that the greatest problems arise, but often with the most popular titles such as *Carols for Choirs*, Fauré's *Requiem*, Handel's *Messiah*, Vivaldi's *Gloria* and similarly popular musicals and operettas. Major collections are frequently overwhelmed with requests from far and wide for this type of material, when it is inevitably also in constant demand from societies within their own boundaries. Unless most library authorities make at least some attempt to provide sets of popular material, it is almost inevitable that the collections of national significance will be unable to cope with providing a service on a national scale. Few, if any libraries can now afford to be self-sufficient, and shared responsibility is the only practical solution to providing a satisfactory service on a wide scale. A regional collection would appear to be the most cost-effective answer to the problem provided a transport system is a practical proposition, but where such conditions are not possible, we have now reached a stage where it is almost essential that some form of co-operative acquisition scheme be established within regions if scarce resources are to be used with optimum effect.

CATALOGUING AND CLASSIFICATION

The theory and practice of cataloguing and classification has been covered in some considerable detail elsewhere and it is not within the scope of this chapter to cover the same ground. There are, however, a number of factors germane to the handling of sets which need to be highlighted, some of which may require modifications or extensions to normal practice. One of the problems of a classification scheme is that even allowing for any inherent faults a system may have, the needs of the personal user, for whom the arrangement may well be quite satisfactory, and the needs of the society user do not always correspond.

In DDC, for example, the literature of drama divides geographically (822 English drama, 832 German drama, and so on) and this is not an unreasonable arrangement for a student requiring play texts and critical material relating to the history of drama. However, this approach is almost totally irrelevant to the needs of most amateur dramatic societies whose prime considerations are usually:

1. the size and nature of the cast (e.g. five women and three men)
2. the type of play (e.g. farce, thriller)
3. the length of the play (e.g. one-act, three-act).

In the same way schools will often have their own distinctive requirements such as the reading age and/or the subject matter of the play. In a conventional classified catalogue it is virtually impossible to comprehend all the possible permutations likely to be required by varying users. It therefore needs to be supplemented by in-house indexes or lists as well as commercially produced catalogues, such as the highly informative *Guide to Selecting Plays* from Samuel French, in order that the relevant material may be isolated. Given a computer system there is no reason why all the signficant data should not be input giving almost instantaneous recall as required. The computer's keyword searching facility, which will respond to half-remembered titles and other imprecisely-formulated information, may be exploited to amplify catalogue entries for both music and plays in order that the users' requirements can be identified with greater precision.

The demands of music groups will often vary according to the type of work involved and, as with drama users, may well be based on different criteria to those of the individual. Operatic societies will often have to make decisions about which show they wish to produce, where the availability of suitable voices will have at least as much influence on the outcome as the intrinsic merits of the work itself. Over and above the problem of human resources, works for the musical stage fall into three fairly easily identifiable categories (which are not necessarily mutually exclusive) in the form of operas, musicals/operettas and works designed for use by young people. These should be clearly distinguished, either by shelf arrangement or by subdivisions in the classified catalogue if the scheme itself does not make such distinctions. The field of choral music will almost certainly reflect the most complex variety of demands a library is likely to encounter, not only because of the size of the repertoire itself but also because of the sheer volume and variety of choral groups in existence. One of the most fundamental divisions that will need to be made is between female, mixed and male voice material. As far as large-scale choral works are concerned, the repertoire for both female and male voices is comparatively small but in the area of small-scale pieces, such as anthems, choruses or partsongs, the demand, especially from ladies' choirs, is likely to be considerable. Whilst many choirs will concentrate on the lighter regions of the repertoire, church choirs can be expected to need items of a seasonal nature, and groups which suffer from the universal problem of shortage of tenors may well be reduced to searching for material available for SAB voices rather than the usual four-part (SATB) items.

Instrumental music for larger ensembles divides fairly easily into broad categories of brass band, wind band, full orchestra and string orchestra but within these classes will be found material whose purposes are quite divergent. Some of them may have been specially written for school or amateur use, possibly by composers of national, if not international repute.

165

Others will consist of arrangements of works designed to be accessible to ensembles who cannot muster the exact resources the composer originally envisaged. A third type will consist of anthologies of simple pieces from almost any source, arranged so that they may be performed by almost any combination of instruments available, with the intention of providing some experience of ensemble playing to performers of limited technical ability. These three species of material may be classed under the heading of school or amateur orchestra and should be easily distinguishable from the standard classical repertoire, most particularly where a work exists in the library in its original form and as an arrangement. Whilst some groups would regard performing arrangements of standard works as almost sacreligious, others would never gain any experience of performing them if they were not otherwise available and the needs of each must be carefully considered. Chamber music parts are most usefully arranged by size of ensemble from duos to nonets, but it is highly desirable that one should be able to identify different types of ensemble in each category so that it is possible to distinguish, for example, what is available for string quintet, wind quintet, piano quintet and miscellaneous combinations of five instruments. Small brass ensembles could be included here but perhaps would be more usefully treated as a separate class quite distinct from brass band sets, which constitute a somewhat specialized category by virtue of their unique instrumentation.

PROBLEMS OF EDITIONS

As we have already suggested above, the problem of differentiating between editions of the same work is a matter of crucial significance in the field of music. There is nothing more frustrating than to supply 50 copies of a major work only to have them returned within days because they were not what was required – not to mention the frustration of the borrower who has received incorrect material. Even though the fault may often lie at the request's source of origin, the librarian has a major responsibility to ensure that sufficient information is received in order that the transaction may be successfully completed. Where a request is ambiguous (and the possibilities for ambiguity are numerous) it should be referred back to source, as the inspired guess has only a fifty–fifty chance of being correct. If requests are received from outlying libraries it will be necessary to devise a request form which can accommodate all the elements necessary to identify clearly the needs of a wide range of societies.

After the composer and title, any or all of the following elements may be required to verify beyond all doubt what a user needs: publisher, editor,

166

nature of the ensemble (e.g. full orchestra, S.S.A. choir), type of scores (e.g. vocal score, set of instrumental parts), version (e.g. concert version, school edition), arrangement/arranger, language of the text, key, opus number/thematic catalogue number or nickname. Not only is it important that a library's catalogue should contain the relevant data to be able to make these distinctions, it is equally vital that different editions of the same work should be instantly distinguishable on the shelves by including sufficient information on the spine (or cover of the score if there is no spine) to identify uniquely all the variant versions of the same title. Four editions of Vivaldi's *Gloria*, for example, can be distinguished simply by including the name of the editor on the spine. The identity of the publisher alone is not sufficiently precise as two of them, the Casella and Malipiero editions are published by Ricordi whilst the Martens and Graulich editions are published by Walton Music and OUP respectively. Sometimes a publisher can be virtual guarantee of an authoritative text, as are the Bärenreiter editions of Bach and Handel, but where a single editor is regarded as a world authority on a composer, such as H.C. Robbins Landon and Haydn, that editor's work may well be produced by several different publishers.

Normally it is unwise to mix editions of the same work because even where every single note is identical, the page numbers will never correspond and almost certainly create a certain amount of difficulty in rehearsals. If a society is in urgent need of a particular work it may accept mixed editions if there is no alternative at the time, but as a matter of principle, a library should not undertake to supply such material without the prior consent of the borrower. Even some of the old Novello pocket editions of choral works do not correspond exactly with the larger format vocal scores of the same work in the matter of pagination and should be treated as if they were quite different versions. At other times the content of scores will not correspond exactly – Vivaldi's *Gloria* mentioned above being one of many examples – and here the hazards of mixing editions increase significantly. Revised editions should also be treated with great caution: the revised vocal score of the Novello edition of Schubert's *Mass in G*, for example, is quite incompatible with its predecessor, a fact which was not acknowledged in the earliest printed copies causing many a problem amongst unsuspecting singers and conductors.

It is not only the musical text which can vary from edition to edition but also, in the case of vocal music, the language of the words as well. This information should also be clearly displayed on the spines of vocal scores in order to avoid the nonsense of supplying a set of Mozart's *Requiem* of which some copies have English words only and others Latin words only. The fact that they originate from the same publishing house and may look superficially identical is no excuse! Similarly it is possible to have

167

two quite different English translations of the same work emanating from the same publisher, such as the two Weinberger editions of Lehar's *Merry Widow*, one by Christopher Hassall originally devised for professional use, and the other by Phil Park and Ronald Hanmer specifically prepared for amateur use. Both of them are tackled by amateur societies but it hardly needs to be said that they are completely incompatible.

Sometimes a work may appear in two or more radically different versions either because of the composer's own intentions or as a result of arrangements by other hands. It may be simply a matter of scale as in Andrew Lloyd Webber's own abridged and enlarged versions of *Joseph and the Amazing Technicolor Dreamcoat* or a question of arranging a work for alternative forces, as in several SSA versions of Vivaldi's *Gloria* and Fauré's *Requiem*, none of which are the work of the composer himself. At other times it is a matter of simplification, allowing works to be performed by resources somewhat smaller than the composer originally intended, as in the arrangements of Handel's *The King Shall Rejoice* or Parry's *Blest Pair of Sirens* which reduce six- and eight-part textures to four making them accessible to a greater number of choirs (even if they may cause a few raised eyebrows in circles where authenticity is a *sine qua non*). On other occasions a work may be telescoped to produce concert versions of varying lengths, of which Bizet's *Carmen* is a typical example, not only changing the scale of the piece but also implying a change of context from opera house to concert hall. The same kind of problems attend the handling of short choral pieces with the additional complication that there is likely to be an even greater variety of voice arrangements, particularly for more popular material, than will be found in large-scale works. They are most commonly arranged for two-, three- or four-part female voices, three-, four or five-part mixed voices and four-part male voices, and although it is very unlikely that all these versions of a single title would be available simultaneously, it is a sobering exercise to consider the implications of page 33 of Malcom Jones' *Music Librarianship* where over seventy different vocal and instrumental versions of Bach's *Jesu Joy of Man's Desiring* are listed. Anticipating all these potential pitfalls should be second nature to a librarian regularly handling multiple copies, so that one's antennae responds to the slightest hint of any ambiguity.

There will be times when it is possible to deduce from the available evidence what is required: it may reasonably be assumed that a junior school will need the unison rather than the SATB version of Horowitz's *Captain Noah and his Floating Zoo* but the longer you deal with such material, the more likely you are to be suspicious about a request that apparently does not tally. Sometimes a ladies' choir really does want *Carols for Choirs 1* (for mixed voices) rather than *Carols for Choirs 4* (for female voices) despite the seemingly conclusive evidence to the contrary! Where there is room for doubt it is safer not to make assumptions but to establish what exactly is required before proceeding in order to avoid wasted effort at one end of the line and dissatisfaction at the other. Information can easily become distorted or garbled during transmission so that a request for Bach's *Magnificat* could refer to one of at least three different settings by three different members of the Bach family, or one for the *Missa Solemnis* might relate to a work by Mozart rather than Beethoven and it should be a matter of professional pride that few, if any such red herrings slip through the net.

TITLE APPROACH

One of the most common approaches to both music and plays is by title, and title entries are an almost indispensible element for the efficient retrieval of information in some areas of the repertoire. It is a strange contradiction, that as far as the classic works in both fields are concerned the author or composer is a factor of prime significance; but the rest of the repertoire comprises works whose titles are often well-known but whose authors or composers often lurk in obscure corners of the user's, or even librarian's consciousness – assuming they were ever there in the first place. The composers of *Bless this House* or *Funiculi Funicula* are hardly household names and often prove difficult to recall, and if one had to make a choice between one form and the other, title entries would have to take precedence in the interests of efficient retrieval, whether or not this ran counter to all principles of cataloguing. The long-term benefits derived from title entries are out of all proportion to the small extra work-load required to produce them in the first place, and with a computer system no additional effort is required whatsoever at the inputting stage because the machine will process the data automatically and recall whatever field is requested with almost instantaneous response. Although they are most useful in the field of more popular material, there are times when they come into their own in the classical repertoire so that it is possible to identify the composer of a setting of *Ave Verum*, for example, whose name a borrower cannot remember, given that the item is in stock in the first place.

Another problem of potentially hidden data concerns anthologies of plays and music. As a general rule collections of plays are more likely to be useful for the individual works they contain (unless the volume has some thematic unity) and will normally not include too many works for analytical cataloguing to be too great a burden. Sometimes plays will only be available in this format but even where this is not the case, they provide a useful supplementary source for items already on loan. Music anthologies, on the other hand, tend to contain small-scale pieces such as anthems, madrigals or partsongs and are valuable for the sheer quantity of material they contain, and as it is not uncommon for up to 50 items to be included in a single volume, the question of analytical cataloguing can present an insuperable problem. The only compromise between all or nothing is to list the contents on the catalogue card and/or photocopy the index pages of each volume and keep them in a separate file so that they may be scanned with comparatively little effort for items which are not otherwise available.

The structure of a building may impose considerable limitations on a library's *modus operandi* and this, in its turn, has implications for user and staff alike. The amount of space available in the public area will not only determine how much material can be displayed there but also in what form that material appears. It is here that the user comes into direct contact with what is available for loan and the importance of this browsing facility cannot be emphasized too strongly. A dramatic or operatic society may be searching for ideas for their next production and encounter several possibilities from which the final choice can be made, or a teacher may be looking for a set of instrumental parts for a non-standard ensemble designed for a specific level of ability. In all cases it would be necessary to examine a range of items before deciding which were the most suitable for the purpose. This scenario is repeated day after day in music and drama libraries by all sorts and conditions of societies, and the output generated by this type of activity is not inconsiderable. If space is severely limited in the public area it may be necessary to display only inspection copies of plays, partsongs, vocal scores and orchestral scores which then can be matched with the corresponding multiple copies or sets of parts when required for use. Where a library fulfils the dual role of serving both personal and group needs – and in most situations this will almost certainly be the case – it may be necessary to have duplicate sequences to differentiate between what is available for individual use and what is available as a set. Much will depend on the scale of the operation, for the smaller the number of sets in stock, the more critical it is to be able to identify them. Where a library has a fairly comprehensive collection it is not unreasonable for the user to anticipate that any request for material from the standard repertoire should stand a good chance of being satisfied, provided it is not in use elsewhere at the same time.

DEFINITION OF SETS; HANDLING

The handling of sets has varying implications stemming from how one defines a set in the first place. It may be a self-sufficient and indivisible unit, such as a set of instrumental parts, or a varying quantity of identical copies, such as a set of vocal scores or plays. It is possible however, to handle play texts and vocal scores in self-sufficient units, so that a play set could comprise a specific number of copies that are only issued in that form or a set of vocal scores only issued in units of ten or twenty copies. It is clearly neither practical nor desirable to display hundreds if not thousands of multiple copies of vocal scores of musicals, operas and large choral works before the public gaze and these are best shelved in the stack, ideally in a single composer sequence so that availability can be checked with a minimum of delay. Small-scale choral pieces can be treated in the same way as vocal scores, with the exception that as they are not sufficiently bulky to stand on a shelf in their own right, the inspection copies will need to be housed in box files from which they may be perused at leisure. Where space in the public area is not at a premium, complete sets of this type of material can be publicly displayed either in box files which can be shelved like scores, or in manilla wallets which can be housed very satisfactorily in filing cabinets, 'spine' upwards. Where a collection of small-scale choral pieces is extensive there is a case for handling them in wallets or boxes of ten or twenty or other convenient quantities, so that each wallet is treated as an indivisible module when it is issued and discharged.

Sets of instrumental parts can be displayed in exactly the same way, with the proviso that the boxes or wallets will need to be of somewhat larger dimensions than those required for most choral leaflets. The advantages of the walleted set are that they can easily be handled by the borrower as self-selection saves staff time, they only occupy a comparatively small amount of space compared with the equivalent number of vocal scores, and a single charging card only is required to represent each unit. The disadvantages are that individual copies can disappear whilst they are on display without the deficiency being immediately obvious, copies can be replaced in the wrong wallets after users have inspected them, and wallets returned from loan incomplete are put out of circulation until the loss is made good. Plays are easy to house by virtue of the fact that they are largely uniform in size and physically diminutive compared with most other types of printed volume, presenting no deterrent to the user wishing to make his own selection from either a collection of inspection copies or complete sets.

If a library has its own bindery, many home-made solutions may be devised for containing sets of copies that need to be kept together as a unit, but even without this advantage, a little ingenuity can work wonders with standard materials available from office supply shops. It is possible, for example, to accommodate a set of instrumental parts, ranging from a trio to a late Romantic symphony, in a document wallet which can be folded to produce a 'spine' of appropriate width. If desired, the spine may be reinforced with adhesive linen tape and lettered as required using a stencil and Indian ink. It hardly needs to be said that this would represent a distinct price advantage over the commercially produced orchestral 'bags' which can be obtained from music publishers and suppliers. Small-scale choral pieces can be treated in the same way in wallets of smaller dimensions, each containing a uniform number of copies. Wallets or folders are most conveniently housed in filing cabinets so that each drawer can be adjusted to support changing quantities of material, but where such material is to be accommodated on shelves it is highly desirable that the containers should be of a much more substantial nature.

There is a widespread misconception amongst non-librarians that working in a music library is but one step removed from the Elysian fields, but it should not be forgotten that the work can at times be physically demanding, especially when handling multiple copies of vocal scores to which the user will not normally have direct access. This throws an extra burden on the library staff who will need to transport the material from where it is stored and, if it is to be sent elsewhere rather than issued over the counter, securely package the copies so that they will reach their destination safely. Thirty bound vocal scores of a musical such as *Oklahoma* weigh around half a hundredweight (25kg) which, in more graphic terms, is the equivalent of a sack of potatoes or half a sack of coal. If the copies need to be sent to destinations other than those on a regional or inter-regional transport scheme, the cost of postage, which would be around £8 (second class) for the example quoted above, can be a factor of some considerable significance, in addition to the staff time expended on a rather labour intensive operation.

There are few short cuts to the time needed to handle sets of music and plays but the labour can be distributed in different ways according to the type of set involved. Self-sufficient and indivisible units such as a set of instrumental parts, or a fixed quantity of partsongs or plays enclosed in a wallet or box will normally require only a single charging card (or bar code label) to represent the entire package, even though the contents of each unit need to be clearly listed on the container which encloses them. When they are returned, however, it will be necessary to physically check every single copy in every set and if any are found to be incomplete, the set is effectively put out of circulation until the deficiency is made good. Sets which are treated as infinitely varying quantities of identical items – both plays and vocal scores are possible candidates for this approach – will require a book card for each individual copy, but will be virtually as time consuming to issue as to discharge. This will create a greater flexibility however, allowing any quantity to be issued. If the set is returned incomplete, the appropriate cards can be matched with the items returned and immediately put back into circulation, whilst the cards for the missing copies remain in the issue. The two systems are interchangeable between different types of material with the exception of instrumental sets, whose constituent parts need to be kept together as a unit, and choral leaflets for which one could hardly justify the labour of processing and issuing individually.

Once a library holds more than one set of the same edition of a particular work, it may become necessary to identify individual sets or individual copies, in order to distinguish between several sets issued to different groups at the same time. The larger and more complex the system, the greater the likelihood that this will become desirable, if not essential; even to the extent of marking every individual score or part. Some of the problems that arise in a large regional system but just as likely to occur to a lesser degree in smaller-scale services are:

1. several sets of the same title are returned simultaneously from different libraries but contain no clue to their source of origin;
2. odd missing copies are returned several weeks or even months after the bulk of the material has been received;
3. odd copies which have been issued to group A are returned with a set of the same title originally issued to group B;
4. sets are returned apparently complete but contain items still outstanding from a previous transaction;
5. sets are returned apparently complete but containing copies which were originally issued separately either to an individual or to the group as inspection copies.

These are just some of the problems that need to be unscrambled on a daily basis, for which the solution is to number uniquely every single play, vocal score, choral leaflet and instrumental part in stock, so that the exact source of origin of every single item returned from loan can be determined by matching the copy numbers with the corresponding records in the issue file. An added benefit of this system is that sets can be discharged by staff without any specialist knowledge. The system really comes into its own with sets of orchestral parts which only need to be sorted into numerical order to establish whether the set is complete or not.

The loan period is an important factor when considering sets of music and plays, for almost by definition, material will be required for a considerably longer time than the needs of the average personal borrower. The only conceivable reason for having short-term loans is to boost one's issue figures artificially as a result of successive renewals over a period of possibly many months! As a general rule plays tend to be required for somewhat shorter periods than music, particularly as it is a fairly common practice for drama groups to borrow several sets of plays for reading purposes before deciding which play they wish to produce. Having made a decision, the group will probably require the chosen title for three or four months during which time the rehearsals will be in progress. With large-scale works, such as musicals or operettas, it is quite normal for sets to be required for a period of six months and sometimes for even longer periods up to a year. There is a case for offering users a choice of loan periods commensurate with their needs, but the larger the system the more cumbersome this will be to administer and it may be necessary to employ a fixed term of, say, three, four or six months. Where this is the case, it is important to determine, at the time the material is requested, how long it will be needed in order to establish whether or not there will be a significant discrepancy between the date the set is due for return and the date to which it will be required. Where requests are received from a variety of service points, the request form should be so devised that this information can be provided at the outset, for there would be little point in reserving a set required for a specific date if that material will continue to be in use well after its apparent date of return.

Whatever system is in operation, forward planning is of the essence if the user is to receive a satisfactory level of service. Unfortunately, the burden of responsibility rests largely with the user rather than the library itself and lack of foresight is a key factor in material not being supplied at the time it is required. It is not uncommon for groups to request sets of music or plays within days of the start of rehearsals in the naïve belief that the goods will be available automatically. If this proves not to be the case there is sometimes almost an implied criticism of the library service rather than self-criticism for this state of affairs. What the library can do, however, is not only accept requests many months in advance but also positively encourage users to adopt this practice as a matter of course wherever this is possible. This will then give time for appropriate action to be taken, whether it be to reserve copies currently on loan, purchase copies for stock, arrange an inter-library loan or establish that the material is only available through other sources. All this requires good communications between a library and its users, an objective that is sometimes easier to propose than to achieve in practice. The library's link with a society will normally be through an individual who will be the designated representative of the group, and establishing a good relationship with that individual will go some way towards resolving actual and anticipating potential problems. In many cases the turnover of representatives tends to be rather frequent so that it is difficult to achieve any continuity, and different individuals will inevitably carry out their responsibilities with varying levels of efficiency creating a constantly changing state of affairs.

Perhaps the most frustrating problem of all in handling sets of music and plays is that of missing copies, especially, as can be the case with instrumental parts, where a set contains unique copies, and is rendered unusable until the deficiency is made good. The situation is aggravated by the fact that some publishers will not supply odd copies of wind parts, as well as the fact that many orchestral works are no longer available for sale. One hopeful sign is that some publishers now offer a special service for producing one-off copies of out-of-print items (provided they hold an archive copy) or will give permission for one to be made if an identical part can be obtained elsewhere. Given this approach, the division between what is available and what is not is somewhat blurred and, as it is impossible to know in advance what can be obtained on this basis, each item will need to be pursued individually. Often borrowers will supply photocopies as replacements for missing parts but, unless these have been duly authorized by the publisher or the edition happens to be out of copyright, they should not be accepted. Copies of the Music Publishers' Association's *The Code of Fair Practice* should be freely available so that users are aware of their legal obligations. Admittedly, it is sometimes difficult to know whether lack of availability is the cause or effect of illegal photocopying but, if one considers the situation in its widest context, it is clear that the extent of the problem far exceeds any causal factors. With vocal scores and plays the loss of copies has potentially less serious practical, if greater financial consequences because the nineteen identical items returned from a loan of twenty can immediately be available for use elsewhere.

The worst aspect of the situation is probably the disproportionate amount of time likely to be expended on sending overdues, sending bills, handling money and re-ordering as well as reprocessing items which have been lost beyond recall. The entire process can drag on for weeks or even months, and if one takes the trouble to cost this process in terms of staff time, stationery and postage, it may well be, for the cheapest items at least, that this expenditure is significantly greater than the face value of the missing items themselves. Given that the items in question have no value other than a monetary one and that staff time is at a premium, one may come to the conclusion that the exercise is a totally uneconomic proposition, even though this might encourage the user to have somewhat less of a sense of responsibility than already prevails. Human nature being what it is, the difficulty of trying to eliminate this problem would seem to be insurmountable. Once a set has left the library the burden of responsibility becomes a much more diffuse affair than that of an individual who borrows a single book and by definition, is personally responsible for its safety.

Some societies have tried to re-introduce the personal element into the situation by charging their members a deposit against the return of items borrowed from a library. The deposit needs to be sufficiently substantial to act as an incentive and if the copies are individually numbered, it is possible to link personal responsibility and particular copies. Unfortunately a library has no jurisdiction over the conduct of a society's affairs but this approach should be actively encouraged. There is also a strong argument for persuading an offending society to undertake the task of replacing missing copies itself, relieving the library of what otherwise would be a considerable chore and placing the onus where it really belongs. The ultimate sanction for societies who cannot keep their affairs in order is withdrawal of the service and this can be a particularly effective stimulus to action when rehearsals for a new work are imminent.

PRESERVATION

An important consideration in a library's long-term strategy is the preservation of the stock's active life for as long a period as possible. It is almost inevitable that sets of music and plays issued to societies will suffer much heavier wear and tear than books in normal domestic conditions. This is not the only concern however, as the physical quality of material published in recent years has shown a marked decline, not so much in the quality of the paper but rather in the durability of the binding. It is not uncommon for quite substantial volumes, such as vocal scores of musicals, to be produced with a perfect binding which is totally insufficient to cope with even normal use. Some of them break apart during their very early life and are candidates for rebinding in only a fraction of the time the very same titles used to last when published with a sewn binding. Similarly many vocal scores are only held together by a pair of staples through sheets of sometimes surprising quantity. Inevitably the inner sheets part company from the rest fairly rapidly and require prompt action if they are not to disappear without trace. Finally there is the spiral or plastic binding which requires the pages to be punched with holes of varying shapes and sizes. The very process of perforation is a recipe for impermanence, but the most unfortunate aspect of this form of binding is that there is frequently insufficient inner margin for rebinding to be undertaken if some of the printed text is not to disappear from view. Sometimes it is possible to purchase unperforated sheets but this would appear to be the exception rather than the rule.

Consequently libraries now need to allocate a greater proportion of their expenditure for the preservation of stock than was necessary ten or fifteen years ago. A library with its own bindery clearly has a head start in this area over those which need to use outside agencies and those in this latter category may well need to spend up to 50 per cent of their purchasing power at various times in conserving the most heavily used material. Currently the average cost of binding a vocal score in cloth is slightly higher than its average purchase price, and although I have no data concerning the working life of rebound material of this type, it is clearly many more times than twice the life of an unbound copy. As such it must be regarded as a sound investment as well as an insurance against the material no longer being available for sale at a later date. The only reservation one might have is that a perfect binding will never produce as durable a product when rebound as a sewn binding, and must inevitably have a comparatively shorter working life for the same outlay. During the last ten years or so music, even more than other forms of printed material, has increased in price at a level somewhat higher than the national average rate of inflation so that, apart from any political factors which may have influenced public spending, it is almost certain that music library budgets will have declined in real terms with very few exceptions. In these circumstances it is tempting to plump for the cheapest option but, in my experience, the cheapest services are unlikely to deliver a product of sufficient durability to withstand the wear and tear to which music and plays are almost certain to be subjected. The only alternative to cloth worth considering is the laminated binding which incorporates the original paper covers of the score or play, and provided the covers are in good condition, creates an attractive and durable product at a slightly cheaper rate than the cloth equivalent.

Colour coding of complete classes of bound scores is not a particularly useful practice as it is virtually impossible to achieve total consistency, apart from the fact that yards and yards of total uniformity does not present an especially inviting spectacle. There are specific circumstances, however, when coding can be a distinct advantage such as:

1. when particular volumes are already associated with particular colours such as the green, orange, blue and red books of the four *Carols for Choirs*;
2. when a series of publications are visually identical such as the 16 volumes of the *Chester Books of Motets* which may be distinguished by binding successive volumes in a different colour;
3. when different editions of the same work can be made visually distinctive by using different colours.

Ideally instrumental parts should be sewn into cloth or manilla covers and housed in a bound portfolio which contains one or two pockets with the opening or openings facing inwards. These can then be shelved in the usual manner. Where economic restraints dictate otherwise, the unbound parts can be enclosed in a manilla wallet of suitable dimensions along the lines suggested previously, and with the possible exception of the most bulky material, this can provide a very satisfactory solution to the problem.

It is tempting to try and retard the disintegration of individual vocal scores and plays by joining the covers to the rest of the volume with strips of self-adhesive tape. Although this undoubtedly puts off the evil day when the two part company, the practice will not only shorten the life of the paper itself but also create problems for the binder who will need to remove the offending material (probably with some difficulty) in order to rebind.

IMPORTANT COLLECTIONS

Major regional collections of sets of both choral and instrumental music available for public use are to be found in Birmingham, Liverpool, Manchester (Henry Watson Music Library), Plymouth (Devon County Library) and Wakefield (Yorkshire Libraries Joint Music and Drama Service). Both Liverpool and Manchester have effectively been providing a national service for many years, with others assuming a similar role in more recent times. Liverpool, Manchester and Wakefield operate a subscription service to libraries and societies outside their own areas, and although the question of library charges inevitably generates a great deal of feeling, it should be appreciated that the traffic is almost entirely one way (in some cases up to 90 per cent of issues going beyond the authority's boundaries), the work load generated is considerable and the charges levied are usually only nominal compared to commercial hire rates. The Wakefield collection is unique in that it operates as a regional service financed jointly by a consortium of library authorities in Yorkshire. The only other direct regional involvement is to be found in the South West where the Devon County music collection is boosted by a financial input from the regional library system and consequently acts as a focus for requests for sets within the South West Regional Library System. The two largest collections of play sets are held by the Yorkshire Libraries Joint Music and Drama Service and Devon County Library, with substantial collections being available in a number of county libraries particularly in the South East, and the library of the British Theatre Association which, after experiencing a succession of financial crises over the years, has now been acquired by the Drama Association of Wales, Cardiff.

BIBLIOGRAPHY

Johnston, A.M. (1979), *Theatre librarianship*, Sheffield: University of Sheffield Postgraduate School of Librarianship and Information Science.

Jones, M. (1979), *Music librarianship*, Bingley, 0 85157 274 X.

Lewis, M. (ed.) (1989), *Sets of Vocal Music: A Librarian's Guide to Interlending Practice*, International Association of Music Libraries, Archives and Documentation Centres (UK Branch), 0 9502339 6 X.

Lovell, L.G. (unpublished), *Play Sets in Public Libraries in England*, 'Typescript tabulating the results of a questionnaire initiated in 1980 by the Director of Cultural Services, City of Manchester concerning the stock and issue figures for play sets'.

Music Publishers' Association, (1985), *The Code of Fair Practice Agreed Between Composers, Publishers and Users of Printed Music* Rev. edn.

Penney, B. (1981), *Music in British Libraries: a directory of resources*, 3rd edn Library Association, 0 85365 739 4.

Redfern, B. (1978-9), *Organising Music in Libraries*, 2 vols, Bingley.

Reed, A. (ed.) (1989), *British Union Catalogue of Orchestral Sets*, 2nd edn, British Library Document Supply Centre/IAML (UK), 0 7123 2044 X.

7

Ephemera

MICHAEL PEARCE

WHAT IS/ARE EPHEMERA?

Much time and effort has been expended on the definition of the word 'ephemera'. If one looks at the adjectival version 'ephemeral', the idea becomes clearer. It is essentially material – in our terms generally printed material in some form or another – which the creator does not intend to have any permanent value or significance. Its whole existence is deemed to be 'one-time'. There is an increasing avalanche of material which we need and/or use, in our daily lives but which once used becomes invalid, useless, and is not used again. We can identify many items that come within this category – tickets, statements from the bank, cards in their many forms, timetables, fruit wrappers, membership cards, labels, blank forms and so on. These all have a job to do, but once having done that job, lose their value and are generally discarded. There is also the increasing amount of advertising material to which we are subjected, from being approached in the street and having leaflets forced into our hands, to the material that comes through the letterbox, from free newspapers to invitations to hear about time-share apartments. A collection of this ephemera looked at in the next century would form valuable primary source material for any researcher considering the social habits, advertising and selling methods of our time.

In 1971, as a direct result of an interest shown in ephemera by the Dainton Committee, which maintained that account should be taken of the 'great quantity and variety of ephemeral material' especially in the social sciences[1], J.E. Pemberton produced a report on ephemera.[2] This probably started the flurry of activity that occurred in the 1970s and very early 1980s, although in 1962 John Lewis has already used the word in the title of his book *Printed Ephemera*[3], and although he did not actually define the word until 1976 in his *Collecting Printed Ephemera*[4], a glance at the pages of the former publication will demonstrate very clearly what Lewis meant by ephemera.

The meaning of the word reaches into what are called 'local publications', or 'minor publications', which do have a sort of ephemeral value, although this may be an overgeneralization, for instance, publications usually found in the back of a church – the parish magazine, and a brief history and description of the church. The magazine has essentially an ephemeral value, in that it is superseded in time by another issue, yet, collected, it forms a detailed social history of the church and parish. The history and description, perhaps only a four-page A5 pamphlet, has a more obvious permanent value but is ephemeral in format. Makepeace[5] suggests that minor publications may be classed in two groups – serials and pamphlets – which bears out the example above.

This leaves newspapers, which in private household terms are ephemeral, as one generally consigns the newspaper to the recycling pile every evening. Libraries are sensitized to the collection and preservation of at least selected newspapers, so that they are collected day by day to create a resource of historical information on all aspects of human life, as the parish magazine informs on continuing life in the church and parish. To librarians therefore, newspapers are not ephemeral in terms of information value, yet they are ephemeral in that each day a new edition of a newspaper supercedes that of the previous day.

In the end, it may well be that trying to define the nature of the subject is wasting time. All librarians should be aware that there is a very large body of, generally, printed information which is not dealt with in the regular way by the accepted bibliographical process. He or she will have to make up his or her own methods of collecting what seems to be of lasting importance to the library yet which has not, and will not, come to notice by way of regular bibliographical publications.

THE IMPORTANCE OF EPHEMERA

The reports by Pemberton[6] and Sturges and Dixon[7] both give clues in their titles to the importance given to the collection of ephemera and minor publications. It has already been suggested why ephemera – it may well be a good idea to use this word for both sorts of material – is important, but it is essential that the importance of this group of material be fully realized. In social science and local history it is primary and raw source material for further and later research. Although the piece of ephemera may have a primary life of only a few minutes or weeks or months, there is a secondary life as a document within a collection of documents of a similar primary use, or a similar subject area, which makes it invaluable as part of a whole reservoir of research material, or at least exhibition material, via of course the demands of graphic designers for inspiration, and media persons for authenticity of sets. Although not dealt with generally in an archival manner, the material is essentially part of a whole continuing archive. Each piece of material may be small in itself, but the totality it helps to create is very important indeed.

One must also remember that ephemera is not just quaint and sometimes naïve material produced in the past. It is all around us, and although all relevant historical ephemera items should be collected as and when they turn up, there is also an ever-increasing flow of ephemera currently being produced, which cascades through our letter boxes. This is the research material of a hundred years' time, and will have the same curiosity and interest value for our descendants as Victorian ephemera has for us today (see also Clinton[8]).

COLLECTING EPHEMERA

The first step in collecting ephemera is to decide what subject, or what geographical area, or what type of ephemera is to be the subject of the collection. There are private collectors who are very specific in what they collect – stamps of a particular country, lump sugar wrappers from France, posters of a particular artist, or theatrically speaking, of a particular artiste. A library may have a subject interest in railways, so that any ephemera to do with railways is grist to the library's mill. But the library may be in a specific area, so that only a certain and restricted railway region is of interest, and ephemera from that region only are collected; or the interest may lie in railway timetables, qualified, or not, by area. For instance the Railway Museum at York collects railway ephemera, old and new. A local studies library on the other hand, may collect a wide range of material in terms of subject, so long as the ephemera has some connection with the particular locality.

With the limits of the collection defined, it is easier to exclude material which comes the librarian's way. This then allows him or her to concentrate on where the sources may be located. For instance, local studies librarians may well find that local printers are willing to supply copies of everything they produce. These items immediately have a twofold interest – the piece of printing in terms of the organization for whom it was printed, and the printer himself as a local tradesman. The emergence of word processing, sophisticated desk-top publishing and laser copiers have made it easy for all and sundry to publish small runs of material which the librarian may miss, so he has to keep an eye open for any possible source. A local studies librarian worth his salt knows what is going on in a locality. Similarly a librarian interested in public service communications may well be able to arrange with British Rail, or National Travel, or local bus operators, to have them supply the library with new timetables at each seasonal change.

Collectors

There are collectors of most things, and there are often associations of collectors which run sometimes to fairs, local societies and periodicals. The librarian would do well to trace any that may exist in the chosen subject.

Antiquarian and second-hand bookshops

Antiquarian booksellers often have items of ephemera in their catalogues. It is important to cultivate a select number who know one's requirements in book titles and in ephemera. In addition, books on the shelves are not unknown to contain bookmarkers slipped in by the last reader, which are in fact tram tickets, offers from local tradesmen, cigarette cartons, or practically anything else one can think of. One of the present writer's best finds was a government notice pushed through each front door at the beginning of the Second World War entitled 'What to do when the air raid warning goes', a copy of which he hadn't seen since 1940. It needs a nose, or sheer good luck, or the gall to flick through books from the second-hand shelves to find treasures. Junk shops, flea markets, and the now popular antique collectors' fairs and car boot sales are also happy hunting grounds.

Public opinion and staff interest

Possibly the most useful way to get material is to sensitize public (especially local societies and schools) and staff interest. If library staff and the public know what is being looked for, it is amazing how many times people will save material (no matter that it is duplicated), and bring all the free advertising material that arrives unbidden through the letter box, as well as older material that has been stored away at home. If members of the public are aware that the library is looking out for ephemeral material, they will think twice about consigning the contents of attics, and deceased relatives' houses to the local tip. The librarian should especially contact local businesses, dignitaries, churches, clubs and so on, for what might be their dross may well be the librarian's gold. Although it is a difficult thing to maintain, a personal contact with as many organizations as possible does help immensely, plus staff or friends who will willingly accept the literature pushed into their hands in the street, or who will deliberately not avoid flag sellers.

Attempting to be comprehensive, even in a small subject area, does seem a daunting task, as so much ephemera is produced. But a sedulous cultivation of sources will bring forth much, which must be dealt with forthwith and not be left to accumulate.

Auction houses

One source of material not yet mentioned is the auction house. As with antiquarian booksellers, it is useful to be on the mailing list of local auctioneers, and to try to get to the viewing day. This can of course be time consuming if one's locality has a number of houses, but also quite exciting. This is partly because, although there may be separately numbered lots which contain ephemera, there are likely to be further job lots. The librarian may well get only a few items, but it is often worth it, and frequently job lots are not heavily bid for and get knocked down quite cheaply. To get an idea of the multifarious sources that exist it is worth looking at Clinton.[9]

STORAGE OF EPHEMERA

The local studies librarian particularly will already be aware of the problems which emerge when handling a wide range of types of material, a problem not unknown to museum curators. Ephemera, by their very nature, do not usually conform to any cosy librarian's requirements of being in standard book sizes. The collection may well include some pamphlets, or other 'near-book' material, but it will be largely single-sided or double-sided sheets, and of a variety of sizes, from poster to small ticket, possibly including photographs taken to demonstrate ephemera which were not detachable. Makepeace[10] has some good illustrative examples of this. It is very difficult to detach posters from billboards, or fly posters from walls, so that photographs are an excellent way of recording them for posterity. It is doubtful if any librarian is going to go to the lengths that fans of Toulouse Lautrec's poster art are said to have gone to, following billposters around Paris, stealthily peeling the posters from the walls before the paste could dry!

184

The librarian is, in all likelihood, going to have to store similar items in more than one sequence to accommodate the varying sizes which will be encountered. Large items, such as posters, are best accommodated in a plan chest, although unless they are protected by large plastic envelopes into which they may be slid, they are likely to suffer from the shuffling about required to extract items from a full drawer. Single-sided smaller items may be put into a scrapbook format, although it is accepted that this format is inflexible, because it is difficult to insert items, and there can come a time when a major rearrangement is necessary. That means that items may have to be taken off the scrapbook sheets, and even though they may have been put in using library paste, this puts them in danger. A more flexible and satisfactory way of dealing with the smaller items is to use chemically neutral manilla envelopes in a filing cabinet. This allows for movement, and for greater and easier subject grouping. Here again there is the problem of shuffling items in and out of the envelope. Greater protection can be assured, and the problem of allowing both sides of two sided items to be inspected (impossible in scrapbooks) can be solved by placing individual items into transparent plastic envelopes which may then, of course, be totally sealed to protect the item as much as possible. Even the rather remote eventuality of someone wishing to look for watermarks would not require the extraction of the item from the envelope. These themselves may be placed in manilla envelopes if required, which will give a better protection to the item involved, and greater rigidity to the manilla envelope, so that it stands better in the filing cabinet. It is also possible to attach sticky labels, on which required information may be written, to the outside of the plastic envelope thus avoiding writing anything at all on the item. Obviously, using this protection tends to bulk out the collection physically, but this is preferable to having it disintegrate due to wear and lack of protection. Box files for storage are unsatisfactory unless they are absolutely full, because when they are stood up their contents tend to slide and bend despite the spring clip provided. Even the clip can cause damage if items are returned carelessly to the box file. A way must be found of storing material in such a way as to give it as much protection as possible, but also to make it easy for users to access.

CONSERVATION

All the problems which librarians have in the conservation of books are repeated in the conservation of ephemera. As has been suggested above, there has to be a balance struck between having the material used – for that is what it is there for – and avoiding over-use in terms of heavy handling. Paper made by hand from rags is very sturdy. However, the problem of conserving books from the time of the invention of, and increasing use of, mechanical and chemical wood-pulp with its inbuilt qualities of self destruction, is a different matter. The poor quality of the paper threatens much bookstock from the nineteenth and twentieth centuries. There were certainly no thoughts of conservation or preservation for posterity in the minds of the nineteenth century publishers as they poured books from their presses to satisfy the appetites of their readers. But at the same time, they generally used an adequately good paper. This was not necessarily so for ephemera. No-one had the faintest interest in preserving these items, which were made to be discarded. Yet at the same time it must be said that one can come across nineteenth century ephemera which have stood the test of time very well, and show little sign of deterioration.

But care is always needed, and plastic envelopes will preserve from dust, poor air and human hands. Material which is showing signs of wear, either through paper decay or through over-use should receive the immediate attention of a qualified archival repair expert. Delay, especially to nineteenth century paper, may be fatal. A good archival repair expert can seemingly bring documents back from the dead, restoring items which have looked to be almost irretrievable. But the expert's time costs money, and if this situation can be avoided it is better to do so.

Home repairs can be done, but nothing extensive is recommended. Items can be cleaned of surface grime, carefully, by the use of white bread kneaded to form a rubber, or by very soft artist's rubber. Simple repairs may also be done using a proprietary library paste. But attempts to bleach out foxing or other marks are best left the expert who can do this and then resize the paper properly. One type of repair material which must not be used is transparent tape. It is not permanent, and leaves a sticky residue which is more or less immoveable and discolours the paper. Also even to approach something with a piece of transparent tape is asking for it to go down on the wrong part of the paper, stick closely and either tear the paper as one tries to get it off, or at least take off the surface, probably with some of the printing attached.

CLASSIFICATION AND CATALOGUING

Dedicated classifiers and cataloguers could have a field day with ephemera. Because each piece of ephemera can be considered from differing subject approaches the important thing is that each should be thoroughly indexed. Intensive classification of a routine nature is more of a hindrance than a help. Some collections of ephemera are part of a larger collection – for example a local studies library – where a classification scheme already exists, and there is a normal catalogue. If this is the case, it is likely that the ephemera will be treated in the same way as the rest of the collection, and at least classified to fit in with that collection. But a higher level of indexing is essential to extract all the use possible from the item, and possibly the cataloguing should be more extensive and descriptive, if only so that the item may be recognized and possibly rejected by a user as being outside his remit before it is pulled out for inspection, thus saving on wear and tear. But for freestanding ephemera collections it is much easier to have either a very broad set of subject divisions such as transport, commerce, leisure, or a set of heading types such as tickets, menus, billheads, trade cards, programmes, depending on the mode of access which the librarian perceives may be required. Within the subject division each item should have a unique accession number by which it may be recognized in the catalogue and in the envelope, drawer, or plan chest. This means that it is immediately retrievable and can be filed by number within the subject. Again cataloguing must be descriptive, and indexing exhaustive. The emergence of OPACS on the scene makes exhaustive indexing worthwhile, and allows members of staff and members of the public, to retrieve on more than one term. It is hardly necessary to detail how much more useful this is than a card catalogue, but if computers are not available card catalogues and subject indexes must be created, and with care and imagination.

To emphasize the point about exhaustive descriptive cataloguing and indexing, a glance at John Lewis's *Printed Ephemera*[11] illustrations shows just how much information there is in a piece of ephemera, and what a wealth of information may be retrieved by good and exhaustive indexing. The illustrations show page after page of retrievable information. For example on pages 173–185, which show trade cards, there is a demonstration of design and style over the years, including some consciously 'designed' cards, which contrast interestingly with what one may call the 'naïve' ones. One press responsible for careful and attractive designs of ephemera was the Curwen Press earlier this century, especially between the wars. For the printing type collection, there is a large selection of types, especially from the Victorians, since they could not resist cramming as many type styles and sizes as possible on such things as trade cards or theatre posters. For a local studies library, there is invaluable information. Not all urban areas have directories which cover them historically, and trade cards can form a basis of a directory of names, occupations and their locations, street names, and sometimes items sold or manufactured and their prices. What Lewis calls 'entertainment notices' (pages 100–112) also yield a plethora of information – names of theatres, plays, authors, actors, type faces again, and aesthetically, the prevailing taste of theatre-goers or music hall goers. The sorts of researchers who can profit by this careful analysis are genealogists, local historians, trade historians, social historians. This is why it is essential for local studies librarians especially to collect current material, as its collection and analysis will allow future researchers to study the present time. Librarians with subject interest (as Pemberton[12] was originally concerned with), should also consider seriously how far ephemera in their subject is actually as essential as the books and periodicals on the shelves – and in the end how much cheaper to obtain. The analytical approach is time consuming at the beginning, but yields dividends eventually in terms of answers, both to the casual enquirer at one end of the spectrum, and to a more structured research approach at the other.

IMPORTANT COLLECTIONS

So far there is no register of collections, so that it is not possible to discover in any specialized reference work whether there is a collection of ephemera on any specific subject. Clinton[13] offers the idea of a National Register of Collections as part of the British Library Reference Division. Pemberton[14] in 1971 proposed a National Documents Library, but only after a National Register of Collections had been formed. Clinton has an excellent description of how the National Register of Collections would operate[15], but it seems that after a lot of flurry, the idea has not been taken forward, largely one assumes as a result of a lack of money. It would be interesting to see the British Library reasserting its legal deposit rights over calendars, labels and so on, and using the material to form a National Documents Library.

The main stumbling block to knowing where to look for collections is that they are not necessarily found in libraries. Because of their nature, ephemera are also collected by museums to form an integral part of their collections, and make very evocative exhibits. It is really a matter of finding out which organization might have a collection, and whether somebody within that organization has or has had the imagination and foresight to make a collection.

One can be fairly certain that a collection of ephemera will exist in the local studies collection of a public library, and that the local museum will also have a collection, possibly of the more visual material. The collection of the local studies library will obviously be of local significance, and be the most important collection of ephemera on the locality. The museum's collection will also very likely have an emphasis on the locality, but its range may be more national and international, as its subject base may not only be local.

National subject collections are harder to locate. Clinton[16] in his appendices, offers a whole range of sources to do with postal work, greetings cards, domestic appliances and housing, and one must expect the more specialized national museums, such as the National Library of Film and Television at Bradford, to make their own collections, as indeed the National Railway Museum has already done, and with which it is proceeding.

There is one outstanding collection of ephemera. This is the John Johnson Collection at the Bodleian Library. Johnson (1882–1956) was the Oxford University Printer, a post to which he was appointed in 1925, after being Assistant Secretary to the Delegates of the University Press from 1914. Before this he held a post which explains his interest in ephemera. He worked at Magdalen College as a papyrologist, a job which took him to Egypt, excavating in winter, and working on the papyrological discoveries at Magdalen in the summer. A good proportion of the papyri which have been discovered are, in fact, ephemera – the throw-away bits of the Egyptian civilization which were, fortunately for us, well preserved in the hot dry sandy soil of Egypt. The involvement with Egyptian ephemera seems to have sensitized him to the ephemera of his own time. To quote from the introduction by M.L. Turner to the exhibition catalogue of 1971:

> More than forty years ago I was spending my winters with large gangs of fellahin digging the rubbish-mounds of Graeco-Roman cities in Egypt for the written materials – the waste paper – of those ages . . . Often I used to look over those dark and crumbling sites and wonder what could be done to treat the background of our own English civilization with the same minute care with which we scholars were treating the ancient. (John Johnson, quoted in M.L. Turner, 1971)[17]

Johnson remained in the post of University Printer until his retirement in 1946. It is interesting that he himself first conceived of the collection as being a museum of what is commonly thrown away, but siting it firmly between museum and library as being also a source of material for work on subjects and/or periods. The collection grew rapidly, received an endowment in 1930 from Constance Meade, after which it was called the Constance Meade Collection, and finally moved to the Bodleian in 1968. It is ironic that at some point when space was tight in the 1930s and 1940s, the Bodleian threw away material, some of which could be called ephemeral; Johnson rescued it, and it eventually made a return to the Bodleian as part of the John Johnson Collection.

There are two outstanding sets of material within the Collection to interest librarians professionally. These are the sets on the history of printed books, and the book trade. Both have great strengths. But there is also a theatrical collection and many other items – flag day flags, tickets, valentine cards, political propaganda to name a few. It is said, and probably apocryphally, that Johnson had a box into which he put each day's accumulation of ephemera, and never threw anything away! Johnson himself, while mentioning six other contemporary collectors of ephemera, says:

> I remember my old friend Sir Emery Walker telling me that he used to keep an old commode in his room with its lifting lid, which was known as 'Proctor's rubbish box'. Day by day all the common discarded papers of life were dropped into the pan of the commode and later went on to Proctor. Proctor kept every railway ticket that he did not give up, and he did not give up a great many, every bus ticket of his daily rounds, every receipt, every paper bag. (John Johnson, quoted in M.L. Turner, 1971)[18]

The collection does have a problem of cataloguing. There is no total catalogue or index, although certain parts are indexed. But the Bodleian does now catalogue what it can for insertion into the general catalogue. Because the collection is catalogued under general headings, there are the usual problems of items which could be placed under more than one heading. Only analytical indexing can overcome this problem. Though rather old now, probably the best description of the collection is John Feather, 1976.[19] There is also the catalogue mentioned above. It is probably worth quoting here Johnson's remarks about the collection, which are reproduced in the 1971 catalogue:

> It is difficult to describe it except by saying that it is everything which would ordinarily go into the waste paper basket that is not actually a book. Another way of describing it is to say that we gather everything which a museum or library would not ordinarily accept if it were offered as a gift (John Johnson, quoted in M.L. Turner, 1971)[20]

It is I think, fair to say that museums and libraries these days are far more aware of the value of ephemera, and realize that gift horses need not be looked in the mouth, and that each small piece of ephemera helps to build an overall picture that contributes to a research collection. A glance at the Contents list of the 1971 exhibition catalogue demonstrates the wide range of the Johnson collection.[21] More information is available in Clinton (1981), Appendix One.[22]

One other more recent collection is the Robert Opie Collection, in the

Museum of Advertising and Packaging. A small part of the collection was displayed in the Victoria and Albert Museum in 1976 under the title 'The Pack Age – A century of wrapping it up'. The collection now has a permanent home in Gloucester, and as the exhibition title demonstrates, it is a collection of packaging based on 25 years of research and collecting by Robert Opie. The collection, which numbers some 300 000 items, is the largest of its kind in the world, and forms not only a wonderfully evocative and colourful demonstration of past packaging, but also a valuable base for research of various natures.

Clinton (1981), Pemberton (1971) and Lewis (1976, pp. 156–7) identify some other important collections. For instance, the British Library has a number of collections, which are listed in the catalogue under that title. But it has much material scattered through the library, which gathered together would form a vast and varied set of collections. The St. Bride's Printing Library has a collection of typographic ephemera. The National Maritime Museum has a collection on naval history, and the National Railway Museum has a collection of railway ephemera. The Smithsonian Museum in Washington D.C. has a collection covering transport, and the Peabody Museum has collections on maritime history, natural history and ethnology. Until a national or even an international register of collections is achieved, intelligent and lateral thinking on the part of the librarian will be crucial in the location of required material. In the UK the *Aslib Directory* may be helpful in the location of some collections.

THE RISE OF BRITISH INTEREST IN EPHEMERA IN THE 1970s

Ephemera had a high profile in Great Britain during the 1970s. In 1969, the Dainton Committee demonstrated a lack of national acquisition of primary material in the social sciences.[23] As a result of this Pemberton did research and published his report in 1971.[24] He was interested in and proposed the formation of the National Register of Collections and a National Documents Library. This did not find any great official favour, and even though Aslib sponsored two conferences of its Social Science Group, and held a working party with the BLRD, nothing really emerged. In a parallel interest, the Standing Conference for Local History and the Local History Group of the LA established the Advisory Committee on Ephemera and Minor Publications. Sturges and Dixon produced their BLRD report on local publications in 1980,[25] and Clinton produced a BLRD report in 1980,[26] one of the results of which was his 1981 book.[27] Since this time, except for Makepeace's book in 1985, there seems to have been little official interest. A demonstration of public interest was the formation of the Ephemera Society in 1975, and the foundation of the periodical, *The Ephemerist*.

THE LITERATURE OF THE SUBJECT

It is important to have a look at the literature of the subject in chronological order. This replaces the usual bibliography at the end of the chapter. It was considered to be more important to have an annotated version, since virtually all the titles mentioned in the bibliography below, have been referenced in the text above. There are further interesting titles, but these may be picked up as references while reading the titles below.

Lewis, J. (1962), *Printed Ephemera*, Cowell. (Reprinted Faber 1969).

A fascinating collection of ephemera divided into sections, and spanning a timescale from the sixteenth century almost to the date of publication. Lewis's interest is essentially in printing and design. He includes an interesting Introduction, and a useful list of typefaces used in ephemeral printing. It was this publication which really whetted public interest in the subject.

Pemberton, J.E. (1971), 'The national provision of printed ephemera in the social sciences: a report prepared for the Social Science and Government Committee of the Social Science Research Council', University of Warwick: University of Warwick. Occasional Publications: 1.

Pemberton was preoccupied primarily in discovering what was being done nationally, and primarily, academically to collect ephemera for research purposes in the social sciences. The report details the result of his researches, and contains his recommendations for a National Register of Collections and a National Documents Library.

Turner, M.L. (ed.) (1971), 'The John Johnson Collection: A catalogue of an exhibition', Oxford: Bodleian Library.

This catalogue of the exhibition held in the Bodleian in 1971 has a very useful introduction (already quoted above in extracts from Johnson's own comments) on Johnson and his life and motives concerning the collection. The introduction is itself an expanded version of a lecture which Turner first gave to the Printing Historical Society at the St. Bride Printing Library. The exhibition (259 entries) was only a miniscule part of the collection, but demonstrated the breadth of its contents. The catalogue is illustrated on most of its double page spreads. There are notes and an index.

Pemberton, J.E. (1972), 'Printed Ephemera in British Libraries', in Aslib Proceedings **24**(3) March.

This is essentially a restatement in a paper given to the Aslib Social Sciences Group, of Pemberton's 1971 report to the Social Science Research Council above, and as such is a more readable abstract of that report.

Standing Conference for Local History, (1975), 'Local history ephemera: a report', SCLH.

A report on local history ephemera and its value.

Lewis, J. (1976), *Collecting Printed Ephemera*, Studio Vista.

This is a progress on the volume of 1962/1969. Here we have another excellent display of examples of ephemera, but they are accompanied by Lewis's thoughts on ephemera, and the ephemera are gathered together in themes, rather than by types as in the previous volumes. There is a short list of collections in Great Britain and the USA.

Feather, J. (1976), 'The Sanctuary of Printing: John Johnson and his Collection', *Art Libraries Journal*, Spring.

This article supplements the introduction by Turner, above, to the Catalogue of the exhibition of the John Johnson collection in 1971. It discusses particularly the printing, booktrade and theatrical collections, and also some of the problems of cataloguing the collection generally.

Pollard, N. (1977), 'Printed Ephemera', in Pacey, P., *Art Library Manual*, Bowker, pp. 316–36.

Pollard is interested in ephemera from an art library point of view, and particularly someone servicing practising artists. There is an annotated list of types of material and brief comments on the acquisition, handling and exploitation of ephemera.

Rickards, M. (1977), *This is Ephemera*, David & Charles.

A slighter companion to Lewis's works, but containing some interesting illustrations, and a readable text which whets the appetite. Ther are some useful pages (46–8) which show the thematic importance of ephemera, and how when properly displayed, they can make a most effective display. The book also deals briefly with handwritten material.

Advisory Committee on Ephemera and Minor Publications (1979), 'Preliminary report', ADCEMP.

A preliminary report on how to deal with ephemera and minor publications.

Clinton, A. (1980), 'Printed Ephemera: Its Collection, Organisation and Access; A Summary Report', BLRD Report 5593, Oxford: Bodleian Library.

A report of a survey done by Clinton for a project entitled 'Preliminary survey of collections of ephemera' conducted under the auspices of the BLRD and the Bodleian Library and directed by M.L. Turner. The report summarizes the survey, and the book below by Clinton is essentially the published report.

Clinton, A. (1981), *Printed Ephemera: Collection, Organisation, Access*. Bingley.

Rather old, but much of what is said about ephemera still holds true. The chapters on control of ephemera are accompanied by some which take themes and discuss and analyse them and their sources. The appendices are also useful for sources, which although they may now be out of date, are good starting points.

Sturges, R.P. and Dixon, D. (1983), 'An Investigation of Local Publications', BLRD Report 5645, Loughborough: Loughborough University, Department of Library and Information Studies.

Investigation, with findings that slight local publications are not noticed by the bibliographical services, but that at the same time many of them are not ephemeral in nature in that they add to the body of local knowledge.

Makepeace, C.E. (1985), *Ephemera*. Grafton/Gower.

The latest book on the subject. Although now a little old, much of what is said in the book remains true. The chapters cover all aspects of dealing with ephemera, from what ephemera is, to how to exploit the collection, and its use. Appendix 1 is a useful list of types of ephemera, and Appendix 2 is a succinct account of the development of official interest, although this appears to have waned. A useful handbook on the subject.

REFERENCES

1. Dainton, F.S. (Chairman), (1969), 'Report of the National Libraries Committee', HMSO, p. 77 paras. 296–7.

2. Pemberton, J.E. (1971), 'The national provision of printed ephemera in the social sciences: a report prepared for the Social Science and Government Committee of the Social Science Research Council', University of Warwick: University of Warwick Occasional Papers: 1.
3. Lewis, J. (1962), *Printed Ephemera*, Cowell, reprinted Faber 1969.
4. Lewis, J. (1976), *Collecting Printed Ephemera*, Studio Vista.
5. Makepeace, C. (1985), *Ephemera*, Gower, pp. 12–15.
6. Pemberton, J., op. cit.
7. Sturges, R. P. and Dixon, D. (1983), 'An investigation of local publications', BLRDD Report 5645, Loughborough University: Department of Library and Information Studies.
8. Clinton, A. (1981), *Printed Ephemera: Its Collection, Organisation and Access*, Bingley.
9. Ibid., chaps 3–6 and Appendices 2–6.
10. Makepeace, C. op. cit.
11. Lewis, J. *Printed Ephemera*, op. cit.
12. Pemberton, J. op. cit.
13. Clinton, A. (1981), pp. 90–95, and Clinton, A. (1980), 'Printed Ephemera: Its Collection, Organisation and Access', BLRDD Report 5593, Bodleian Library. 1980. pp. 17–22.
14. Pemberton, J., op. cit.
15. Clinton, A. (1981), pp. 90–95.
16. Clinton, A. (1981), pp. 95–119.
17. Turner, M.C. (1971), 'The John Johnson Collection: a catalogue of an exhibition', (introd.), Bodleian Library, p. 7.
18. Ibid., p. 10.
19. Feather, J. (1976), 'The Sanctuary of Printing: John Johnson and his Collection', *Art Libraries Journal*, Spring, pp. 23–32.
20. Turner, M.C. (1971), p. 11.
21. Turner, M.C. (1971), p. 4.
22. Clinton, A. (1981), pp. 95–8.
23. Dainton, F.S. (1969), p. 77. paras. 296–7.
24. Pemberton, J. op. cit.
25. Sturges and Dixon, op. cit.
26. Clinton, A. (1980).
27. Clinton, A. (1981).

8

Slides, microfilms, microfiches

JOHN KIRBY

THE MATERIAL

Slides, microfilms and microfiches are all photographic or quasi-photographic media, storing information in the form of text or visual images on film. Although all three media share this superficial similarity there are also major differences which affect the use to which each is put. Production of 35mm slides is within the capabilities of almost anyone with a suitable camera; the manufacture of microfilm and microfiche generally requires a much more complex process, with access to expensive machinery and specialist operation. Perhaps the most substantial differences lie in the area of use to which each format is put. Slides are frequently used for projection to a large audience, for example in a classroom or lecture theatre. Microfilm and microfiche can be projected but are far more likely to be used for individual study and research. Differences in the material used to make the slides or microforms result in slides deteriorating more quickly, which again affects the use to which the medium can be put.

All these media have major disadvantages as carriers of information. They deteriorate easily and are extremely vulnerable to damage. They are also vulnerable to replacement by new technologies and although it would be rash at this stage to predict the demise of either slides or microform in the immediate future, there must be questions over their future in the face of developments in CD-ROM, videodisc and other computer-based systems.

THE SLIDE

It is the ability to project slides, to show visual material to a group of people, in a lecture for example, coupled with the almost infinite flexibility of selecting specific required images, that makes the slide such a popular and enduring medium for providing information. The user can choose which images he or she wishes to show and project them in whatever order seems appropriate. Multiple projectors allow slides to be put onto the screen side by side for the purposes of comparison of the images. The pictures can be left on the screen for as long or as little time as is required, within reason, and the medium is so flexible that this time period can be adjusted during the actual lecture. Once the sequence has been selected for a particular occasion however, it is difficult to use the slides other than in a linear pattern as it is generally not easy to jump about at random within the set of slides; but judicious use of duplicate slides and more than one projector can ameliorate this minor difficulty. The slides can be projected to a very large audience or can as easily be viewed by an individual. No other medium has yet been developed that will fulfil all of these criteria within reasonable cost parameters, and the slide has been in use for many years with successful results. Like the book, its demise has often been predicted but so far nothing has taken its place. Whether that superiority will last is unclear.

The videodisc or other form of digital recording of visual images may well make the slide obsolete in the future as this system can offer even more flexibility, but the present costs place it beyond the reach of most slide users as a viable tool. The ability to make slides easily and cheaply and the individualization of a teaching resource, is surely a flexibility that few slide users would be prepared to forego. Until we can make our own videodiscs at low cost, edit them, add to them and project the resultant images with high definition, the slide must remain supreme, despite its faults, as a medium of image storage and communication.

But against the inherent usefulness of the slide as an information carrier is a major disadvantage. Slides are not permanent records; they deteriorate with time and with use as the chemicals in the emulsion on the film change. Moreover they may not be a totally accurate record, even when they are first made. The colours on photographic film may vary considerably from the original, depending on the light, the process used, the type of film, and in time, with use. Exposed to the light, the colours will fade unevenly. Even infrequent use will alter the slide's colour balance.

The physical nature of the medium is also vulnerable to damage. Slides melt if exposed to undue heat. Even leaving them in the projector for too long can lead to meltdown. Moisture too can cause the emulsion to bloom and the plastic of the transparency is easily scratched.

For these reasons slides must be considered as an ephemeral medium. Although the quality of slides has improved in the last twenty years there is still no guarantee that they will last for long. The user has only to look at old slides to see how much deterioration can take place. It is essential to be aware of these limitations and to keep them in mind, as it can affect decisions on how the slides will be used and stored.

Slides are generally used to provide visual images in the absence of the real thing, or because the actual object cannot be viewed except through another medium. For example, slides may be used in a lecture on painting and show examples of an artist's work from galleries scattered over the world. Clearly it would be impossible to view these artworks in any other way in this context. Similarly, slides of a medical condition are a replacement for seeing the real thing; the slides can be viewed as often as required, the disease may be met with only rarely. Industrial processes can be illustrated by slides where it would be too dangerous for a human being to go. These are perfectly valid uses of the slide as a means of conveying information. It must be stressed however that the slide image is a *replacement* for the real thing and that it may contain inaccuracies which create a false impression in the mind of the viewer. The brilliant colours of the projected slide, the translucence of the image, the large size of the picture on the screen all conspire to a surrogate reality. Students who have seen certain paintings only through slides have been known to be disappointed when they saw the original works of art. They found them smaller, duller, less lambent, often with very different colours. This falseness, or potential falseness, of the slide can easily be demonstrated by collecting a variety of slides of the same subject from a number of sources; the variations will soon be clear.

Despite these strictures the slide is a valuable tool. It is probably the cheapest means of building a collection of colour images in any subject field and at the present time the flexibility of use far outweighs the disadvantages inherent in the physical make-up of the medium.

Acquisition of slides

Slides can be acquired in a variety of ways. The making of slides is a skill that can be easily gained by anyone with a reasonable aptitude with a camera and minimal equipment. Some form of copy stand and portable lights are a useful accessory if the librarian intends taking many slides from books. The user can photograph the real thing or may copy an existing picture. The former is always preferable but may not always be possible. Copying an existing picture of the object exacerbates the colour problem; a slide of a postcard of a painting in an art gallery is not a slide of the painting but a slide of a reproduction which will itself almost certainly contain imperfections. Nevertheless copying existing images may be the only way to obtain slides. The original may not be available; it may be a long way away or in a place where photography would be impossible. It may no longer exist. Graham Sutherland's portrait of Sir Winston Churchill, now destroyed, can only be known to us through reproductions. It may be of an image of an event which cannot be repeated or which happened in the past. Slides of the Crystal Palace and the Great Exhibition of 1851 can only be made from illustrations and photographs taken at the time. For these and many other reasons, including convenience, slides will be copied from other visual material, even other slides. The legality of this copying under the laws of copyright and any restrictions that may be placed on subsequent use of the slides should be checked thoroughly.

Obviously the other major way of obtaining slides is through purchase. Sources vary enormously between different subject areas. Those subjects which have always used slides, for example art history, have a variety of commercial and institutional sources; art galleries and museums generally sell slides of the works of art in their collections. Each librarian must seek out potential sources in his or her subject field as no truly comprehensive guide exists to suppliers of slide material.

It is generally stated that, bearing in mind the strictures on image quality, the librarian would be advised to buy slides only on approval, so that the standard of reproduction may be judged. This counsel of perfection may not always be possible or practicable. Unless one is very familiar with the insects of South America it may be difficult to assess whether a slide of a Brazilian beetle is precisely the right colour or not. The museum from which the slide came may be unwilling to send it half-way round the world without pre-payment. It is often necessary to buy without seeing the slides in advance. Since they are generally fairly cheap it may not be a major disaster if they turn out to be of poor quality. Sometimes it is necessary to consider the advantages of having a less than perfect image as an alternative to not having the image at all.

Acquisition may be of individual slides or a set of slides packaged by the publisher. The latter has the disadvantage that the librarian may have to purchase a number of slides that are not required, in order to obtain those that are. On the other hand it is probably simpler and quicker to order a set of slides of the sights of London than to agonize over which views of the Houses of Parliament or Tower Bridge are most effective. As always selection of material is a matter of taste, the needs of the library users, financial considerations, and all the other factors that librarians weigh up in their minds when they buy anything.

As with other forms of material that are not subject to adequate bibliographic control, the librarian should always be on the look out for potential sources of supply and should not hesitate to employ as imaginative a range of acquisition techniques as possible. For example asking friends and colleagues to photograph what they find on the beach may produce a far more effective set of slides on pollution than any that can be purchased.

Classification and cataloguing of slides

The classification and cataloguing of slides can be problematical. Is each slide to be treated individually? Are they to be made up into sets? What sort of access will be provided to users and how will the slides be stored? How much knowledge will potential users have and how many of them will there be? All these factors can affect decisions on the possibilities for slide cataloguing.

If the slides are to be made into sets, they can be put into plastic wallets in some form of binder and treated in exactly the same way that the library catalogues and classifies its books. The set can be shelved at an appropriate class number alongside books on the subject. It can be catalogued as a book; to all intents and purposes it *is* a book. This approach has some tempting advantages and in certain libraries may well be appropriate. It may be the only way that some libraries would wish to handle slides for loan. In most cases however there are significant problems in treating slides in sets. The flexibility of the slide medium positively encourages the user to select for him or herself, those images he or she wishes to show from the collection. Users may not wish to take out several sets just to choose a few images from each. The librarian would also not want this to happen. Several sets would be out on loan precluding the use of any of those slides by others. There is also the problem of slides being replaced in the wrong sets! Most people who wish to use slides will wish to select and make their own *temporary* set for immediate use. The management of the collection needs to cater for this.

Does this mean therefore that every slide must be treated as an individual piece of library stock, with its own catalogue record? Perhaps, perhaps not! Before looking at the various options it is necessary to consider how the slides will be stored, in what arrangement, and how the collection will be accessed. These factors will influence the level of cataloguing that will be required.

Whatever form of cataloguing or storage is used, each slide should be labelled so that it is identifiable. The amount of data that is squeezed onto the limited space of a slide mount will vary from library to library but may include title, class number or subject heading, accession number, source of image. The use of a typewriter with a very small font can make this a neater job than handwriting.

The slides can be arranged in accession number order. Access to individual slides can then only be through the catalogue so records of each slide will be essential. What form these records take will depend on the library's practice, but since there will be no browsing facility there should be as many access points as possible through the catalogue. AACR2 provides guidance on the cataloguing of slides. Obviously this means of cataloguing is expensive but it does provide very precise access to specific slides if it is done well, and this may be what the library users require.

The other main type of storage is by subject so that the slides are in a self-indexing system. The slides are stored under subject headings or classification numbers. To find what is available on a topic the appropriate heading is found and with it the slides on that topic. With this system minimal cataloguing is necessary. As slides can be duplicated cheaply it is possible to store them under a variety of subject headings so allowing multiple access. Some form of cross-referencing and guiding would also be useful, and clearly adequate instruction in the use of the subject headings or classification scheme used will be necessary.

One factor in deciding what storage and cataloguing will be appropriate for a slide collection will be the librarian's knowledge of the potential users of the collection. Where considerable expertise can be presupposed it may be necessary to provide also for specific retrieval, since the users may frame their requests in terms of individual images required. Where less knowledge of the subject can be expected in the user group, more browsing facilities may need to be provided. This is only a broad generalization; even the most expert user may also wish to browse and given the importance of browsing as an activity in selecting material it should be facilitated where possible.

Between these extremes there are a number of variations and the librarian is referred to specialist literature on the subject in order to decide which is most appropriate in a particular library. Some general points are worth bearing in mind. Slides are cheap and likely to be ephemeral. Their use and size make them vulnerable to loss and damage. Descriptive cataloguing of visual images is extremely difficult and is also expensive. Rarely will words give an adequate description of any but the most unsophisticated picture. The user will almost certainly wish to select material on the basis of seeing the slides. Visual material in a library is often of interest to more than one group of users and it can be difficult to cater for this variety of need through the catalogue; a Gainsborough painting is of interest to art historians but may also be used to illustrate costume, social status, architecture, transport etc; sometimes the background will be of greater interest than the main subject of the picture. In an attempt to overcome this problem various systems have been devised to classify visual images, for example *Iconclass*. Not surprisingly all are complex and likely to be expensive to apply.

Having decided on the arrangement of the collection the librarian must exercise control on its use. Since it is certain that the users will wish to borrow slides, some form of issue system will be necessary. The simplest is to count how many slides the user borrows. Beyond this are various more rigorous systems of recording loans. Each slide may well have a card which has on it the details of the slide. This can then be put in the place of the slide borrowed. Such a simple record could also indicate who had borrowed the slide. This could work quite well in a small library where the number of users is limited. It is a little cumbersome, in that a card has to exist for each slide. More simply a blank card could be put in the place of the slide and a list made of which slides a user has borrowed. As slides are generally borrowed in large numbers, it is essential that any circulation system be simple and cost-effective. It may be enough to record that a borrower has 20 slides on loan for example, with the library keeping no record of individual slides. This may appear to be heresy to librarians used to keeping detailed control of their collection, but the value of establishing elaborate systems to keep track of items costing only a few pence each is debatable. If a catalogue record has been made for each slide it should be fairly simple to issue slides by linking this record to a unique number. Small barcode labels are available which would enable a light-pen to be used for issue and return; making the control of the collection simple and straightforward using one of the existing computerized circulation systems. Again there is a spectrum of approaches and the librarian msut decide which one is best suited to his or her particular circumstances.

Preservation of slides

The ephemeral nature of slides and their fragility has already been noted. A number of systems of physical management are possible to minimize deterioration while at the same time maximizing access for use. Because of the quality of the slide format it would be unwise to view this medium as a suitable one for archival purposes. Rather it should be a case of preserving the slide for as long as possible but with no expectation that it will be for ever.

Slides are normally obtained in card or plastic mounts. While these may be adequate for personal collections or occasional use the librarian may wish to protect the slide further by using glass mounts. Such mounts solve some problems but also cause others. They can trap moisture which leads to damage of the emulsion on the transparency. In some ways glass mounts are more suceptible to damage than unprotected slides in that the glass can break easily. Finally the cost of the additional mounts may be more than the cost of the slide itself. Glass mounts undoubtedly can add to the life of the slide, but whether the additional cost is more productive than say, providing more copies of the slide is perhaps questionable.

Slides should be protected from heat, light and damp as far as possible. The ideal environment would probably be in a day refrigerator but since few librarians, and probably fewer library users, would relish this climate a compromise has to be reached. Certainly slides should not be stored where they are exposed to the light. Some form of closed cabinet seems necessary. They can be arranged in shallow drawers; this method is particularly useful if they are stored in accession number order. Collections which allow self-indexing and self-selection by users are better stored in transparent wallets which can be hung in filing cabinets of some kind. Wallets which contain 24 slides can then be viewed on a light-box or simply held up to the light and the required images chosen. This method also reduces the handling of individual slides. Both these systems allow for expansion of the collection; additional drawers or wallets can be added as appropriate. There are other slide storage systems available but these are generally rather cumbersome. The display unit type often seen in art galleries is really not suitable for libraries, exposing the slides to too much light and restricting access.

Viewing of slides

Finally, in addition to storage facilities the slide collection will need some form of viewing equipment. A light-box or light-table on which a number of slides can be viewed and sorted with perhaps a small projector or hand-held viewer may be adequate. Clearly the amount of such equipment will depend on the particular needs of the library.

MICROFILMS AND MICROFICHES

Microfilms and microfiches are very similar to each other in most points except format. Microfilm is a roll of film similar to that in a camera. Standard sizes are 35mm and 16mm, but 8mm is sometimes used and there are also a number of unusual sizes which may be encountered. Microfiche is a rectangular sheet containing frames of information. It may be produced photographically, like microfilm, or it may be generated from a computer file – COM, Computer Output on Microfiche. Library catalogues on microfiche are produced in this way.

Microfilms and microfiches may contain visual images or text or both. Unlike slides there is relatively little flexibility in their use. Of the two, microfiche is easier to use if there is a need to select frames of information in a random sequence, as when checking a booklist against a library catalogue for example. Microfilm can only be read in a linear manner and moving from one part of the film to another involves winding and rewinding the film. As a means of storing information, microfiche is probably a more efficient method, particularly if the information is broken up into individual items. It is easier to identify the correct microfiche and then select the frame within that, than to search for specific frames on microfilm. Even with motorized viewers it can be very tedious to search microfilm.

Microfilm and microfiche have had an important place in libraries for the storing of specific types of information. Material held on microform takes up less storage space than paper copies. This can lead to a saving in storage costs or a more efficient use of available space. Archival material or otherwise unobtainable items can be put onto microfilm or microfiche and so made available to any library at a reasonable cost. This is particularly valuable for an academic library which can purchase archival material and make it accessible for a larger number of people than might be able to see the original. The *Mass Observation Archive* held at the University of Sussex, for example, can be bought on microfiche so this key research on 1930s and 1940s Britain can be studied anywhere in the world. Journal backruns lend themselves particularly to storage on microfilm or microfiche. In their hard copy they take up a lot of room, often they are referred to relatively little so are expensive to store, and they are frequently difficult to obtain in their original form. Microfilm or microfiche copies solve these problems; complete sets can be purchased and stored in a small space. By the same token microfilm and microfiche can be used to store rare or fragile items so that the microform copies can be used instead of the original to save wear. Alternatively, microfilm and microfiche copies of journal backruns can be used for permanent storage and the library users given daily use of the paper copies which can then be discarded after a period.

Acquisition of microforms

The librarian should seek to get on mailing lists for microform publishers. Because the technology needed to produce microfilm and microfiche is in most cases more complex than that needed for slides there are far fewer potential sources of supply. It is possible to produce microfiche in-house using a system where negatives from standard photographic film are slotted into 'microjackets' and microfiche produced from these masters, but this system is not really suitable for mass-production and the quality of the finished item is not as good as the more conventionally-made microfiche.

Classification and cataloguing of microforms

There seems little reason not to classify and catalogue microfilms and microfiches in the same way as books, even if they are stored in a different place. AACR2 provides substantial detail on cataloguing. There are some problems however. Microforms are often issued as sets. They may even contain copies of many individual volumes. The librarian is then faced with the choice of cataloguing the set as one item, or cataloguing each of the constituent parts separately. Such sets frequently include a printed index or guide to the contents. It may be adequate to catalogue the set and rely on the use of the printed guide to obtain information on the contents. This method, although it may be a pragmatic solution to avoiding the need to catalogue perhaps several hundred separate items, does demand that the library users are aware of what is likely to be in the microform set. This may be acceptable for the researcher who is prepared to look at a variety of sources on a topic, but is rather hard on the user who is looking for a specific document, particularly if he or she is not an expert in the subject. Despite the amount of work involved it would be better to catalogue each identifiable bibliographic record within the set. The maintenance of handlists, catalogues, guides and so on separate from any main library catalogue is a recipe for their being overlooked and not used.

Whatever strategy is adopted for cataloguing and classification of microfilms and microfiches, it is essential that there is a clear indication in the catalogue record of the medium and its storage location; particularly if, as is usually the case, the microforms are stored separately from the main sequence of the bookstock. This information should also include any internal arrangement within a set of microform.

Because of the nature of the format it is common to store microfilms and microfiches in their own units where they can be kept in conditions suitable for their conservation. It is possible to keep microfiche in folders and in these cases it would be possible to shelve the folder with other material at the appropriate classification number. On the whole this approach only works well for fairly small sets, containing perhaps only one bibliographical entity. More usually microform sets are too large for this approach or contain multiple titles and have their own internal arrangement, often dictated by the publisher. In some cases there seems little logic to this arrangement, others may be arranged by date of original publication, classification of some kind, or date of fiche production; some even use a combination of these. The Chadwyck–Healey microfiche of art exhibition catalogues are arranged by a code which indicates year of fiche production, gallery or museum, then a running number to indicate a particular publication; for example, 3.041.004. In general it is probably better to house the microforms near the equipment needed to view them. This will reduce the need of the user to search for the necessary machine.

Preservation of microforms

Although boxed microfilm can be kept on shelves, storage of both microfilms and microfiches is usually in drawer units of some kind. Here they can be stored away from dust, with a reasonable chance of avoiding major temperature fluctuations. Like slides this medium should be stored away from heat which is the most damaging physical factor. Scratching of both microfilms and microfiches can be a problem, though unless the marks are serious the text or images are generally legible when viewed on the reader, as the magnification blurs the scratch and reduces its appearance to some extent. As with most library materials the very act of touching microfilms and microfiches with bare hands can cause long-term damage from the acids and oils in human skin. Items that are expected to be kept for a long period should therefore be handled by the edges only and touched as little as possible. More ephemeral articles such as library catalogues which will be updated by new editions at regular intervals need less care. For these uses the medium is fairly robust.

Viewing microforms

Microfilm and microfiche readers are available in a variety of shapes and sizes. Some can be used to project the information onto a screen; more usually the equipment is supplied with an inbuilt screen onto which the image is projected from behind, through a series of mirrors. The screens are semi-translucent and are either blue or 'white' in colour. The blue screens are good for viewing text and are commonly used for the display of library catalogues. Used with an appropriate level of light source and with negative images, the letters light on a dark background, they are not too tiring on the eyes. Where the microform contains visual material or is a positive image, that is, dark letters on a light background, then a 'white' screen should be used. More light reaches the eyes of the user than with negative film so it is supposedly more tiring to use. As positive images are generally more natural to read, like dark print on light paper, it may be less offputting to view this form of microform even if it is more tiring in the long run. Since the microfilm or microfiche producer will be the decider of the negative or positive form it is likely that the library will have both; negative images can be viewed on a 'white' screen but positive images do not appear well on a blue screen. If only one machine is purchased, it should be with a 'white' screen.

It is possible to purchase equipment which is dual use and can be changed to show either microfilm or microfiche. While such machines may have a use in a small microform collection they should be avoided if possible and specialist viewers obtained. There seems to be some law of nature that results in the attachments for the wrong format being on the machine whenever one goes to use it!

The resultant irritation to the library user, if not to the librarian, is a further barrier in the effective exploitation of this medium. There is no doubt that there still exists user resistance to microfilms and microfiches. While this may simply be due to lack of familiarity with the format which is not one that is encountered much in daily life, there is also the need for the machine interface in order to view the information. This undoubtedly gets in the way of ease of use. The medium is not as user-friendly as a book, and the librarian must be aware of this and the need to take positive action in the guidance given to potential users. Clear details in the catalogue are the first step in encouraging the use of microfilms and microfiches. Good guiding to the microform storage and labelling so that it is easy to find individual items is also essential. Whereas it is easy to look along a shelf of books to find the required title once one is in the right area of the stack, browsing in microfilms or microfiches is virtually impossible. Equipment that is easy to use should be chosen, and instructions should be with each machine. If necessary the librarian should write these and ensure that they are both clear and logical and that they omit information that the library user will not need, such as how to service the equipment. This may appear obvious but it is a simple practice which is inadequately handled by many librarians; pointing to the microfilm reader and saying 'there it is' may not encourage the user to feel happy about looking at microforms for the first time.

Since the medium may appear confusing and difficult the librarian should aim for a positive approach. Talking enthusiastically about the major research tool which the library owns and which just happens to be on microfiche will probably have better results than a mere mention of the medium in a library introduction session. The assumption that most people will need help with using the equipment and even finding what they want, will lead to a better service even though it may be more expensive in staff time and effort. But like most other special collections the exploitation of this part of the stock will need particular attention from the librarian, and if he or she is not prepared to invest such time then it should be questioned whether it is worth purchasing the material in this medium in the first place.

While many library users will be satisfied by simply viewing the item on the microfilm or microfiche reader, others will want a paper copy to take away. Reader–printer machines are available for both microfilms and microfiches; in most cases attachments mean that one machine can serve both formats. The strictures above apply to these dual-use machines but it may not be economical to buy one for each format. Quality of output is extremely variable. Factors that affect quality include the amount of use the machine gets, the process used to print the copy, and of course the quality of the microform image itself. Microfilms or microfiches of old typewritten material may appear slightly fuzzy as the original letters were slightly blurred. When such material is copied again on the reader–printer the distortion can be exaggerated and made even less easy to read. Negative microforms should be copied if possible so that the resulting image is a positive one, as it will be much more legible in most cases. While some reader–printers copy onto plain paper, many still use a paper coated with chemicals. Often library users find this unpleasant to handle and the images will fade in time, particularly if exposed to the light. This problem can be overcome by making a copy of the copy on a photocopier using plain paper, but as this then becomes a copy of a copy of a copy of the original the resultant loss of quality can be judged! Certainly quality of the image and ease of operation will be the major factors in influencing library users on the value of microfilms and microfiches as media they are happy to use.

The future of microforms

Given that much material held on microfilms and microfiches is in the form of text there must be a question mark over the future of these media for information storage. Text can easily be held on a computer file, and the searching facilities for specific items within the file or by keywords for related material must make computerized storage a much more attractive option. The added flexibility of manipulating the data, of accessing it from a variety of locations not necessarily in the library itself, and of producing printout quickly and cheaply, highlight the benefits of the computer databank or CD-ROM over microform for data storage. The library need not own material providing that it can buy the disks or have on-line access to data, which can be held anywhere in the world. Provided that such access is fast enough and cheap enough there would be little need for the library to possess little-used research or archival material, unless visual material was needed which could not be stored adequately in digital form. Not all subjects lend themselves to this computerized approach; art history for example, but for many other topics the use of remote databanks is already superceding microform collections. In the case of library catalogues produced on microfiche or microfilm, it has always been accepted that this was an intermediate technology. The logical move from the rigid structure of the microform catalogue to the multiple access provided by online catalogues for library users is fast becoming the norm as the costs of computer terminals and central processing units come down.

Computerized storage and access is the key to the future, or rather non-future, of both slides and microforms. Because there are so many items in libraries in these formats there will undoubtedly be an inertia factor working against the introduction of any system that would replace them. There will probably be a need for libraries to continue to have machines for utilizing slides, microfiches and microfilms for many years to come, but it must now only be a matter of time before the increasing availability of digital storage of both text and images change the ways that libraries store this data. As the price of production reduces and the appropriate technology becomes more widely available manufacturers will increasingly publish material in computerized form. Already there are signs that this is happening, with the availability of major bibliographical tools on CD-ROM as well as in microform and paper copies.

IMPORTANT COLLECTIONS

Collections of slides are less common than those containing microforms. Examples of slide collections can be found in most academic institutions which have any courses on art or design and such collections are often highly developed; but they can also be found in many other libraries, indeed any library which has any need for the storage of visual material may contain some slides, even if only a small number. Microfiches and microfilms are even more pervasive and examples can be found in almost every library which contains a reference or research collection.

BIBLIOGRAPHY

'Guide to microforms in print'. (1988–   ), Meckler.

Gwinn, N.E. (1987), *Preservation Microfilming; Guide for Librarians and Archivists*, American Library Association.

Irvine, B.J. (1974), *Slide Libraries; A Guide for Academic Institutions and Museums*, Libraries Unlimited.

Pacey, P. (1977), *Art Library Manual; A Guide to Resources and Practice*. Bowker. Includes chapters on slides and microforms.

Simons, W.W. and Tansey, L.C. (1970), *Slide Classification System for the Organisation and Automatic Indexing of Interdisciplinary Collections of Slides and Pictures*, Council on Library Resources.

Teague, S.J. (1985), *Microform, Video and Electronic Media Librarianship*, Butterworth.

Van de Waal, H. et al. (1981–), *Iconclass; An Iconographic Classification System*, North-Holland Publishing Company.

Wassermann, E.S. (1989), *Microform Marketplace; An International Directory of Micropublishing*, Meckler.

9

Recorded sources, visual and audio

PATSY CULLEN

INTRODUCTION

Collections of recorded material, both sound and visual, have an important and distinctive role to play in providing access to people and events which would otherwise be lost. A printed source can preserve the words that were spoken but only a film, video or sound recording can give the tone of voice, the nuances of intonation and the overall context of an event. Recordings have a unique ability to bring back the past and to enable the listener/viewer to experience, albeit vicariously, events and places impossible to experience in reality. Microphotography, used in medicine, can allow us to see inside the deepest recesses of the body, while techniques of digital imaging, as used on the Voyager space mission enabled us to see in vivid colour and detail the surface of Jupiter and the extraordinary features of its moons.

Recorded materials are also unique in that they are 'opaque': unlike a book or a photograph they have to be 'read' with the aid of equipment. This quality of opaqueness means that much greater explanation must be provided by librarians in order to enable full use of the material. Catalogues and indexes of recorded material must provide much more detailed interpretation than those for printed sources and it is in this area that the development of computerized information retrieval techniques have proved such an advantage.

FUNCTION OF LIBRARIES OF RECORDED MEDIA

There is no common unifying factor underlying the role of the various media libraries. Specialist libraries of film, video, or recorded sound are well established and exist to collect, organize, use and conserve that particular medium. One can make a useful distinction between material held in entirety to be used again as a complete programme, what may be described as the documentary approach; and material to be used in part – sequences of sound or images, or in the case of film, individual shots in the production of other programmes. Public libraries and academic libraries at all levels of the educational system now hold collections of complete recorded documents, whereas the organization and retrieval of sequences of recorded material is mainly the province of specialist film, video and sound libraries.

THE MATERIAL AND ITS PROBLEMS

What is remarkable about collections of recorded material is the diversity of forms covered by such an apparently simple heading. Recorded sounds and images have been in existence for about a hundred years, but the media upon which those sounds and images are preserved have changed considerably. Alternative formats have been invented which do the same things: sound recordings have progressed from wax cylinders to discs, to magnetic tape and now to optical compact discs and DAT (digital audiotape). New technologies have been created which allow completely new media to be developed, such as interactive videodisc, which by combining still and moving images with sound and computer software allows the user a hitherto impossible control over access to the vast amounts of information stored on the disc. Whilst some commentators predict an eventual 'convergence of technology', meaning that in the future all our existing recording techniques will be replaced by reliance on a single, all purpose medium, (the one most commonly mentioned is the optical disc) at present we are faced with a proliferation of formats, each presenting the librarian with its own problems of selection, acquisition, storage, retrieval and preservation, and each requiring its own particular equipment configuration for playback. This latter problem adds to the difficulties of archival collections, where not only have the preservation needs of the materials to be addressed, but suitable equipment must be maintained in order for access to remain possible.

Other general issues affecting recorded sound and image collections are security and copyright. Security has two meanings here: preservation of the material free from damage, and prevention of unlawful removal. In open access collections both these must be faced. In the past libraries have been over-zealous in their attempts to deal with both problems, which has led to locked collections, over-strict procedures and an inevitable reluctance on the part of the potential user to brave the hazards for the sake of a simple videotape. If the decision has been made that material is unique, fragile because of age or extremely valuable then of course the most stringent measures must be taken to preserve it. This must mean that such material is in fact removed from public access completely and use is only made of copies. If, however, recorded material forms part of a general collection it must be made easily available and security measures tempered to the requirements of open access. The second question, unlawful removal, is best addressed by including recorded materials in a general electronic security system such as Knogo or 3M, both of which can be used successfully with such material.

The complex restrictions of copyright legislation have for years been the bane of librarians responsible for media collections of all kinds. The long awaited Copyright, Designs and Patents Act 1988 has brought a number of major changes, not all of which are fully evident yet. The statutory infrastructure which will control the rights of producers and users is not, at the time of writing, established. The basic principle however, remains the same: the purchaser of any form of recorded material has no right, without the prior permission of the copyright holder, to reproduce it in the same or any other form. This is not the place for detailed examination of the provisions and restrictions of the Act, and readers should refer to the Act itself, its associated statutory instruments and to commentaries appearing in the professional press.

FORMS OF SOUND AND VISUAL RECORDINGS

Ciné film

Characteristics

Individual images are arranged vertically in sequence, the impression of movement being given by the speed of projection (normally 24 frames per second). Ciné film is usually stored on open reels, but old 8mm and Super 8mm films can be found in a variety of cartridges or cassettes.

Applications

Thirty-five mm is used for theatrical film distribution, 16mm has been the traditional format for non-theatrical distribution, that is, education and training. Eight mm and Super 8mm are used for home movie making and, in their cartridge and cassette forms, for educational purposes. These latter

213

have been almost entirely superseded by video. Sixteen mm ciné films are still used for showing to large groups, but developments in projection and other forms of televised display are likely to replace this too.

Physical construction

Acetate base, emulsion coating, optical and magnetic sound tracks.

Formats

8mm, Super 8mm, 16mm, 35mm, 70mm.

Replay

Each format requires a specific projector. Film passing from one reel to a second, take-up reel, goes through a 'gate' where light from a bulb shines through the individual frames and the image is projected through a lens system onto a distant screen. Magnetic soundtracks are read by a head similar to that on a tape-recorder, while the patterns on an optical track are converted into sound by a photo-electric cell. An amplifier and loudspeaker(s) enable the soundtrack to be heard by the audience.

Specific problems

Feature films produced before 1951 were shot on nitrate stock. This material is chemically unstable, highly combustible and will eventually crumble away entirely. Any such material *must* be kept in highly controlled conditions and be transferred to modern safety stock as soon as possible. Without transfer it will either rot or will have to be destroyed, so conservation is constrained not only by resources but by time. Modern safety stock carries its own problems; the base material can deteriorate, and the emulsion is prone to scratching and dirt, which are almost impossible to correct.

Videotape (inc. cassette/cartridge forms)

Characteristics

A moving image is recorded as an electronic signal onto magnetic tape, which for most purposes (except 2-inch broadcast masters) is in cassette form. As a general rule, the wider the tape, the better the quality of the recording. Magnetic tape can be recorded instantly – no processing is required before it can be used – and also wiped and re-recorded. Editing is carried out electronically: the tape is not physically cut and spliced as in the case of film. The 'eraseability' of videotape can be a disadvantage as poor storage and use conditions can lead to loss of the signal. It can also of course be corrupted deliberately.

Applications

Broadcast television programmes of all kinds: news, documentary features and drama productions. In-house production of publicity, educational and training materials in industry, commerce and academic institutions. Off-air recording. Video cameras, especially the compact formats, have virtually replaced film for non-professional recordings.

Physical construction

Polyester tape of various widths with a magnetic coating such as chromium oxide. Several tracks are recorded simultaneously: a sound track, a visual track, a cueing track and the control track which monitors all the recorded information.

Formats

2-inch broadcast tape. Cassette: Philips 1500 (obsolete); ½ inch VHS, Beta (different playing speeds); ¾ inch Umatic (High and Low bands); compact tapes: VHS -C.

Replay

The signals recorded on tape are played back on a videocassette recorder using either a standard television receiver using the aerial (RF) socket, or through a monitor using a direct video signal. VCRs use a helical scan system, which means that the tape travels across the record/playback heads at an angle; this gives the largest possible recording area. When recording the signal can originate from an RF aerial, a video camera, or another VCR. Search facilities on VCRs mean that the tape can be scanned quickly either forward or in reverse. The tape can be paused, but the quality of the image is usually poor and repeated use at the same spot can cause damage.

Specific problems

Incompatibility of tape formats and recording systems: tapes recorded on

the USA standard NTSC cannot be replayed on the UK standard PAL. SECAM recordings (France and Eastern Europe) are PAL compatible but with colour loss.
Sensitivity to magnetic fields.
'Print through' in archival storage.

Audiotape

Characteristics

Audiosignals can be recorded on either open reel or cassette tape. Open reel is now used exclusively for professional recording or by hobbyists, having been replaced by cassette for all other applications. Open reel recorders allow a choice of recording speed, and the higher the recording speed the better the quality of reproduction. Audiocassettes run at a single speed of 4.75 centimetres per second (1⅞ ips). The latest development in audiotape is DAT (Digital Audiotape) which promises the quality of a CD with the record/erase advantages of tape.

Formats

Open reel mono; open reel stereo; (compact) cassette; DAT.

Applications

Music, spoken word, talking books for the visually handicapped. Open reel is the preferred format for archiving because of its superior quality.

Physical construction

Polyester tape coated with ferrichrome (chromium dioxide and iron oxide) magnetic layers. Either open reel or cassette.

Replay

Open reel tape passes from the source reel on the left to a take-up reel on the right, passing in the process across whichever of the three heads has been selected. These are the record head, the replay head and the erase head. In a cassette player the principle is the same, but a single head is used for both recording and playback. Sound input can be from a microphone, radio signal, CD or record player, or another electronic source such as an electric guitar. Output can be via headphones or through an amplifier to one or more speakers.

216

Specific problems

As for any magnetic media, the problems are unwanted erasure, corruption from other magnetic sources, and 'print-through' of the signal during storage. Audiotape can stretch and the lead ends are particularly prone to damage. Failure of the cassette mechanism itself can also be a problem.

Optical discs

Characteristics

Twelve-inch and 4¾ inch silver discs with a characteristic mirror finish.

Applications

Twelve-inch videodiscs are now most often used for education and training applications, often interfaced with a computer to produce interactive video programmes, of which the BBC Domesday discs are perhaps the best known. The smaller discs are used for high quality digitized music recordings (Compact disc or CD), digital data storage (CD-ROM) and most recently video images plus music (CDV).

Physical construction

A hard polymer base is given a reflective aluminium coating and finished with a transparent protective layer. Twelve-inch videodiscs are often double sided, in other words two discs are bonded together back to back. CDs and CD-ROMs are single sided and in either case it is the underside of the disc which is read. Information is encoded as a series of pits of variable length and spacing arranged on a spiral track. Although types of optical disc exist which can record information (an example is the WORM – Write Once Read Many times), at the time of writing it is best to regard them as pre-recorded media.

Formats

Videodisc, compact disc, CD-ROM, CDV, CD-I.

Replay

Each format requires a dedicated player but in each case the discs are read from the centre outwards by a small laser. Output is to a video/computer

217

monitor in the case of videodisc and CD-ROM, and through an amplifier to speakers from CDs.

Specific problems

Optical discs seem to be highly durable, but they are too recent a development for definite conclusions to be possible about their long-term life. Pressing faults can cause problems, although improved quality control should pick these up at source. Contrary to popular myth, optical discs do need careful handling as finger prints and other surface marks can interfere with the ability of the laser to read the coded data.

Vinyl recordings

Characteristics

Black PVC discs, 7 inches and 12 inches in diameter.

Applications

Music and spoken word, increasingly being superseded by CD.

Physical construction

The signal is held in grooves on the surface of the disc, with one channel recorded on each side of the groove for stereo recordings.

Formats

Sixteen rpm (obsolete), 45 rpm, 33⅓ rpm, 78 rpm (obsolete).

Replay

Discs are played on a turntable and read from the outside to the centre. The signals are read by a diamond or sapphire stylus and converted by the cartridge into electrical impulses, which are then amplified and transmitted as sound through the speakers or headphones.

Specific problems

Discs are easily damaged, especially by scratching and warping due to heat or incorrect storage, or by dirt building up in the tracks. A worn stylus or one that is incorrectly aligned can also cause damage.

ACQUISITION

The acquisition of printed materials in the UK is facilitated by such factors as legal deposit, systematic bibliographical control and a well-organized system of publishers, distributors and booksellers. The acquisition of sound and video recordings has no such supporting infrastructure, making identification, selection and acquisition a frustrating and often time-consuming business.

To take these missing elements one by one: there is no system of legal deposit for any kind of sound or visual recording in this country. The national archives themselves must either buy or rely on donations from the relevant industries. In some cases these donations are obtained under systematic arrangements such as the special deposit arrangement between the National Sound Archive and the British Phonographic Industry, in others the national archives must rely on the generosity of either individual collectors or industry.

The bibliographical control – or lack of it – of audiovisual materials in general is a constant source of complaint and a major obstacle to the comprehensive development and maintenance of collections. It is, of course, closely allied to the absence of legal deposit. However, of all the media, it is perhaps sound and visual recordings which are best served in bibliographical terms.

For availability of film and video in the UK the publications of the British Film Institute provide the essential information. The *British National Film and Video Catalogue* (first published in 1963 as the *British National Film Catalogue*) is a quarterly record of films and videos available in the UK. It is classified by subject and extensively indexed. For materials produced for degree level teaching by British institutions of higher education, the annual catalogue of the British Universities Film and Video Council is a valuable and authoritative reference source. Music sound recordings are well served by the various Gramophone publications: *Classical Record Catalogue* (quarterly); *Popular Music Catalogue*; (six-monthly) and *Spoken Word and Miscellaneous Catalogue* (annual). The establishment of the British National Discography should go even further towards the systematic control of at least this particular medium. There is an inevitable degree of overlap between the existing bibliographical sources, and there are also omissions, so in order to establish comprehensive coverage (or as near as possible) it is essential to collect the listings of individual publishers/producers/distributors.

The case of music recordings can be set aside for the moment because the pattern of publication and distribution is comparable with that of printed materials, but visual recordings are more complex. Film is more often hired than purchased and there are a number of large distributors, each with their particular strengths, and each producing their own catalogues listing films (and videos) plus hire and purchase costs. These include Guild Sound and Vision, Concord Films, and Albany Video Distribution. Next come the large producers/publishers such as the television companies. BBC Enterprises is the sales arm for BBC programmes on video and videodisc, and sound recordings of all kinds. The individual independent TV companies also have educational and/or sales departments and will provide catalogues on request. The position is similar with large industrial concerns such as Shell, BP, BNF and British Gas, all of which produce educational materials. These are always of a high standard of design and production, but care must be taken about their possible bias. The universities and polytechnics produce a great deal of valuable material which must be purchased direct. Art galleries and museums have also entered the video production market in recent years, these include the Institute for Contemporary Arts, The Mall, London SW1Y 5AH and The Design Council, 28 Haymarket, London SW1. Professional bodies such as those of probation officers and social workers also produce their own high quality training materials which are then made generally available. Then come the enormous number of small, independent, production companies of which the following are good examples: Team Video Productions, Canalot 222, Kensal Road, London W10 5BN; Cinema of Women, 31 Clerkenwell Close, London EC1R OAT, and the Leeds Animation Workshop, 45 Bayswater Row, Leeds 8. Keeping track of such a diversity of sources is a lengthy job, but publications such as the *Good Video Guide* and BUFVC's *Distributors Index* can be enormously useful.

It is now possible to buy video recordings at a number of high street retail outlets, as chains such as W.H. Smith, Virgin, and Woolworth sell feature films and music videos. Care must be taken in buying from retailers that there are no restrictive conditions attached to the sale, which would prevent the use of the material in a library context. This is a complex legal area, where the best advice must be 'caveat emptor'.

Hire or purchase are not the only ways of obtaining recorded material; off-air recording is a common way of building up a collection. The 1988 Copyright Act gives educational establishments the right to record all broadcast output. This can be done freely where no licensing agreement exists, otherwise it must be subject to the terms and conditions of the licence. The Open University licence scheme administered by Guild Sound and Vision is probably the best known, and details of new, blanket licences are currently eagerly awaited. Unfortunately no such rights or licences apply to the non-educational sectors.

CLASSIFICATION, CATALOGUING AND RETRIEVAL

The most significant difference between collections of print and those of media materials is the opacity of the latter, which makes the provision of a detailed descriptive catalogue essential, since this has to provide a substitute for the actual document for selection purposes. Essential information on this substitute document will include first, that concerned with playback, such as the kind of equipment required, how long the recording lasts, and whether it is in colour. Second, unlike print material, recordings may exist in different versions. These may be due to the technical processes involved in their production, such as negative and positive film, or because of differently edited versions. Third, aspects to do with the audience must also be covered: the language and country of origin, the intellectual level and approach adopted.

The retrieval methods employed in the management of collections of sound and visual recordings will depend on a number of factors, including whether the collection is open or closed access, whether whole documents or parts of documents are to be retrieved, whether the collection is free-standing or forms part of a larger, mixed-media library.

The provisions of AACR2 are generally accepted as suitable for the description of items in a mixed-media library where an integrated catalogue is required. They are not appropriate (nor were they ever intended to be) for specialist single media collections, where the materials are likely to need much greater description in order to identify very short sequences, or even, in the case of film, single shots. Even in collections where the retrieval of whole documents is the main requirement, the level of description will generally be greater than for print.

The responsibility for the publication of an item of print material is usually simple to establish, but audiovisual materials are produced by groups of people rather than individuals, and each member of the group has made their own particular, individual contribution to the finished product. This means that catalogue entries must identify each person involved; for example in the case of film this will include the director, producers, actors, cinematographer, editor, and composer of the soundtrack.

A further difference between print and non-print materials is the lack of an equivalent to the title page, where key information is recorded in a standard form. It can often be difficult to establish such details as the duration of a recording, its origins or its date of production from the material itself and extensive background research may be necessary.

The subject analysis and subsequent classification of sound and visual recordings is complicated by their frequent lack of specificity. A given recording is likely to have a number of possible subject applications which

221

makes precise allocation within a classification scheme difficult. Closed access collections can avoid this problem since they are likely to be arranged in accession number or other administratively convenient order rather than according to subject content. Where classification is required, UDC has been found to provide greater flexibility than say DDC, and is used to classify materials in the *British National Film and Video Catalogue*. Subject indexing using keywords is probably the most useful approach, as several subject descriptors can be applied to each catalogue record. Single subject collections can make use of existing specialist thesauri, while mixed collections can adapt standard lists of subject headings such as Library of Congress or Sears. It is in this area that computer-based systems have so many advantages over other retrieval devices, making possible the fast and efficient retrieval of a given item or of a number of linked items.

CONTROL OF USE

There is always tension in any library system between the demands of access to information and the need to protect stock from misuse and damage. This tension is even greater when the material concerned may be very difficult to replace or physically fragile. Wherever possible in such cases it is advisable to make viewing or listening copies on video or audiocassette, thus preserving the original. Where this is not possible (because of copyright restrictions for example) then use may have to be restricted, with procedures established for thorough checking of the material whenever it is used, and the recording of any damage. Obviously any such damage must be repaired as soon as possible, but if this cannot be done and the material remains useable even though of poorer quality then some form of damage report must be attached to the item concerned.

Loan collections must have some method of recording issues and returns, and in a mixed media collection it is most efficient to have a single system covering all media. Issue systems are a useful source of statistical information about the collection, and whatever system is chosen should be able to provide a history of the item in terms both of frequency of use and of users.

Reference only collections similarly need a way of determining what has been used, by whom and when. Shelf markers which show the position of items in use simplify shelving, while a simple form can be retained as a permanent record to provide a history of usage. Reference collections, and to a lesser extent loan collections, will require good playback facilities and a booking system is likely to be necessary.

No collection of recorded material in the UK has yet committed itself to new technology for all these administrative functions to the extent of the French. At both the *Videothèque de Paris* and the *Médiathèque de l'Institut du Monde Arabe* the entire process of identifying, selecting and replaying visual recordings has been totally automated, using extensive databases linked to robotized retrieval equipment. The user selects and watches the material from his seat in the viewing hall and the recordings themselves are not touched by humans at all. Similar automated approaches to recorded material are taken at the public library (BPI) in the Pompidou Centre and in the *Médiathèque* at the *Centre des Sciences et de l'Industrie*, La Villette. In Paris the initiatives have come about because of a firm commitment by national and local government to the importance of sound and visual recordings in the commercial and cultural life of the city, supported by the provision of a high level of public funding.

CONSERVATION AND PRESERVATION

Maintaining any collection of materials is problematic, but the maintenance of sound and visual recordings has its own specific difficulties. In addition to the general lack of national policy on the preservation and conservation of library materials, the lack of funding for such activities, and an apparent lack of awareness that they are actually necessary, there is our inability to predict what will happen in the future to many recorded materials. Film, both nitrate and safety stock, has proved to be surprisingly volatile, and while new formats such as optical discs appear to be highly stable we simply do not yet know what their active life is likely to be. There is already evidence that the printers ink used in the production of certain CDs can eat into the disc's protective coating and damage the reflective layer. A further problem is to establish the principle that sound and video recordings should be preserved at all, and then to decide what, out of all the material possible should be retained for future generations. Finally, there comes the question of who should be responsible.

All these issues are clouded by the nature of sound and visual collections in this country, the absence of legal deposit and the lack of a 'copy of last resort'. The major national collections do, of course, play a major role in the preservation of recordings, but their collections do not cover everything. It is highly possible that the last remaining copy of a key recorded document could be in the collection of a public or a university library. It therefore becomes essential that all libraries which have substantial collections of this nature develop a policy on at least the conservation, and where necessary the preservation, of its materials. Such a policy should define the distinction between conservation, meaning the maintenance of materials in good order, whilst allowing their continued use; and preservation, which means in addition the restoration and, where necessary, transfer from one material to another, in order to preserve the original content and also to preserve the original carrier. A disaster plan, which envisages a 'worst case scenario' and sets out strategies for prevention, damage containment and restoration is an essential part of collection management, not only for peace of mind but in many cases because such a plan is required by insurers.

Successful conservation of recorded materials, that is, their maintenance in good working order, requires an appropriate environment, suitable storage conditions and proper handling. What then constitutes an appropriate environment for sound and visual recordings? The greatest environmental hazards for all these materials are temperature, dust and humidity. In addition, magnetic fields threaten video and audio tape, while light will fade colour film. Changes in temperature will cause the base medium to expand and contract, with damaging consequences for the carrier coatings. Dust particles will scratch film emulsion, clog record grooves and damage magnetic coatings. High humidity levels encourage fungal growth and mould. Recommended environmental levels for recorded materials vary: film is best maintained at a constant temperature of 12°C with 50 per cent relative humidity; video and audiotape can be kept at a higher temperature of 21° and 40–60 per cent humidity. The essential factor however is stability, and for most collections (except film) a constantly maintained working temperature of 20°C will provide a suitable environment. Optimum conditions for archival preservation will incorporate air conditioning and filtering. Storage conditions must in general provide protection from dust and light sources and must accommodate the specific needs of the different media. Optical and audiodiscs should be stored vertically with adequate support to prevent warping or pressure from surrounding discs. Film is normally stored flat in metal canisters. Magnetic tape can suffer from 'print-through' or ghosting if not used regularly, so conservation of this material must take into account the need to run tapes through at intervals, and to transfer recordings to new tape every 10–15 years. The final factor to consider is handling of the material. Archival preservation requires the production of copies for use so that the original is not compromised, but in a working library it is likely that the originals will be used. Well-trained staff, well-maintained playback equipment and clean surroundings for use are good preventative measures against damage.

IMPORTANT COLLECTIONS

Major archival collections in the UK can be grouped as national and regional, and then subdivided by medium. The two principal collections are the National Film Archive and the National Sound Archive. The NFA was established in 1935 and is funded by the BFI. It aims to provide 'a representative selection of all film and television shown in the UK' covering feature films, documentaries and television. The film and video archives of the Imperial War Museum are also of national importance. Both archives provide viewing facilities. Scotland and Wales have their own film archives which document their particular cultural and linguistic heritage. There has been a growth in recent years of regional film archives devoted to preserving the recordings of particular local areas. Two of the best known are the North West Regional Film Archive, based in Manchester, and the East Anglia Regional Film Archive in Norwich. Not in the public domain, but with collections of immense national significance, are the BBC Film and Videotape Library and the Visnews Library. The BBC collection is maintained principally to support the Corporation's own programme output, although some material is available through the NFA. Visnews is a commercial company which holds newsfilm for sale to production companies, but its size and conservation policies entitle it to be considered as a major national collection.

The National Sound Archive (NSA) had its origins in the private British Institute of Recorded Sound, founded during the 1940s. In 1982 it became part of the British Library. The NSA collects sound recordings of all kinds and is international in scope, although British material is a particular responsibility. Listening facilities are provided at the NSA headquarters in London and also at the British Library at Boston Spa, West Yorkshire. The Imperial War Museum also has a nationally important collection of sound recordings dealing with the social, economic, historical and military aspects of war. Listening facilities are available and the Museum also makes copies and compilations of sound recordings for sale.

Mixed media archive collections are much less well established but are developing in order to document particular areas of interest. The Graves Medical Audiovisual Library is nationally and internationally known for its postal loan service of, in many cases, specially commissioned audiovisual materials for the support of medical education and training. It also has an archival role and keeps copies of all its programmes. Collections which support the arts are a growing area and examples include the National Resource Centre for Dance, based at the University of Surrey and the National Arts Education Archive at Bretton Hall, near Wakefield, West Yorkshire.

225

All such collections have a dual role, in that they combine the collection and exploitation of their materials for education, research or commercial purposes, with a policy of archival conservation. The smaller organizations, despite their national (and in many cases international) importance, survive on minimal and insecure financial support, which obviously affects the level of their activities and the extent to which they can fulfil their objectives. In all too many cases the preservation of nationally significant and unique material is threatened by lack of funds.

BIBLIOGRAPHY

British National Film and Video Catalogue, British Film Institute. (quarterly).

British Universities Film and Video Council, 'Catalogue of Audiovisual Materials in Higher Education', B.U.F.V.C. (annual) (microfiche).

British Universities Film and Video Council, (1987), *The Distributor's Index*, B.U.F.V.C.

Butchart, I. and Fothergill, R. (1990), *Non-Book Materials in Libraries*, 3rd edn, Bumpley.

Cornish, G.P. (1986), *Archival Collections of Non-book Material*, British Library.

Cornish, G.P. (1988), 'Audiovisual Archives in the UK', *AVL* **14** (1) February, pp. 17–23.

HMSO (1988), 'Copyright, Designs and Patents Act 1988'.

HMSO (1989), 'Copyright: The Copyright (Librarians and Archivists) (Copying of Copyright Materials) Regulations 1989', (Statutory Instrument 1989 no. 1212).

Harrison, H.P. (1973), *Film Library Techniques*, Focal Press.

Harrison, H.P. (1986), 'Audiovisual Archives', *AVL* **12** (3), August, 133–41.

Harrison, H.P. (1987), 'Conservation of Audiovisual Materials', *AVL* **13** (3), August, pp. 154–62.

Hendley, T. (1985), *Videodiscs, Compact Discs and Digital Optical Discs*, Cimtech.

I.C.A. Video, *Good Video Guide*, Institute of Contemporary Arts, The Mall, London SW1Y 5AH.

International Federation of Film Archives (1986), *Preservation and Restoration of Moving Images and Sound*. Brussels: FIAF.

Pinion, C.F. (1986), 'Legal Deposit of Non-book Materials', Library and information research report 49, British Library.

Researchers' Guide to British Film and Television Collections (1985), rev. edn, BUFVC – 50 UK regional archives.

Thorpe, F. (ed.) (1988), *International Directory of Film and Television Documentation Centres*, 3rd edn. St James Press. 104 collections in 47 countries.

Weerasinghe, L. (ed.) (1989), 'Directory of Recorded Sound Resources in the UK', British Library – results of 1984 survey on NSA database: national Register for collections of recorded sound including private collections accessible via the NSA.

USEFUL ADDRESSES

Albany Video Distribution, The Albany, Douglas Way, London SE8 4AG.

BBC Enterprises, Villiers House, The Broadway, Ealing, London W5 2PA.

BFI, 127 Charing Cross Road, London WC2H OEA.

BUFVC, 55 Greek Street, London W1V 5LR.

Cinema of Women, 31 Clerkenwell Close, London EC1R 0AT.

Concord Films, 201 Felixstowe Road, Ipswich IP3 9BP, Suffolk.

The Design Council, 28 Haymarket, London SW1.

Guild Sound and Vision, 6 Royce Road, Peterborough PE1 5YB.

Institute for Contemporary Arts, The Mall, London SW1Y 5AH.

Leeds Animation Workshop, 45 Bayswater Row, Leeds 8.

Team Video Productions, Canalot 222, Kensal Road, London W10 5BN.

Index